AFTER EMANCIPATION

After Emancipation

Racism and Resistance at the University of Virginia

Edited by Kirt von Daacke and Andrea Douglas

University of Virginia Press
Charlottesville and London

University of Virginia Press

Printed in the United States of America on acid-free paper

First published 2024

1 3 5 7 9 8 6 4 2

Library of Congress Cataloging-in-Publication Data

Names: Von Daacke, Kirt, editor. | Douglas, Andrea N., editor.
Title: After emancipation : racism and resistance at the University of Virginia / edited by Kirt von Daacke and Andrea Douglas.
Description: Charlottesville : University of Virginia Press, 2024. | Includes bibliographical references and index.
Identifiers: LCCN 2023037510 (print) | LCCN 2023037511 (ebook) | ISBN 9780813949253 (hardcover) | ISBN 9780813949260 (paperback) | ISBN 9780813949277 (ebook)
Subjects: LCSH: University of Virginia—History. | Racism—Virginia—Charlottesville—History. | Slavery—Virginia—Charlottesville—History. | Racism in higher education—Virginia—Charlottesville—History. | Segregation in higher education—Virginia—Charlottesville—History. | Charlottesville (Va.)—Race relations.
Classification: LCC LD5678 .A65 2024 (print) | LCC LD5678 (ebook) | DDC 378.1/9820755481—dc23/eng/20230814
LC record available at https://lccn.loc.gov/2023037510
LC ebook record available at https://lccn.loc.gov/2023037511

Cover art: African American demonstrators outside the White House. Photograph by Warren K Leffler, 1965. (Library of Congress Prints and Photographs Division)

Let any man now claim for the Negro, or worse still, let the Negro now claim for himself, any right, privilege or immunity which has hitherto been denied him by law or custom, and he will at once open a fountain of bitterness, and call forth overwhelming wrath.

—Frederick Douglass, 1883

CONTENTS

FOREWORD

Books, like people, have many origins. Let me trace one line of origin for this book.

In 2003, Brown University president Ruth Simmons appointed a committee to investigate and publicly disclose Brown's historical relationship to slavery and the transatlantic slave trade. Simmons also asked the committee to organize public programs that might help students and the nation to think in reasoned, rigorous ways about the meaning and significance of that history in the present. "Understanding our history and suggesting how the full truth of that history can be incorporated into our common traditions will not be easy," she acknowledged. "But, then, it doesn't have to be."

I had the privilege of chairing the Brown committee. I learned many things in the process—not least that when you are publicly identified with an inquiry into America's racial past, you will receive a lot of emails. I still have them, from all manner of people, sharing their thoughts about race, slavery, and the wisdom of excavating an uneasy past. While a few praised Simmons for her courage, others expressed bewilderment, indignation, even rage. "You disgust me, as you disgust many other Americans," wrote one correspondent. "Slavery was wrong, but at that time it was a legal enterprise. It ended, case closed. You cite slavery's effects as being the reason that black people are so far behind, but that just illustrates your ignorance. Black people, here and now, are behind because some can't keep their hands off drugs, or guns, or can't move forward, can't get off welfare, can't do the simple things to improve their life. . . . They don't deserve money, they deserve a boot in the backside over and over. . . . Can your ignorant research, and can Ruth Simmons, too."

The furor provoked by the committee's appointment soon faded—people who rush to judgment also tend to have short attention spans—and we were able to go about our work. Public programs were substantive and illuminating, and the historical research was revelatory. As a scholar of African American history, I imagined that I appreciated slavery's foundational role in American history, but I did not know that thirty members of the governing board of the College of Rhode Island, what later became

Brown, owned or captained slave ships; that enslaved Jamaicans subsisted on salt cod harvested off Rhode Island's shores; or that the streets of Newport were literally paved with a duty on imported slaves. Slavery, I learned, was not some excrescence on the Atlantic economy. It *was* the Atlantic economy, and New Englanders were as much a part of it as their neighbors to the south.

Perhaps more important than the history lesson, the initiative at Brown provided a model for—and a challenge to—other colleges and universities. At this writing, more than eighty other schools, mostly in the United States but also in Canada and the United Kingdom, have undertaken similar investigations. The University of Virginia stands prominently in their ranks. What was once derided as a "hypocritical race hustle" by a Black woman with "an agenda"—again quoting some of the Brown committee's early critics—is now widely accepted as a basic institutional responsibility.

And how could it be otherwise? We are talking, after all, not about bakeries or barbershops but about universities, which are (to borrow a phrase) "peculiar institutions," with their own distinctive purposes, values, and responsibilities. Universities are truth-seeking: they exist to produce and disseminate knowledge of all kinds. They are fundamentally irreverent, questioning orthodoxies, encouraging dispute, demanding that every assertion, whether about the nature of a subatomic particle or the meaning of a poem, be supported by reasoned argument and specific evidence. Perhaps most important, they are historically minded, celebrating their own histories and traditions while also acting as repositories of humanity's collective past. As the Brown committee wrote in its report, to live and learn at a university "is to be a member of a community that exists across time, a participant in a procession that began centuries ago and will continue long after we are gone. If an institution professing these principles cannot squarely face its own history, it is hard to imagine how any other institution, let alone our nation, might do so."

Given my experience, I have watched the efforts of other universities to confront their own historical entanglements with slavery and other forms of racial injustice with considerable interest. Each initiative has been different, reflecting both the specific histories of particular institutions and the array of political pressures that they face in the present. As President Simmons noted, facing the "full truth" of history is an inherently demanding task, but the challenges that we faced at Brown, a private institution in New England, were very different from the challenges that confronted colleagues at, say, the University of Alabama, where a faculty member advocating an institutional apology for slavery was threatened with violence, or the University of North Carolina, where the state legislature passed a law to forestall the removal of a campus memorial honoring the Confederacy.

In few places are the stakes of this kind of historical reckoning higher than they are at the University of Virginia, which launched its President's Commission on Slavery and the University in 2013. Like Alabama and UNC, UVA is a public institution, the educational flagship of a state whose capital was once the capital of the Confederacy. The campus and the surrounding countryside are peppered with monuments and memorials hearkening back to the Confederate era, including a recently removed equestrian statue of Robert E. Lee in Charlottesville's Market Street Park—the monument at the center of the deadly 2017 "Unite the Right" rally. If one needed proof that such monuments are not mere expressions of "heritage," innocent of racial meaning, one need look no further than Market Street Park, where armed white supremacists, some in Klan robes, marched beneath swastikas and Confederate battle flags chanting, "You will not replace us."

The initiative at UVA also commands our attention because of the institution's distinctive history. As anyone who has spent an hour on the grounds knows, the University is, in a more than figurative sense, a product of the vision of one man, Thomas Jefferson, a man whose soaring paeans to liberty and equality continue to stir the breasts of human beings all over the world—and also a man who, over the course of his life, owned 607 human beings, including at least 6 who were his own children. Slavery was a pervasive presence at "Mr. Jefferson's University," and it shadows the grounds to this day. Yet until very recently, visitors to UVA would have had little inkling of this, so thoroughly had slavery's presence been erased from collective memory. Jefferson himself contributed to the erasure, designing his "Academical Village," as he had his home at Monticello, to keep the enslaved people on whom the operation depended safely out of view. Thus while students traversed the porticoes and manicured lawns, lifting their eyes to the elegant, Palladian-style Rotunda (designed by Jefferson as a "model in architecture of the purist forms of antiquity, furnishing to the student examples of the precepts he will be taught in art"), a legion of enslaved people grubbed in basements and walled "gardens," cooking the food and emptying the privies of these masters-in-the-making, scrubbing their clothes and chopping the wood that warmed them in winter. Some continued to serve even in death: their cadavers would be dissected by medical students in the University's "Anatomical Theatre," also designed by Jefferson.

In the life of every institution, as in the life of every individual, there are things that we remember and cherish and other things that we deny, extenuate, and forget. Thanks to the President's Commission on Slavery and the University, some of the latter things have been brought into the light. Tour the grounds today and you will learn not only about Jefferson's vision but also about the enslaved people whose unremunerated toil underwrote it. You will also see a new memorial to enslaved workers, inscribed with the names of nearly a thousand of these forgotten founders, a fraction of the estimated five thousand enslaved men, women, and children who labored at the University.

As a historian, I am chary of metaphors, but it is hard not to see Jefferson's long, sometimes anguished struggle to square the circle of slavery and freedom, race and equality, as a metaphor for our nation's ongoing struggle to realize the "self-evident" truths that he so eloquently proclaimed. In the same way, I believe that the effort of the University of Virginia to acknowledge and accept responsibility for its past carries a message for all Americans, reminding us of who we are and whence we have come but also reminding us of the possibility, the promise, of change.

In contrast to most of its peer institutions, the University of Virginia did not stop with slavery. Even before the initial commission completed its five-year term in 2018, UVA president Teresa Sullivan launched another venture, the President's Commission on the University in the Age of Segregation. The essays in this book—they are stories, really—grow out of that commission's work. Written not only by faculty members but also by students and community members, the essays explore the University's racial history in the century following emancipation, a century that produced moments of extraordinary progress and hope but also more than its share of horrors: the onset of formal segregation and disfranchisement; the terror of lynch law; the birth of eugenics and the rebirth of the Ku Klux Klan; "massive resistance" to integration; and the invention of so-called urban renewal, a concept that legitimated the removal of long-established Black communities abutting the UVA campus—communities whose members had labored at the University for generations, in some cases all the way back to the time of slavery. In the report that we submitted at Brown, we wrote earnestly about slavery's enduring legacy, reminding readers that the University's complicity in racial injustice did not end with abolition. Committees at other universities have done the same. But few, if any, institutions have had the courage to do what UVA has done: to bring the story of racial exclusion and injustice—and the questions of institutional responsibility that come with it—right down to the present day.

Read the stories. While specific in their details, they are all expressions of a singular commitment: to confront the past in all its beauty and its pain, the gracious and the grievous, and to accept the burden and responsibilities entailed by each. Some of the stories are inspirational. Some are shameful. But they all are true. And truth, as Thomas Jefferson once observed, "is great . . . and has nothing to fear from the conflict."

James T. Campbell

ACKNOWLEDGMENTS

The histories presented within this volume often interpret new archival research conducted by Dr. Ashley Schmidt and student research interns. Schmidt's leadership of a massive research project included far more than spending time in the archives and supervising the interns' work. She managed that while working as the sole staff person handling a breadth of administrative projects created by the commission—scheduling meetings, planning large- and small-scale events, organizing conferences, coordinating a growing consortium of universities coming to terms with institutional racism, and even annually shepherding a high school summer immersion program on the afterlives of slavery, from initial design to completion. Her activities and the team's work under her guidance have allowed us to create a repository available to academic and lay scholars. Much of that material informs the historical essays in this volume, *After Emancipation,* as well as the commission's many achievements since 2019. We have been so fortunate to have her as a partner in this work for the past several years.

We also thank our team at the University of Virginia Press for believing in the possibilities of this volume, even when all we came to them with were thirteen *UVA Today* online essays and an idea about how to turn them into a community conversation across time and space. History Editor Nadine Zimmerli's guidance in shaping the volume and willingness to stand up for our broader vision of how the volume would differ from most edited volumes, along with Senior Project Editor Wren Morgan Myers's astute editing of both scholarly essays and community reflections, made each contribution immeasurably better.

We have endeavored over the past several years to detail both the University of Virginia's role in creating and maintaining the decades-long age of segregation and the local Black community's enduring commitment to dismantling those very systems as they continually sought the full fruits of American freedom. On that journey, we have learned just how many people truly deserve credit not just for this book but for the shared community truth-telling project from which it arose. We dedicate this book first to all those unsung heroes who survived more than one hundred years of racial discrimination after 1865, and especially to those who persisted in challenging white supremacy in all its manifestations.

They were housekeepers, undertakers, preachers, teachers, merchants, maids, laborers, barbers, insurance agents, grocers, nurses, a doctor, and a dentist—all local residents who pushed for change as they sought citizenship rights and equality of access to education, employment, health care, and housing. Too many people to identify individually here, but we still call many of their names: Isabella and William Gibbons, Burkley Bullock, John West, John Twine, George P. Inge, Dr. George Ferguson, Charles Coles Jr., Nannie Cox Jackson, Ernest and Ethel Allen, John Bell, Virginia and Fellisco Hardy, William Kenney, T. J. Sellers, Randolph White, Gregory Swanson, Sandra Wicks, Charles E. Alexander, Raymond Dixon, Regina Dixon, Maurice Henry, Marvin Townsend, William Townsend, Roland T. Woodfolk, Ronald E. Woodfolk, French Jackson, Donald Martin, John Martin, Wesley Harris, and William Harris, to name but a few.

This book would also not exist without those who bravely signed a charter petition in 1918 establishing a local NAACP chapter, nor without the men and women who toiled as maids and orderlies who forced the university to pay Black workers better wages. They, along with the "hidden nurses," ultimately compelled the university to desegregate its hospital. Every moment, both large and small, of dismantling some aspect of Virginia's apartheid state has behind it a story of heroic persistence in demanding better. Change at UVA after the 1960s also cannot be understood without acknowledging the continuing commitment of students, faculty, and community members in the late twentieth and early twenty-first centuries to challenge white supremacy in all its contemporary manifestations. This book is dedicated to those unsung heroes.

After Emancipation grows out of the University of Virginia President's Commission in the Age of Segregation's truth-telling and community-focused goals. The commission, composed of university affiliates and community members, demanded—energetically and with goodwill—that the institution not shy away from its difficult histories. We thank them, and by extension, all the members of our twenty-first century community who continue those long traditions of challenging white supremacy in all its contemporary guises. Their work continues, and we all stand on the shoulders of the generations who preceded us in working to make our community and our society more open, equitable, and inclusive.

AFTER EMANCIPATION

Introduction

Twenty-First-Century Truth-Telling

> One is astonished in the study of history at the recurrence of the idea that evil must be forgotten, distorted, skimmed over. The difficulty of course with this philosophy is that history loses its value as an incentive and example. It paints perfect men and noble nations, but it does not tell the truth.
>
> —W. E. B. Du Bois, *Black Reconstruction in America*

Du Bois's trenchant 1935 critique of accepted scholarly accounts of Reconstruction serves today as a clarion call in a time when truth remains contested and the possibility of writing an unimpeachable narrative about American race relations seems increasingly daunting. In Virginia in 2022, one of newly elected governor Glenn Youngkin's first acts in office was to declare war on "divisive" history and Critical Race Theory. He even established a tip line so that teachers who dared to teach truthful narratives about American race relations could be reported. The University of Virginia President's Commission on the University in the Age of Segregation (PCUAS) and the volume we present here, *After Emancipation: Racism and Resistance at the University of Virginia,* thus feels ever more urgent and necessary. The ideologies that give rise to today's mistrust of truth-telling, now disguised behind disingenuous calls for national unity and parental choice in schools, run deep through the history of the University of Virginia.

On March 3, 1865, U.S. military forces passed through Albemarle County for only the second time during the Civil War, this time as a conquering army. On that afternoon, the Civil War had been raging for nearly four years, with most of the military action in Virginia happening away from Charlottesville, Albemarle County, and the University of Virginia.

The institution, the third largest college in the United States at the time, had remained open throughout the war, often with only a few dozen students in attendance. For over two years, University medical faculty had been running Charlottesville General Hospital, taking over school and town buildings as they worked to provide medical care for wounded Confederate soldiers, supporting the war effort against the United States that raged on battlefronts often only thirty miles or so from town. At that point, the school had for decades operated powerfully as an incubator for pro-slavery thought.

Eleven years before Virginia seceded, UVA students responded to the national debate over the possible extension of slavery into territories acquired in the Mexican-American War by calling for secession. They hyperbolically claimed that "from the entire North has gone forth the fiat, that the area of African slavery shall never be extended." The student Southern Rights Association worriedly asked, "Hemmed in on all sides, deprived of the liberty of expansion, and surrounded by a cordon of free States, what Southerner can fail to see, as the inevitable result of such a policy, the certain downfall of an institution [slavery], with whose safety and preservation, are indissolubly interwoven all [white Southerners'] interests, . . . sympathies, and hopes[?]" They answered by calling on slave states to secede from the United States, having "within our own borders all the elements of a great and flourishing empire; save us from those who rob us of our rights, and we will speedily become one of the first nations of the world."[1] Thus, faculty, students, and townspeople had long (and defiantly) supported slavery and what became the Confederate cause.

That day in March 1865 was different, though. Gone were the giddy days four years earlier when, as student Randolph H. McKim remembered, "so general was sympathy with the Southern cause" that there was "a sudden explosion of excitement" and "one after another of the leaders of the young men mount[ed] the steps [of the Rotunda] and harangue[d] the crowd in favor of the Southern Confederacy."[2] For those at the University in 1865, that fateful March day was one of resignation and capitulation to the United States military. UVA professors John B. Minor and Socrates Maupin headed to the entrance of the University and waited nearby, "prominently displaying a white flag of truce" as they anticipated the arrival of an occupying army. According to Minor, they beseeched the officer in charge that "no defense of Charlottesville was contemplated. . . . The town was evacuated . . . and [they] requested protection for the university, and for the town." That army came as an occupying and conquering army, not as an army of emancipation, and only remained in the area a few days after the mayor and UVA professors surrendered, "delivering up the keys of the public buildings."[3]

Despite the army's short stay and disinterest in emancipating anyone, it was the beginning of freedom for 52 percent of the local population, who had been held in bondage until then. Local white reaction to secession, to that occupation, and to the end of the conflict tells us so much about the University. To a great extent, that reaction also reveals enduring white Virginian attitudes about the war, slavery, and society. For instance, alumnus McKim spent his postwar life "combining his impeccable Confederate *bona* fides" with decades of Lost Cause activism, including orating at the University's 1906 dedication of Rotunda tablets memorializing students who had enlisted in the Confederate war.[4] Those reactions also expose quite a bit about enslaved people's understanding of the war and its meaning. Professor Minor noted at the time that the departure of U.S. military forces also meant the departure of hundreds, if not thousands, of enslaved people who understood those days in March 1865 to be a moment of liberation as they followed the army out of town. After enslaved man Henry self-emancipated and left Minor, Minor disparaged Henry and other enslaved people as "poor misguided creatures . . . I lament it on [their] account more than my own."[5] Similarly, teenager Sarah Ann Strickler, who was a student at the Albemarle Female Institute in Charlottesville and a young "Confederate partisan," was incensed by the occupation and complained of having to "submit to their [U.S. soldiers'] insolence." She, too, noted what amounted to a mass self-emancipation by enslaved people in Albemarle: "Two of our maids went off with their brethren," following the U.S. military as they departed the area.[6]

Regardless of the failure of the Confederate military effort, the surrender of Robert E. Lee's army at Appomattox just over a month after U.S. Army forces decamped from Charlottesville, and the onset of emancipation in 1865, white Virginians remained stalwart in their commitment to the vision of white rule that had led them to secession. As Frederick Douglass remarked about post-emancipation America, "Let any man now claim for the Negro, or worse still, let the Negro now claim for himself, any right, privilege or immunity which has hitherto been denied him by law or custom, and he will at once open a fountain of bitterness, and call forth overwhelming wrath."[7] For example, UVA alumnus Robert Garlick Hill Kean, writing in June 1865, complained that "on some farms the negroes quit work in a body" and then often "became insubordinate" as they demanded land as well as wages for their work. Echoing Thomas Jefferson's 1814 statement that African Americans, "by their habits rendered as incapable as children of taking care of themselves," would in emancipation become "pests in society by their idleness, and the depredations to which this leads them," Kean similarly understood "manumission after this fashion . . . as the greatest social crime ever committed on this earth," an event that would lead to African American "want, vice, crime, . . . disease, the jails."[8] Professors Minor and Maupin, Robert Kean, Randolph H. McKim, Sarah Strickler's husband and Confederate veteran Robert H. Fife, students returning to UVA, and most other white Virginians agreed and committed themselves to re-creating or reconstituting the world they had wagered and lost in the Civil War. *After Emancipation* highlights the ways in which the University of Virginia remained a breeding ground for thought dedicated to that project—reclaiming, maintaining, and justifying white rule in Virginia for decades after 1865.

By the early twentieth century, the University of Virginia, Charlottesville, and Albemarle County had reimagined themselves as an idyllic landscape steeped in a heroic Revolutionary era. A 1926 pamphlet extolled Charlottesville (with its "National Shrine, a great university") as the site where Founding Father Thomas Jefferson ultimately honed the ideas that made him a "mighty son of Old Virginia in drafting the Magna Charta [*sic*] of American Independence."[9] The pamphlet further described the University of Virginia as "for a century the predominant force in Southern education," adding that it had been "founded, built and spiritually created by Thomas Jefferson." In lauding Jefferson, the pamphlet also noted that there were "a number of old mansions" in the area "of unusual beauty," all "designed in whole or in part by Thomas Jefferson." Absent in the decades of mythologizing about Jefferson, the University of Virginia, and Central Virginia was an acknowledgment that the countryside of "mansions" was in fact a landscape sustained by human bondage. Also absent was any recognition of more than half the local population: the enslaved people who shaped and fired every brick in the Academical Village, terraced the Lawn, dug cellars and foundations, carved stone for the Rotunda, tended gardens, cooked meals, maintained classrooms, managed laboratories, and otherwise maintained both the University and all those "mansions."

After Emancipation represents an important intervention and correction to that long history of mythologizing the past at the University of Virginia, in Charlottesville, and in Virginia. The essays collected here

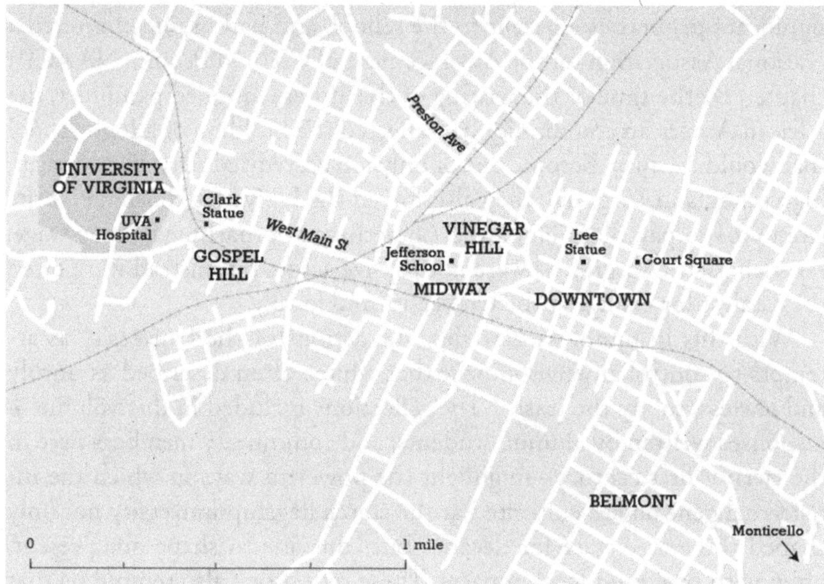

Charlottesville in 1963. (Nat Case)

tell a fuller story about the century after 1865, elucidating the University's intellectual commitment to white supremacy across generations that shaped not only the local community but the state and beyond. Taken together, they build upon scholarship that has examined other elements of this history not fully covered here. *After Emancipation* thus seeks to extend the fine research of others on, for example, eugenics at UVA, the destruction of Charlottesville's Vinegar Hill neighborhood in the 1960s, and the Black student experience at the University since the 1960s.[10]

This volume also alters the narrative by acknowledging the resistance, resilience, and energy of African Americans during Reconstruction and during the Jim Crow era. It further makes explicit the role of African Americans in this exchange: the University's ideologies were enacted upon a community of now free people who, just two years after emancipation, would exert their political clout through universal suffrage. In a letter to city leaders written in 1867, Black community members demanded, among other things, that the newly enfranchised never again be deprived of the vote.[11] Moreover, as whites were writing their Arcadian narrative, the African American community had created a Piedmont Industrial Land Improvement Company, which led to the purchase of significant properties adjacent to the school, and had in 1918 chartered a National Association for the Advancement of Colored People (NAACP) chapter. By the time of the writing of the aforementioned pamphlet, the African American community had effected the building of a high school that would, by 1929, become one of only ten accredited African American high schools in Virginia. They also forced the University hospital by the late 1940s to pay Black employees something approaching a living wage. As such, Black Virginians were not passive actors but instead were often the catalyst for change at the University and locally.

With this in mind, we can view the actions of the University as attempts to control an environment that whites often described as unruly and lawless, to say the least.[12] The reflections included in this volume—responses written by alumni, students, and community members here in the twenty-first century—highlight the powerful ways in which the intellectual genealogies cultivated at the state's flagship university not only shaped the entire state for decades but continue to shape our present, often with profound local impacts. These reflections also remind us that the University of Virginia and Charlottesville today have changed and diversified in important ways while simultaneously highlighting just how much work remains to be done to dismantle the afterlives of slavery.

In 2013, visitors to the University of Virginia could find neither any significant public acknowledgment of enslaved people at the University nor any commemorations of African American lives at the school. The historical fact of nearly two hundred years of African American presence at the school was largely hidden or ignored. Students walking from the two main libraries to the Rotunda, to the Lawn, or just strolling through on their way to the "Corner" commercial district, just northwest of the school, passed a reconstructed brick garden wall with a plaque that had been there for over sixty years. The bronze marker—part of that Arcadian narrative—hailed Thomas Jefferson as the man who "designed and built" those very walls. If, perchance, students found their way to the Rotunda's cryptoporticus, and then stopped to read an inscription on an archway threshold in that subterranean passageway, they would have found brief mention of enslaved people at the University in another plaque more interested in realizing "Thomas Jefferson's design for the University of Virginia." Similarly, there existed no official institutional history that did much more than acknowledge Jefferson's founding role and discuss long-serving professors and administrators from the college's first 150 years or so. UVA president Teresa Sullivan, responding in 2013 to recommendations from student groups, alumni, and Dr. Marcus Martin, the chief diversity officer, created the President's Commission on Slavery and the University (PCSU). That commission's charge was simple: research the history of slavery and the enslaved at the University before 1865; hold an educational conference; publish a report; and consider appropriate memorialization.

So much has happened since then president Sullivan issued that charge. For six years, the first commission remained the driving force behind much of the work to uncover, educate, and move toward some reconciliation with the University's difficult past. Inspired in a way by Pauli Murray's words—that "slavery had done such violence to the human spirit that the very memory of it was intolerable long after people had outlived it" and that "true emancipation lies in the acceptance of the whole past"—the commission inaugurated a process of community engagement, listening, atonement, and public education that is still ongoing both at UVA and now at more than ninety schools in several countries.[13] That historical reckoning, however, extended only to the end of the Civil War.

A lot has changed since 2013, even if much work remains to be done in examining post-1865 history, both at the University and in the local area. During the slavery commission's tenure, American race politics exploded. The Black Lives Matter movement was born. White nationalist Dylann Roof murdered nine Black people at "Mother Emanuel"—Charleston's Emanuel African Methodist Episcopal (AME) Church. Following this horrible mass shooting, South Carolina removed its Confederate flag from the state capitol building. Danville, Virginia, just over one hundred miles from Charlottesville, similarly removed the Confederate flag from city property. That year would prove to be a flashpoint for a resurgence of the white supremacist alt-right movement. The symbols of the Confederacy, so beloved in the University's secession period and mythologized endlessly there through decades of Lost Cause celebrations, once again became contested space. During that period, the city of Charlottesville also created a Blue Ribbon Commission on Race, Memorials, and Public Spaces (BRC) to examine the city's history and landscape as part of a process to make recommendations about public memorials in the city. That project focused on twentieth-century public installations owned by the city that were hallmarks of the age of segregation, but its work indirectly shed light on the University of Virginia's own complicated landscape of Lost Cause memorialization and uncritical celebration of white supremacists from the school's past. To fulfill the promise of that vital work,

Statue of Robert E. Lee in downtown Charlottesville (removed 2021). (Sanjay Suchak)

acknowledging and atoning for enslavement in institutional history, the University of Virginia would need a blue-ribbon commission of its own.

In 2017, after the BRC released its report recommending recontextualization, removal, or relocation of several statues, white supremacists led by the alt-right repeatedly descended on Charlottesville's public spaces, ostensibly to rally in support of Lost Cause statues of Robert E. Lee and Stonewall Jackson. Those statues, situated in what were whites-only parks for decades (and, in at least one case, on land where a Black neighborhood known as McKee Row once stood), represented monumental celebrations of white rule. Twenty-first-century white nationalists wanted that celebration to continue as they sought once again to claim those public spaces as places where only white people would be welcome.

The Ku Klux Klan, under heavy police protection and countered by a much larger group of antiracist demonstrators, marched to Charlottesville's Jackson statue in July 2017. A month later, a new generation of white supremacists, often heavily armed, descended upon the University and Charlottesville. Those alt-right events, largely organized by two University of Virginia alumni, turned Charlottesville into a battleground for two days. Hundreds marched through the University of Virginia grounds, finally attacking a small group of students and local residents protecting the Jefferson statue on the north plaza of the Rotunda. The torch-bearing white nationalist mob came to claim Thomas Jefferson as their intellectual ancestor—someone similarly committed to white rule and to a vision of the United States as a white republic. That mob attacked the students and locals who stood in peaceful resistance to them. The mob returned to Charlottesville the next day to reclaim Robert E. Lee as another of their intellectual forebears. With area residents and University alumni among their ranks, they also sought to reclaim the park as a whites-only space. At each terrible moment that summer, those committed to an inclusive and equitable twenty-first-century America led peaceful counterprotests and often outnumbered the alt-right demonstrators. When it was over, after armed white nationalists repeatedly attacked those counterprotesters, dozens who resisted the white supremacists had been grievously injured, and four people had died.

Shocking and terrible as it most certainly was, the event served as a painful reminder that although many locally evinced a commitment to diversity, equity, and inclusion, the legacies of slavery and what Du Bois defined as the "new state serfdom of Black folk" are still all around us—they shape our communities, they shape contemporary inequality, they shape people's worldviews.[14] Without a doubt, "slavery had established a measure of man and a ranking of life and worth that has yet to be undone." The University of Virginia, responding to the PCSU's insistent reminders about the long shadows cast by slavery and racism, moved quickly to establish a second commission focused on the next one hundred years that would seek to understand how slavery's "perils and dangers still threatened and that even now lives hung in the balance."[15] In summer 2018, retiring president Teresa Sullivan and her successor, James P. Ryan, agreed to establish the President's Commission on the University in the Age of Segregation (PCUAS). This new commission would continue the work of the PCSU, spending several years examining a century of the school's history after 1865.

The PCUAS officially launched in fall 2018 as a shared community project led by both the University and the executive director of the Jefferson School African American Heritage Center. Such a shared framework represented an implicit admission that the extensive history of town-gown relations had long been defined by the University's power to ignore the community or bend the community to its will. Several years of listening and engagement had made it clear that empowering the community to tailor the commission process was a necessary precursor to the work that would follow. This new commission dove into a much more expansive research project focusing on post-emancipation and Jim Crow–era history. Working on multiple fronts, the PCUAS sought to document white supremacy at the University from 1865 into the 1960s, to attempt to create an intellectual genealogy of alumni and their impact on public policy as they largely remained committed to white rule over that same time period, and to demonstrate how that intellectual genealogy was in many ways a continuation of the one developed by Jefferson and his contemporaries as they created Virginia's first public university. This new commission also aimed to assist the Jefferson School African American Heritage Center in its continued quest to document more fully the history of Black Charlottesville after emancipation. The strength of this collaboration lies in bringing UVA into direct dialogue with the community within which it resides and upon which it acts, thereby enabling the community to shape the commission's direction and work.

In anticipation of UVA's main library repository closing in 2019 for a massive renovation project, the team dove first into scanning a century of student publications and local newspapers before the stacks there were demolished. The commission made great progress by the end of 2019 and prepared to turn to the official University archives in 2020. The novel coronavirus pandemic arrived in March 2020, however, closing libraries and sending everyone home to socially distance. The pandemic also exposed how Black Americans have been "disproportionately affected by the pandemic in the United States and are not having their right to health fulfilled," a painful but powerful reminder of the ways in which the afterlives of slavery continue to shape the present.[16] That summer, the murder of George Floyd in Minneapolis captured national attention and, for some white Americans, may have represented a new understanding of the disparate impacts of policing in Black communities and on Black Americans—and how those impacts can be traced back to the era of slavery and measured, horrifically, in police shootings and murders of unarmed Black people.[17] Floyd's murder triggered a national wave of protests, complete with renewed demands for cities and universities to take down Confederate statues and remove the names of racists from buildings.

Over that summer of 2020, the Memorial to Enslaved Laborers at the University of Virginia became a site of repeated silent protests, with masked and socially distanced participants kneeling in honor of George Floyd and in support of Black lives. In September, Albemarle County removed the "Johnny Reb" standing soldier statue from the courthouse lawn in downtown Charlottesville. Renewed calls for UVA to remove the George Rogers Clark statue (a monument to Native American erasure, if not genocide) and the Frank Hume Memorial Fountain (a monument to a Confederate soldier and spy), to contextualize or remove the standing soldier in the Confederate cemetery on University property, to rename buildings named after enslavers and racists, and to more fully come to terms with its own built landscape echoed loudly across the grounds.[18] The pandemic may have continued to rage on well beyond that summer, but the calls for change did not diminish. By the end of 2021, transformations in the landscape were evident: the George Rogers Clark monument had come down, and the fountain was covered up as a team worked to remove the inscribed tribute to Frank Hume from the structure.

The PCUAS research project and charge have remained centered on the long history of racism at the school from 1865 to 1965, but the entire commission unanimously demanded that the research and educational effort should, in light of events locally and nationally since 2017, focus on anti-Black racism's local and regional manifestations as well as the University's evolving role in its design and maintenance. As Saidiya Hartman argues, "If slavery persists as an issue in the political life of Black America, it is not because of an antiquarian obsession with bygone days or the burden of a too-long memory, but because Black lives are still imperiled and devalued by a racial calculus and a political arithmetic that were entrenched centuries ago." Current events had brought into painful focus the reality that what we were researching and teaching traced the long "afterlife of slavery—skewed life chances, limited access to health and education, premature death, incarceration, and impoverishment" that define the experiences of so many American people of color today.[19] Thus, the commission had to ask: How did racist ideas honed by faculty and students at the University go on to shape public policy and therefore have injurious and destructive effects on Black Virginians?

Current events soon demonstrated just how important our research was. Several months into the commission's first year, a political scandal erupted in Richmond. Images emerged that allegedly showed Governor Ralph Northam either in blackface or in a Klan costume in his 1984 medical school yearbook. Soon afterward, his Virginia Military Institute (VMI) undergraduate yearbook picture also surfaced. At VMI, with its long history of Lost Cause mythologizing about Confederate military acumen, Northam had the nickname "Coonman" as a cadet, almost certainly referencing a racial slur from the age of segregation. Days after these accusations, Attorney General Mark Herring admitted that he had worn blackface while a student at UVA. In October, police murders of unarmed Black Americans once again became national news after

Atatiana Jefferson was shot to death in her own Texas home by a police officer. Racist lampooning, a century of falsehoods about the Confederate cause, and police violence against unarmed Black Americans are all part of the long afterlife of slavery—an insistent story about cultivating and maintaining white supremacy.

Soon, in response to those revelations about the Virginia governor and attorney general, yearbooks became a source of intense scrutiny, and UVA's *Corks and Curls* yearbook became the subject of particular focus. In spring 2018, before the new Age of Segregation commission had even been formed, Professor Kirt von Daacke taught a Pavilion Seminar at UVA that had students examining yearbooks. Those early research findings were quite revealing: the UVA yearbook had at least a half-century of brutal racism as the wallpaper of student life. Through print images alone, the honing of the ideologies and practices of white supremacy at Virginia's flagship state university was plainly visible. In fall 2018, the commission began a systematic examination of all the yearbooks, and by January 2019 it had thousands of images from the yearbooks alone, not to mention from other student publications. The vast majority of that material was vicious and anti-Black. The yearbook's name, originally a pair of terms for doing well or performing poorly in class that dated to 1840 or earlier, had by the 1880s become a winking double entendre, both for the older term and then for the racist practices of blackface minstrelsy (applying burnt cork to the face and donning a curly-haired wig). The yearbooks and other student publications confirmed the wisdom of the commission's decision to remain focused on that long history of anti-Black racism, but they also revealed so much more.

Our research quickly exposed a University community that was not only committed to developing and promoting the Lost Cause ideology in the years after 1865 but also deeply invested in wholesale racism in a wide variety of forms: blackface theatrical and musical performance, anti-Black "race science" investigations, eugenics, an emerging late nineteenth-century commitment to one-party rule by a white Democratic Party, shaping public policy to perpetuate white rule, a penchant for mob violence, and (especially after 1902) reclaiming public space as whites-only space. The records also often revealed a concomitant commitment to misogyny, to antisemitism, to removal and erasure of Indigenous peoples, and to racist lampooning of other ethnicities and nationalities deemed foreign and non-white. Thus, those many forms of marginalization and domination need to be understood as threads in the institution's and in white Virginia's long commitment to white supremacy. To fully trace the contours of anti-Black racism here, we must simultaneously address the patriarchal, nativist, and elitist assumptions of the nearly all-white flagship state university.

After Emancipation revises and reprints essays from the first public acknowledgment and education effort by the PCUAS: UVA and the History of Race. This series of thirteen articles appeared online in *UVA Today* between summer 2019 and spring 2021. McGregor McCance of UVA Communications was instrumental in shepherding this challenging series from idea to published reality. The series, and this volume, were never intended to interpret every event from 1865 on—they do not present a total history. Instead, taken together, they highlight some significant and difficult historical themes and challenge readers to connect those pasts to our twenty-first-century world.

Although we could not tell every story, we have endeavored to tell the truth, in plain terms, about aspects of the institution's difficult history: mythologizing about the causes and the meaning of the Civil War, articulating the Lost Cause, racist lampooning of Black Americans, engaging in racial terrorism, erasing Native Americans from U.S. history, marginalizing and othering Asians and Asian Americans, creating and enforcing racial segregation, producing "scientific" knowledge in support of a priori racist beliefs, and resisting school integration. Taken together, those ideas and practices represent the continuation of an intellectual genealogy dating back to the school's founding in the early nineteenth century that shaped the University, and Virginia, for decades after 1865. Those threads run from Thomas Jefferson and his contemporaries through generations of students and faculty. They also stretch geographically, spreading ideas and practices far beyond the University grounds.

This volume also emphasizes the persistence of Black Virginians and underscores the fact that they were not defined by their oppressors. Instead, they built community organizations, schools, businesses, and churches, and in those ways they resisted the ideologies of the age of segregation. Generation after generation strove to achieve the full fruits of freedom in America. The essays in this volume make no attempt to be comprehensive; there remain many other stories to tell that will further broaden our understanding of Charlottesville's and the University's complicated history. The President's Commission on the University in the Age of Segregation's research and community engagement is meant to continue building upon the foundational work of the slavery commission as it fearlessly follows truth wherever it may lead—and the University remains at the beginning of that work even today. Much more research, acknowledgment, and education await.

Finally, this volume listens to the voices of twenty-first-century people of color. It allows those people most affected by the University's interventions to comment on the results of its marginalizing activity. Now that we are telling the truth and acknowledging this history, the research has revealed much more fully the University's important and extensive role in shaping and perpetuating white rule for so long. *After Emancipation* attempts to move just such a conversation forward by pairing revised versions of the original *UVA Today* essays with reflections from community members.

The format, a sort of call-and-response between truth-telling history pieces and contemporary community reflections about history, meaning, and identity, is deeply informed by the work of Professor Rhondda Robinson Thomas, our friend and colleague at Clemson University who authored *Call My Name, Clemson: Documenting the Black Experience in an American University Community*. Her fine book, centered on her research and personal experience in studying Clemson's fraught history, includes response passages from descendants, students, alumni, faculty, and staff. Although this volume lacks an individual journey weaving through the whole book, it was nonetheless inspired by the power of Thomas's formula. Even without a single authorial voice and experience at its center, we hope this volume's essays and community reflections further the conversation about what comes after acknowledgment and atonement. *After Emancipation* ultimately seeks to expose directions in which the commission, the University, and the nation might move if we are to make meaningful amends in the twenty-first century.

Notes

1. Address of the Southern Rights Association of the University of Virginia, December 19, 1850, Jefferson's University—The Early Life, accessed January 29, 2022, http://juel.iath.virginia.edu/node/343?doc=/juel_display/addresses/Public/SRA.
2. Randolph H. McKim, *A Soldier's Recollections: Leaves from the Diary of a Young Confederate, with an Oration on the Motives and Aims of the Soldiers of the South* (Norwood, Mass.: Plimpton Press, 1910), 1–2, https://docsouth.unc.edu/fpn/mckim/mckim.html.

3. Report of Maj. Gen. Philip H. Sheridan, U.S. Army, commanding expedition, in *The War of the Rebellion: A Compilation of the Official Records of the Union and Confederate Armies* (Washington, D.C., 1880–1901), ser. 1, vol. 46, pt. 1, p. 477. Sheridan's report stated that his army "would remain two days at this point [Charlottesville], for the purpose of resting, refitting, and destroying the railroad."
4. Steve Longenecker, "Randolph H. McKim: Lost Cause Conservative, Episcopal Liberal," *Anglican and Episcopal History* 87, no. 3 (2018): 266–67.
5. See Anne Freudenberg and John Casteen, eds., "John B. Minor's Civil War Diary," *Magazine of Albemarle County History* 22 (1964): 45–55.
6. Diary of Sarah Ann Graves Strickler Fife, March 6, 1865, Special Collections, University of Virginia Library.
7. Frederick Douglass, speech on the occasion of the Twenty-First Anniversary of Emancipation in the District of Columbia, April 16, 1883, in *Frederick Douglass: Selected Speeches and Writings*, ed. Philip S. Foner (Chicago: Lawrence Hill Books, 1999), 658.
8. Thomas Jefferson, letter to Edward Coles, August 25, 1814, Founders Online, accessed January 29, 2022, https://founders.archives.gov/documents/Jefferson/03-07-02-0439; Edward Younger, ed., *Inside the Confederate Government: The Diary of Robert Garlick Hill Kean* (New York: Oxford University Press, 1957), 208–10 (diary entries dated June 1 and June 27, 1865).
9. *Historic Beauty in Charlottesville, and Albemarle County Virginia* (Charlottesville, Va.: Chamber of Commerce, 1926), 3.
10. Gregory Michael Dorr, *Segregation's Science: Eugenics and Society in Virginia* (Charlottesville: University of Virginia Press, 2008); Scot A. French, Hannah Brown Ayers, and Lance Warren, *That World Is Gone: Race and Displacement in a Southern Town,* directed and edited by Hannah Brown Ayers and Lance Warren (Field Studio, 2010); Claudrena Harold, Black Fire at UVA, https://blackfireuva.com/.
11. Letter from Committee of the Colored People to Col. Thos. J. Randolph, May 13, 1867, *Charlottesville Chronicle,* May 25, 1867. See Scot French, "African American Civic Activism and the Making of Jefferson High School," in *Pride Overcomes Prejudice: A History of Charlottesville's African American School,* ed. Andrea Douglas (Charlottesville, Va.: Jefferson School African American Heritage Center, 2013), 35.
12. The McKee block (also known as McKee Row), owned by African American freedman and millionaire John West, was described as a "forlorn rookery" consisting of "ramshackle housing" where "boys from the area were hanging around the Levy Opera House," disturbing its white patrons. As early as 1912, white locals called the street "an eyesore to the whole town" while already seeking to evict Black residents by purchasing all of the lots there. See C. B. McKennie letter, April 26, 1912, in Records of Charlottesville,

Virginia, Law Firm of Perkins & Perkins, Special Collections, University of Virginia Library. The Albemarle County Board of Supervisors passed a resolution in 1914 "to give the city the street adjacent to the courthouse between Jefferson and High Streets." The thirty-foot-wide dirt alley, used principally for horse sales and hitching racks, was offered on the condition that the city should purchase "the old McKee property" and "erect on it a public school for white children." See "A Guide to the History and Gardens of Jackson Park," accessed January 27, 2022, https://stowekeller.com/Portfolio/CityParks/JacksonPark/JacksonPark_History&Gardens.html.

13. The PCSU worked steadfastly to create permanent, visible results: the naming of two new buildings after enslaved people, permanent interpretive exhibits centering the lives and labor of the enslaved at the University, two major conferences on slavery and universities, meaningful rituals of remembrance, four years of community engagement, a multiauthor interdisciplinary book on slavery at UVA, an annual summer camp for high school students (UVA's Cornerstone Summer Institute), a consortium encouraging other schools to do similar work that has grown continuously for several years, and a significant memorial that was completed in 2020. The University has also updated the plaque on the garden wall, which used to claim that Thomas Jefferson designed and built the garden walls. It now correctly acknowledges the role of enslaved people in building and maintaining the school for half a century.
14. W. E. B. Du Bois, *Black Reconstruction in America* (New York: Free Press, 1998), 128.
15. Saidiya V. Hartman, *Lose Your Mother: A Journey along the Atlantic Slave Route* (New York: Farrar, Straus and Giroux, 2007), 6.
16. Marita Vasquez Reyes, "The Disproportional Impact of COVID-19 on African Americans," *Health and Human Rights Journal* 22, no. 2 (2020): 299–307.
17. "Fatal Force," *Washington Post*, updated January 7, 2022, https://www.washingtonpost.com/graphics/investigations/police-shootings-database/.
18. University of Virginia President's Commission on the University in the Age of Segregation, "Memorialization and Mission at UVA," Report to President James E. Ryan, March 2020, accessed January 28, 2022, https://segregation.virginia.edu/wp-content/uploads/2020/06/Memorialization-and-Mission-at-UVA-Committee-Report-March-2020.pdf.
19. Hartman, *Lose Your Mother*, 6.

Truth-Telling and Coming to Terms with UVA's Hard Histories

MCGREGOR MCCANCE

In September 2019, *UVA Today* launched a special series that brought to light the work of those who have researched the role of the University of Virginia during the decades of racial segregation in the nineteenth and twentieth centuries. These are stories of discrimination and oppression. They are also stories of inspiration and determination. Together, they contribute to the University's efforts to explore and present a more complete account of its past so that it can better fulfill its values in the future.

The *UVA Today* series featured stories written by faculty authors and by researchers who serve as members of the President's Commission on the University in the Age of Segregation (PCUAS) or who conduct research as part of the commission's responsibilities. Established in 2018 at the direction of then president Teresa A. Sullivan and supported by President Jim Ryan, the commission complements the findings and recommendations of the President's Commission on Slavery and the University (PCSU), which concluded its formal work in 2018.

For *UVA Today*, the new series provided an opportunity to support the work of an important University initiative and to bring forward a form of storytelling that differed from its traditional approach of staff-written articles. Some of the content addressed uncomfortable topics and presented difficult facts about the institution during the era of segregation. Our intention was not to inflame but to contribute to the University's commitment to fully and honestly examine that part of its history by sharing stories that came out of this research with our full audience.

UVA Today interviewed Kirt von Daacke, assistant dean and professor of history; Andrea Douglas, director of the Jefferson School African American Heritage Center; and Louis Nelson, vice provost for academic outreach and professor of architectural history, via email to discuss the work of the commission and the *UVA Today* series (Douglas and von Daacke cochaired the commission). They answered collectively.

Q. What's the mission of the President's Commission on the University in the Age of Segregation (PCUAS)?

A. Our mission is to explore and report on UVA's history during the era of segregation and examine the enduring legacies of that past, especially as it connects to the Charlottesville-Albemarle community. By design, we are continuing the path-breaking work of the President's Commission on Slavery and the University by taking that research at least through the century after the Civil War.

In the spirit of the first commission, we are focusing on community engagement, education, and memorialization as part of an open process informed by the restorative justice model. This means we are not just telling a more accurate history, but we are telling our shared story as truth-telling and the first step toward atonement.

UVA is committed to telling its own story with the rigor and integrity that we expect of our students. If we wish to be a university that is both great and good, we must be a university that can look clear-eyed at our own history no matter how ugly. Only when we are honest about our past can we look to our future with great expectations. Our students deserve nothing less.

Q. Is the research uncovering facts or stories that have not been told or widely known? Will these stories surprise people?

A. The commission's first job, as we see it, is to collect all the amazing historical research on UVA and the Charlottesville-Albemarle area that's been done over the past couple decades and to concentrate that research in a single location. Some of the necessary research has already been done by faculty and graduate students who were at UVA well before the commission was founded.

As well, so much work has been done by community members and organizations in the past few decades. Our job is first to collect as much of that existing work and begin to stitch it all together in telling multiple complicated and interconnected stories that change our understanding of UVA and its past.

We are doing that work now and will also fill in the research gaps as necessary. Many of our institution's difficult stories have indeed been told, but UVA has not promoted that work publicly as part of a truth-telling project until recently. We do think that many people will find the history we uncover and share surprising; we all have a lot to learn about the history of our institution from the Civil War to the modern era.

Response
A Reflection on the President's Commissions, Their Work, and Telling the Truth

COUNTESS HUGHES

I GRADUATED FROM the University of Virginia in 1986 and then again in 1988 with a graduate degree in counselor education with an emphasis in higher education. I have been working at universities ever since, including now at UVA. After I graduated from UVA, I learned that my ancestors were slaves at Monticello for many generations and that my grandfather was born in Albemarle County. He was born free; his father was not. Something must have been pulling me here because I knew nothing about UVA when I decided to attend.

The work of the President's Commission on Slavery and the University and the President's Commission on the University in the Age of Segregation is personal to me. The hard work and the research being done are incredible. We must consider fully the past to make decisions in the present that will positively impact the future of all at the University and all in the community.

The information provided in these essays about UVA and about those who attended, taught, and led UVA's involvement in things like the Lost Cause propaganda, the KKK, and eugenics was disturbing—but not necessarily surprising. It was sad to have it in front of my face, in black and white, that my alma mater and prior students could be involved in something so detrimental to a group of people. At the same time, it was inspirational to read how Black people like Burkley Bullock, who was born a slave, eventually came to own 75 acres of land and founded a company with eight other men to extend aid to persons of limited means so they could purchase homes. This reminded me of my ancestor who, in 1865, was given an acre of land by Thomas Jefferson Randolph to build a church but also came to own 130 acres of his own land. Inspirational stories of triumph in the face of adversity.

UVA students, leaders, and faculty have also been the face of change for the University of Virginia. Reading how Colgate Darden, UVA's third president, was the first to envision a school that educated not just the top tier of elite white men was a bright spot (and led to my being able to attend UVA). For his efforts, people burned crosses in front of the president's house on Carr's Hill. It is not easy for anyone trying to go against what is considered the norm. Are those people burning crosses that much different from the people, organized by alumni, walking down the Lawn with burning tiki torches?

Students like Staige Blackford, the editor of the *Cavalier Daily*, supported integration and the changing of the student body. Students like Gregory Swanson, UVA's first Black student, made it possible for me to be here and inspire the current calls for change.

I like to believe that we are beyond some of the things that happened in the past, but then I read about how the expansion of the University and the healthcare system contributed to the razing of working-class Black neighborhoods in Charlottesville such as Vinegar Hill and Gospel Hill. I am conflicted, because if the University had not expanded and allowed the admission of Blacks and women, I would not be the person I am today.

So I ask: Can we look at how that razing compares to today's gentrification and how we can avoid yesterday's mistakes? Today, UVA is working to be a part of the solution, but I can't help but think that if information that is available now had been available and widely distributed earlier, we might have saved some of the affordable housing that has been redeveloped so we would not have to re-create those opportunities. I worry that we will continue to make the same mistakes and harm future generations as we have in the past.

These stories of discrimination and oppression, inspiration and determination, are as old as time. Such stories have been told over and over. They are being told again. Some who read the stories will be angry or surprised because the history they know will be upended—or things they did not know will be revealed. For some, things that they already knew are now in print for all to see. As Kirt von Daacke, Andrea Douglas, and

Louis Nelson put it, "Only when we are honest about our past can we look to our future with great expectations." It is great to know that people are interested in—and dedicated to finding—stories that have not been told publicly. Why were they not heard in the 1800s, 1900s, 2000s? For the same reason that Thomas Jefferson kept my ancestors enslaved yet talked about equality. It is hard to go against the grain of society. It is hard to be brave and counter the narrative and share your privilege.

Will knowing these stories make people want to do better? I hope so. This history has been UVA's since its founding. Sometimes I think that Thomas Jefferson is outraged and red-faced, knowing that the descendant of his gardener has two degrees from his University, but then I would also like to think that better angels would prevail and he would admit his failings and short-sightedness and would want to make amends.

Maybe people who have not noticed these stories in the past will notice them now. I hope they will want to read a truth they have not heard in the past. Maybe a more extensive truth will help people understand and motivate us to do more to make a better future. Only time will tell. We will keep telling the stories until there is concrete and meaningful change.

The Lost Cause through Judge Duke's Eyes

ELIZABETH R. VARON

Why did Charlottesville's white citizens choose to erect a statue to Confederate general Robert E. Lee in 1924—nearly sixty years after the Civil War? One clue can be found in the personal papers of Judge R. T. W. Duke Jr., held at the University of Virginia's Albert and Shirley Small Special Collections Library.

Duke—who literally presided over the Lee and Jackson monument dedication ceremonies as the designated "chair" of each event—was a fixture at Confederate Memorial Day celebrations and monument dedications all across Virginia in the early twentieth century. He was known for his fiery defense of slavery and attacks on emancipation and Reconstruction. The record of Duke's public role as a Confederate memorialist, when read together with his extensive private diaries and memoirs, provides a window into the "Lost Cause" creed—and into the University's role in promulgating it.

Duke was born in Charlottesville in 1853. His father, R. T. W. Duke Sr. (1822–1898), attended UVA as a student and then served on its Board of Visitors. A successful lawyer, Duke Sr. served during the Civil War as a colonel in the Confederate army, and, after the war, in the U.S. Congress, where he protested against extending citizenship rights to African Americans. The younger Duke attended UVA from 1870 to 1874, studying law under John B. Minor and editing the *Virginia University Magazine*. Duke Jr. then embarked on his own legal career, serving as judge of the Corporation (Circuit) Court and as commonwealth's attorney for Albemarle County in the early twentieth century.[1]

Duke Jr. was reared on the dogma of the Lost Cause, the pro-Confederate interpretation of Southern history that prevailed among white Southerners in the decades after the Civil War. According to this mythology, slavery was a benign institution; secession was a constitutional defense of state sovereignty; the wartime emancipation of the slaves was a travesty; the Yankee victory in the war was a triumph of might over right; and the postwar experiment in Black citizenship was a failure, necessitating the "redemption" of the South by former Confederates. The essence of the Lost Cause was that the Civil War was not truly lost and could yet be won by new forms of racial proscription and segregation. Duke's extensive memoirs are a compendium of Lost Cause talking points. Of slavery, Duke wrote that his own family's treatment of their slaves "was so kind," and the slaves' affection for their owners "so sincere," that he "never saw any of the 'horrors' of slavery—so called."

But other passages in Duke's memoirs contradict such claims of kindness and affection. The Duke household's "Mammy," an enslaved woman named Rose, he remembered as so "impatient of control" that she "required firmness in handling." The cook Jane was bought by his father in 1859 for $1,000, Duke recollected, to "save her" from the slave traders; as the historian Walter Johnson has noted, slaveowners often rationalized the act of buying human bodies as a benign way to "save" them from the market. Jane, Duke noted disapprovingly, was the first of the family's slaves to leave Charlottesville when freedom came at the end of the war. In further portrayals of the enslaved, Duke recalled that the housemaid Maria was so rebellious that his father sold her in 1858 or 1859. In these passages, Duke adhered to the dehumanizing chattel principle, whereby slaves were defined as property. But he also unwittingly revealed the discontent of the enslaved and their resistance to white control.[2]

When Duke wrote of secession and the Civil War, he expressed his implacable loathing of Northerners, Lincoln, and the Republican Party. In his passages on Union general Philip Sheridan's occupation of Charlottesville in March 1865, Duke vented his wrath at the Union soldier who led a raiding party that looted the Duke family's foodstuffs. "I would like to kill him even now," Duke fumed, "forty two years after the event—and I would like to do it slowly and with deliberation."

Duke's indignation at the Confederate surrender was somewhat tempered by his joy at Lincoln's assassination. "Lincoln was to us," he

"The Freedman's Bureau," drawn by Alfred R. Waud, *Harper's Weekly*, July 25, 1868. (Library of Congress)

remembered, "a clownish ape, who had brought on the war" and "stolen our slaves."[3] In recounting the war's immediate aftermath, Duke derided the Union soldiers and Freedmen's Bureau officials who were stationed in Charlottesville to facilitate the transition from slavery to freedom. The Union provost marshal provided the Duke family a guard to help it protect its property from theft, but the guard, a "puritanical down-easter," was not to Duke's liking, as the Northern man "sat a great deal with the negroes—read to them [and] prayed in most unctuous tones with them." In an anecdote meant to illustrate his preference for the old ways over the "new order of things," Duke related how a local white man gave a "good sound flogging" to a freedman, tasked with removing worms from tobacco plants, who "shirked his work" and became "saucy."[4]

Congressional Reconstruction, instituted by the Republicans in 1867, Duke deemed "the worst crime in the history of civilization," for it enfranchised African American men such as James T. S. Taylor, the Union army veteran who represented Albemarle County at the Virginia Constitutional Convention of 1867–68 (he was one of 24 Black men among the 104 delegates). The purpose of Reconstruction, Duke insisted, was to place the South "under the heel of the negro"; he trafficked, in other

Virginia Constitutional Convention of December 1867–April 1868, with twenty-four African American delegates attending. "The State Convention at Richmond, Va., in Session," *Frank Leslie's Illustrated Newspaper,* February 15, 1868. (Library of Virginia, https://www.virginiamemory.com/online-exhibitions/items/show/602)

words, in the Lost Cause myth of Reconstruction as a "tragic era" of "black rule"—a myth that flies in the face of the fact that even at the height of Congressional Reconstruction, Blacks were underrepresented in Southern politics. In Duke's worldview, former slaves had no place whatsoever in Virginia politics.[5]

Duke rejoiced in the 1877 overthrow of Reconstruction by ex-Confederates and sought to prevent the return of Black people to political life. He campaigned, for example, against the Readjuster movement, which tried to fuse disgruntled white farmers and marginalized Black voters in Virginia into a new coalition. Duke's politics went hand-in-hand with his Confederate memorialization activities. He became a popular speaker on the Confederate circuit and at Democratic Party events in Virginia in the early twentieth century, and he used both settings to hurl blame at the North and cast the Confederacy as faultless. At a tribute to the Confederate dead at Richmond's Oakwood Cemetery in May 1908, Duke defended the "deathless memory of an immortal cause," proclaiming that "slavery was right and emancipation a wrong and a robbery."

"Truth is Truth" and "must be fearlessly told," he cried out, adding, "Let it hurt who it may."

Duke repeatedly vowed in his speeches that he would never forgive the Republican Party—the "miserable hounds who fastened their fangs upon our throats and humiliated the prostrate South for the negro." Such sentiments won him acclaim from Democratic voters across the state. The *Richmond Times-Dispatch* declared in 1920 that "as a public speaker Judge Duke has no superior on the hustings or rostrum in all the broad bounds of Virginia."[6] Duke's long career as a mouthpiece for Lost Cause politics secured him a conspicuous place in the Jackson and Lee monument ceremonies in Charlottesville. Jurists like Duke made ideal marshals and orators at Confederate memorial events, as they could cloak the proceedings in the authority of the state. Duke appeared before audiences at Confederate events as "the Judge": a man who represented the legal regime of Jim Crow, which refers to laws enacted after the Civil War that enforced racial segregation.

On the evening of October 18, 1921, to inaugurate the Jackson ceremonies, Duke delivered an "address of welcome on behalf of the City of Charlottesville and County of Albemarle" to an assembly at the Jefferson Theater. On October 19, the day of the Jackson statue dedication, Duke

Unveiling of the Stonewall Jackson monument, 1921, Court Square, downtown Charlottesville. (University of Virginia Albert and Shirley Small Special Collections Library)

"presided over the exercises of the unveiling" and accepted the Jackson statue, a gift from local philanthropist Paul McIntire, on Charlottesville's behalf.[7] Duke played an equally visible role in the Lee statue's unveiling three years later. He served on the "Reunion Committee" of the local Sons of Confederate Veterans chapter that helped choreograph the monument dedication. Throngs of attendees gathered on May 20 to hear speeches by various ceremonial "commanders," such as W. McDonald Lee, a member of the Ku Klux Klan who described Union soldiers as "hired mercenaries" and proclaimed, "I believe them wrong today, sixty years after the war."

Duke moved to center stage on May 21, "Robert E. Lee Day." He participated in a massive procession that snaked its way through Charlottesville to the new Lee Park downtown. After "the multitude assembled about the statue," Duke was the first man they heard from as he assumed his role as the "presiding officer" of the day's events, welcoming a series of speakers who made the case that Robert E. Lee, a "Victor over Defeat," represented "the moral greatness of the Old South." In what the local paper called the "most dramatic moment" of the unveiling, Duke brought to center stage three-year-old Mary Walker Lee to pull the cord unveiling the monument. Duke introduced her, to the roar of the crowd, as "the great-granddaughter of the greatest man who ever lived."[8]

Duke's career not only reveals the racial animus at the heart of the Lost Cause creed but also reflects UVA's role in promulgating Lost Cause propaganda. UVA was an incubator for Lost Cause ideology, just as it had been an incubator for proslavery ideology and secessionism. The very term "Lost Cause" was coined in 1866 by Edward A. Pollard, who attended UVA in the late 1840s and became an influential editor and proslavery ideologue; his 1866 book *The Lost Cause: A New Southern History of the War of the Confederates* offered a defiant defense of slavery and secession, establishing the template that Duke and countless other UVA students and faculty would follow in glorifying the Confederacy.

Prominent Lost Cause spokesmen with UVA ties include Confederate veterans Robert E. Lee Jr. and Randolph H. McKim (former students), the influential writer Thomas Nelson Page (who had attended the UVA School of Law), and faculty member Charles Venable, who served during the war on Robert E. Lee's staff. Through figures such as these, UVA lent its institutional prestige to the Lost Cause creed.

Even as he rode the lecture circuit as an unreconstructed rebel, Duke himself remained very active and visible in University affairs as an officer in the Alumni Society and as a mentor and employer for UVA law

Postcard depicting the 1924 unveiling of the Robert E. Lee statue. (University of Alabama Libraries Special Collections)

students.[9] Moreover, UVA was central to the pageantry and propaganda of the monument unveilings in Charlottesville. Prominent among the featured speakers at the Stonewall Jackson unveiling was UVA president Edwin A. Alderman, who described Jackson as a "great Christian warrior." Alderman ceremonially presented the Jackson statue, on behalf of McIntire (himself a UVA alumnus), to Duke.

Among the many other alumni who participated in the program of events were Richard Heath Dabney, a professor of history at UVA and outspoken segregationist, and E. Lee Trinkle, the Democratic nominee for governor. Trinkle proclaimed, on an unmistakably political note, that Virginia would be "careful that the evil days of reconstruction shall not return."[10]

Three years later, UVA was the staging ground for the Lee unveiling ceremonies. The procession to Lee Park began at the Rotunda, and it included not only Governor Trinkle, assorted city and county officials, and the police and fire departments but also UVA faculty, officers, and students. Alumnus M. Ashby Jones of Atlanta gave the chief address, in which he referred to the "dark days of 'Reconstruction'" as "worse than war," and he celebrated the subsequent "social triumph of the South" as a "reincarnation of the spirit of Lee." Edwin Alderman was again a featured speaker, this time declaring Lee a "faultless" man who had become a "majestic ideal to a whole land." The festivities closed with a reception and "Grand Ball" in Memorial Gym.[11]

Southern whites were "conscious that the rituals of black memory represented a form of cultural resistance," the historian W. Fitzhugh Brundage has observed, and whites therefore "ensured that public spaces conspicuously excluded any recognition of the recalled past of blacks." One could never glean, from R. T. W. Duke's versions of the past, that Blacks had outnumbered whites in Albemarle County during the Civil War era, or that Blacks experienced the Union army's arrival in the city in March 1865 as a moment of liberation, or that more than 250 Black men born in Albemarle County fought in the Union army.

The Lost Cause creed sought to distort the South's complex history. We at modern-day UVA have a profound responsibility and unprecedented opportunity to recover that history in all its complexity.[12]

Notes

1. "Death of Editor-in-Chief: Judge R. T. W. Duke, Jr.," *Virginia Law Register,* April 1926, 757–60; Michael Peter Charles Smith, "Richard Thomas Walker Duke (1853–1926)," *Dictionary of Virginia Biography,* http://www.lva.virginia.gov/public/dvb/bio.asp?b=Duke_Richard_Thomas_Walker_1853-1926.
2. R. T. W. Duke Jr., "Recollections" (hereafter Duke Recollections), Duke Family Papers, Special Collections, University of Virginia Library, 1:17–26.
3. Duke Recollections, 1:216–17; 2:34–35.
4. Duke Recollections, 2:46–51.
5. Duke Recollections, 4:73–78.
6. Duke Recollections, 4:136–37; *Richmond Times Dispatch,* May 10, 1908; October 27, 1909; May 27, 1920.
7. *Charlottesville Daily Progress,* October 19, 1921; *Staunton News Leader,* September 22, 1921; "The Jackson Monument at Charlottesville, Va.," *Confederate Veteran,* February 1922, 44.
8. John S. Patton, ed., *Proceedings of the 37th Annual Reunion of the Virginia Division of the Grand Camp U.C.V.* (Charlottesville, Va.: Michie, 1924), 1–6, 13–15, 20–21, 39–41; Brendan Wolfe, "History Writ Aright," http://brendanwolfe.com/lee-monument/; *Charlottesville Daily Progress,* May 19, 20, 21, 1924.
9. Caroline E. Janney, "The Lost Cause," *Encyclopedia Virginia,* https://www.encyclopediavirginia.org/Lost_Cause_The; on Duke's alumni activities, see the *University of Virginia Alumni Bulletin* for the years 1894–1924.

10. *Proceedings of the Thirty-Fourth Annual Meeting of the Grand Camp Confederate Veterans Department of Virginia* (Petersburg, Va.: Presses of Frank A. Owen, 1922); *Staunton News Leader,* September 22, 1921; "The Stonewall Jackson Monument," *University of Virginia Alumni News,* September 1921, 327; *Charlottesville Daily Progress,* October 19, 1921.
11. Patton, *Proceedings; Charlottesville Daily Progress,* May 21, 1924; *University of Virginia Alumni News,* May 1924, 222–24.
12. W. Fitzhugh Brundage, *The Southern Past: A Clash of Race and Memory* (Cambridge, Mass.: Harvard University Press, 2005), 6–10. On African American soldiers from Charlottesville, see, for example, William Kurtz, "A Word on Methods: Recovering the Stories of Black Virginians in the Union Army," from the John L. Nau III Center for Civil War History blog, January 3, 2017, http://naucenter.as.virginia.edu/blog-page/401.

Response

The Man of My Dreams

A Letter to Judge R. T. W. Duke Jr.

WES BELLAMY

July 19, 2021

Dear Judge Duke,

When most people hear the phrase "You are the man of my dreams," adulation, euphoria, joy, and a sense of pleasure are usually associated with it. While I have never physically seen you—your face, your beard, your eyes, your stature, your tone, the overall embodiment of who you were and what you stood for as an individual—you are the person whom I have dreamt about for nearly five years. It is you, not Robert E. Lee, who has visited me in my dreams. It is you whom I am now proud to inform, "You lost."

According to Professor Elizabeth Varon's essay, you "literally presided over the Lee and Jackson monument dedication ceremonies as the designated 'chair' of each event" and were "a fixture at Confederate Memorial Day celebrations and monument dedications all across Virginia in the early twentieth century." You were "known for [your] fiery defense of slavery and attacks on emancipation and Reconstruction."

Born in Charlottesville in 1853, you attended and graduated from the University of Virginia and would undoubtedly have been one of the many people who argued on the side of "Wes Bellamy is destroying MY community/city/state." It is plausible to believe that you would have considered me to be an individual unworthy to be in your presence, one who should be given the same treatment as cattle. It was you who stated emphatically in your travels across the commonwealth, speaking at great length and with incomparable passion, that Robert E. Lee was the greatest man to ever walk the earth. It was you who often paraded around the Commonwealth of Virginia, your home city of Charlottesville, and Albemarle County proclaiming that the Confederacy had not lost the Civil War, that Reconstruction was an abomination, and that the white race would always reign supreme.

It is also plausible to believe that you passed down your thoughts, ideology, and inherent beliefs in white supremacy to your children, grandchildren, colleagues, friends, family, and generations to come after your death. In my dreams, in my reality, in my world for five consecutive years, I have come face-to-face with you and your offspring of covert and overt white supremacists. For my ancestors, I am proud to say that on the surface, once again, we have won.

After the removal of the Robert E. Lee statue erected in 1924, I stood on the pedestal vacated by the man on his horse. I, a Black man who has made Charlottesville his home, did the unthinkable. However, this victory is not just symbolic; it is tangible and only one step on the path to equity, liberation, and making our community "ours," not just "theirs." I remember the early days of this journey to remove the Confederate statues in our city and the pain, which often included condemnation by older Black folk. I cannot state how many times I have heard, "Wes, leave *them* people statues alone." "Ain't nobody worried about them statues. We got other stuff to deal with." Or "Wes, you stirring up stuff and going to get yourself and them pretty little baby girls of yours hurt. You going to get us all hurt." In reality, they weren't concerned with the removal of the statues. Their utterances were in fact the mirror image of the inner confidence that your offspring were imbued with. Black folk in our community have always been proud. Black folk in our community have always been willing to stand up. Black folk in our community have always looked out for each other. Black folk in our community have also often lived in fear of what "could" happen if we boldly go up against the status quo.

When you go up against the Judge Dukes of the area, "they" make an example out of you. They take your job away—as happened to me and Eugene Williams, a Charlottesville civil rights hero. They take your "prestigious" positions away—as was attempted in my situation, when in 2016 I faced a concerted campaign seeking to force my resignation from Charlottesville City Council and from Albemarle High School. They try to do everything in their power to break you down and make an example out of you in order to show the others that "they better not ever get out of line like the last one." Those sentiments and messages are painful reminders that white supremacy is still prevalent in communities with ties to the Confederacy. Those hateful ideas apparently run rampant across our nation as much today as 50, 100, or 150 years ago. But what happens when Black people win? This victory is for all marginalized communities. We have nothing to lose but our chains, and when we fight together, we win.

I saw you in my dreams for years, and in each dream, you lost. For years, I dreamt of standing on the same pedestal where Robert E. Lee's statue resided. On Sunday, July 11, 2021, that dream became a reality. In *our* Charlottesville, we have accomplished the unimaginable. Not just with statue removals but with tangible resource reallocation to address issues revolving around equity in our city. We have elected the first Black woman to serve as mayor. We have had two Black people serve on the city council for the first time in history. We have held the University of Virginia accountable for its shortcomings, and we continue to do so with bold community collaboration.

In *our* Charlottesville, we accept all challenges. Even those that come from the Confederates. I am proud to stand in *my* city a little battered, a little bruised, and having lost a couple of battles . . . but undefeated in all acts of war. #NewCville

Thanks, Judge Duke. I haven't had that dream in a week.

Dr. Wes Bellamy

Blackface and the Rise of a Segregated Society

ASHLEY SCHMIDT AND KIRT VON DAACKE

In 1867, just over two years after the Civil War ended in defeat for the Confederacy, the University of Virginia had returned to full enrollment. Former Confederate soldiers and those too young to have fought—490 students in all—had come back to the school. In December, the student editors of the *Virginia University Magazine* opined about the "humiliation of living in these days of Conventions and Freedmen's Bureaus" and complained about "negrophilism"—their term for attempts to include African Americans in the state constitutional reform process.[1] This malice was a response to state and local politics at the time. At a meeting in April 1867, white political leaders led a failed attempt to court Black voters by pointing out the advantages of white rule. During the meeting, Fairfax Taylor, a vocal supporter of the rights of freedmen to vote, serve on juries, and attend the University, won over many of the Black men in the audience.[2] Ultimately, Taylor's son, James T. S. Taylor, would win election as a delegate representing Albemarle County at the State Constitutional Convention in Richmond.[3]

Isabella Gibbons, who had been enslaved just a couple of years earlier and was then working as a teacher in the local Freedmen's School, noted: "We have lived to see the fortieth Congress and to behold a change of affairs. The rebels begin to see the error of their way at last. . . . They say 'the colored people are not only free but have a right to vote. . . . They [the freedpeople] are a good people, and so fond of their old masters, they will do what we want they should. Most of them love us, and have forgotten what happened while they were slaves. They know we are their friends.'" Gibbons keenly observed the local reality when she explained, "This is a grand story for them to tell, but let us answer them. Can we forget the crack of the whip, cowhide, whipping-post, the auction-block . . . ? Have we forgotten . . . those horrible cruelties . . . ?" "No, we have not," she added, "nor ever will." Despite the best hopes of Gibbons, the Taylors, and thousands of other freedpeople, the reality was that white locals remained committed to white rule and enraged by the reality of Black freedom.[4]

Student publications in the decades after the Civil War evinced a growing preoccupation with rationalizing what they termed "white rule" as the natural and proper state of affairs. An April 1868 article entitled "The Future Rulers of the World" posed the question, "What nation . . . will be the ruling power and direct the civilization of the world?"[5] The writers answered their own question, asserting, "It is plain that it will be the Caucasian race." The editors of the issue agreed, reminding readers that "we will *never* submit to negro rule."[6] Mythologizing about the "Lost Cause"—a post–Civil War, pro-Confederate interpretation of history—was accompanied by mocking dehumanization of African Americans through blackface minstrel shows and other stereotypes, all of which fed into a white supremacist ethos supporting the rise and continuation of the segregated state.

UVA student publications increasingly peddled in degrading characterizations of African Americans. By the early 1870s, the *Virginia University Magazine* began mentioning "negro minstrels," "dusky minstrel[s]," and "nagar minstrels" in fictional works mocking freedpeople or imagining enslaved life before the general emancipation. At the same time, scattered references to traveling theatrical "minstrel troupes" also began to appear, including one in 1872 about Joe Gaylord's Minstrel Troupe, which visited Charlottesville: "The pleasure-seekers of the town, were highly entertained for two evenings with the jig-dancing and stale jokes of this motley company."[7] Beginning in the 1830s in New York and spreading to most northern and midwestern urban areas by the 1860s, blackface minstrelsy by the 1870s was a nationally popular form of entertainment for white Americans.

By 1879, if not earlier, students at UVA had regularly begun putting on blackface performances. That year, the student magazine announced: "To our great joy we hear it authoritatively announced that the students will before long give another minstrel-show."[8] These theatrical groups routinely performed in blackface, which by the late nineteenth century "was an established theatrical practice . . . in which white men caricatured blacks for sport and profit. It has therefore been summed up by one observer as 'half a century of inurement to the uses of white supremacy.'"[9] White performers combined burnt ground cork with water and petroleum jelly as skin-darkening makeup for a popular culture entertainment that dehumanized African Americans and "reinforced widely held" white supremacist beliefs.[10] They were indeed popular with UVA students and local whites alike: "Our minstrel-shows are by far the best entertainments ever offered to the Charlottesville public."[11]

In the 1880s, as blackface performance grew in popularity locally, students continued to rationalize white supremacy. One student in November 1882 argued, "That the negro is not the wiser of the two races requires no great degree of insight to perceive; that the white race, for the most part Anglo-Saxon, is the wise one, appointed by divine right to rule, is known and acknowledged by all men. So, rule they will, till the end of time."[12] Only a year later, in a piece entitled "Plea for a Race Distinction in the United States," a student reminded readers that "this country was discovered by a white man . . . its government made by and for white men, and, until the late unpleasantness, it remained a white man's government."

Echoing the dehumanizing work of blackface performance, the student continued: "Since then four million negroes have been made citizens, and as the experiment demonstrates, they are unable to appreciate citizenship, and lamentably fail to exercise this great prerogative aright."[13] The magazine's editors in April 1884 also highly recommended Thomas Nelson Page's "Marse Chan," a fictional Lost Cause story of a faithful former slave "in Ole Virginia," which they described as a "touching little story of Virginia life in *ante-bellum* days, as told by an old negro."[14] Page (UVA Law 1874), along with Joel Chandler Harris, were the Plantation School's "literary stars in the late nineteenth century, publishing books or serialized works, traveling to speaking engagements around the country, and topping the A-list of social, literary, and political functions." UVA students emulated their work regularly.[15] Just over a year later, the magazine published "The Darkeyad, a heroical poem, celebrating the never-to-be-forgotten events of the late dread conflict of the races." This long-form poem imagined an ongoing war between students and African Americans, ultimately promising that "rage now fills the student breast, / Their thirst of vengeance knows no rest."[16] Blackface performance, rationalizations for white rule, Lost Cause fabrications, and prose dehumanization of African Americans went hand-in-hand.

The central role blackface performance played in student life became even clearer in 1888, when students began publishing a yearbook. The yearbook name, *Corks and Curls,* referenced UVA student terminology for classroom and examination performance that dated back at least to the 1840s. In the local UVA parlance, "corking" meant that a student did not know the answer when called upon in class or did poorly on an examination—"Perhaps our fellow-students can better understand our feelings when we say, 'we never felt as if we never could be *corked.*'" "Curling" was unexpectedly answering correctly in class, delivering a first-rate oration, or acing an exam, as student William Ramsey described it: "The final examinations are nearly upon us . . . but I am trying to 'curl' and if I fail it will be because I don't know the thing."[17]

By the late 1880s, however, the choice of the yearbook name *Corks and Curls* almost certainly functioned as a double entendre referencing blackface minstrel performance, white supremacy, and Lost Cause mythologizing. Ernest Stires, the yearbook editor credited with naming the yearbook, was himself a member of the Glee Club, which regularly performed in blackface across the country. The inaugural edition of the yearbook concocted a fanciful story about the title, describing a yearbook-naming competition. The fictional student who won the imaginary contest, Leander Fogg, received a chromolithograph—an expensive colored image—of Henry Martin, a freedman who worked as a janitor and bell ringer at the University. There almost certainly were no chromolithographs produced in Charlottesville in the 1880s—and definitely not one depicting Henry Martin. Instead, the "prize" was all about race. To students at that time, Martin was thought of as the "faithful slave," both a Lost Cause character and a minstrel archetype. They understood Henry Martin as their own version of "Marse Chan"'s loyal body-servant. The faithful slave trope contended that "enslaved people appeared faithful and caring not because they had to be or were violently compelled to be, but because their fidelity was heartfelt and indicative of their love for and dependence on their owners."[18] The contest winner also received two moot court ballots. The moot court regularly engaged in theatrical performances of legal cases, especially those that touched on the law of slavery or the emerging body of law codifying white rule. Those mock trial events routinely involved students performing in blackface.[19] Thus, the yearbook name and the completely fictional naming competition were clearly winking nods both to long-standing student vernacular about classroom performance and to blackface minstrelsy and Lost Cause mythology.

UVA students took part in a commonplace performance of white supremacy through their use of blackface imagery. Blackface became

Three University of Virginia Glee Club members posing in blackface at Holsinger Studio in Charlottesville, 1917. (University of Virginia Albert and Shirley Small Special Collections Library)

popular with white communities because it "produced a form of racism that meshed well with the modern racial state . . . by linking racism with pleasure" at the turn of the twentieth century.[20] Minstrel cartoons, racist jokes, and photographs of actors performing in blackface saturate the UVA yearbooks from the first issue, in 1888, until about 1940. In these publications and performances, students dehumanized Black individuals by projecting white supremacist notions about Blackness. They depicted African Americans as grotesque, comical, bizarre, and unfit for civilization. The pervasive nature of blackface at UVA, in Virginia, and more broadly in the United States helped maintain and perpetuate white rule.

In 1906, UVA alum Nevil G. Henshaw ('98) wrote *The Visiting Girl*, a "comic opera," for the Arcadians, a UVA drama club.[21] The play follows Thomas Jefferson's ghost as he returns to the University with his cousin Richard Jefferson and his enslaved man Pompey. The character of Pompey served as a mechanism for Henshaw to join the Plantation School in depicting Pompey as the minstrel stereotype of the faithful slave. Through Pompey's character, Henshaw commented on African Americans in post-Reconstruction Charlottesville without detracting from his main focus—the white characters.

Throughout the play, Henshaw utilizes the naïve and dedicated slave caricature of Pompey to draw comparisons to what he views as the problems with Black society in Charlottesville in 1907. During the play, Pompey reports back to Jefferson about what he finds while exploring the Black neighborhoods in Charlottesville. Initially, Pompey believes that the world has improved without slavery. The first time Pompey returns to the stage, he explains that he has met an African American man named Ezekil Brown, a janitor working for one of the University's fraternities. Brown had shown Pompey around and invited him to a bazaar happening in Vinegar Hill, a center of the Black community in town. As Pompey is leaving, however, a white student warns him to be careful: "He [Ezekil] may take your money but he will never take your life."[22] For Henshaw and the audience, the joke is clear—that Ezekil, himself a criminal and hustler, must be armed when taking Pompey to Vinegar Hill, a Black neighborhood plagued by crime and violence. In the play Ezekil represents another minstrel stereotype: African American men as dishonest criminals. Charlottesville's Vinegar Hill appearing as the center of the local failure of Black freedom and citizenship surely confirmed the white audience's racism.

Henshaw's play also introduces another minstrel character on stage: Flo, an African American domestic servant, is offered up by her white boss as a companion for Pompey as he heads to the Vinegar Hill bazaar. When Pompey returns from the bazaar "walking slowly and sadly wearing a suit of students [*sic*] clothes too small for him and a variegated appearance," Henshaw highlights multiple stereotypes all at once. Pompey claims Flo ran off with someone else when they arrived, pointing to her sexual promiscuity as a Jezebel (a stock minstrel show character);[23] a group of Black men took advantage of Pompey during a dice game and stole all of his belongings; and Ezekil stole a white student's clothing from a fraternity house for Pompey to wear.[24] Pompey concludes by saying that his initial reaction to a new society without slavery was wrong: now, he does not think the world has improved at all, that "twont be long before hits the edge and tumbles off into nuffin."[25] Here, Pompey functions as both the faithful slave and a comical buffoon, while Ezekil and the other men function as examples of Black criminality.[26]

The Arcadians performed *The Visiting Girl* to rave reviews wherever they went, including at several alumni events across the region. The show was hailed as "just the kind of production which appeals to the college man."[27] The Arcadians produced another Henshaw play, *King of Kong,* that they gave in blackface during the 1909–10 school year. The drama club performed in many spaces, including at Cabell Hall and the Charlottesville Theatre, located along West Main Street in the Vinegar Hill neighborhood. They also took the show on the road—performing *The Visiting Girl* and *King of Kong* regionally in Petersburg, Richmond, Norfolk, Roanoke, Staunton, and Washington, D.C., as well as in several cities in other states.

Other student groups, including the University Glee Club, also routinely performed in blackface and engaged in other forms of racist cultural misappropriation. As a regular part of their performances, the Glee Club would don blackface as the "Janitor Quartet" and sing minstrel tunes, including "Massa's in the Cold, Cold Ground," which featured these lyrics: "Massa make de darkeys love him, / Cayse he was so kind, / Now, dey sadly weep above him, / Mourning cayse he leave dem behind." In 1917, the Glee Club performed *Oh Julius!*—again, with actors in blackface. The Glee Club even put on a revival of the 1907 Arcadian production of *The Visiting Girl* during its 1920–21 theater season. The Glee Club also performed regionally and in radio broadcasts, such as one in 1936 that included minstrel songs.[28] And as part of an ongoing Lost Cause commitment to cultural misappropriation, they and other collegiate vocal groups performed songs from Black musical traditions, including "Negro Spirituals," at least through the 1930s.[29]

News headlines show that these old models of racist expression continued well beyond the 1930s, even if they were not discussed as regularly in student publications as they had been in earlier years. For decades, fraternities and sororities continued to hold parties honoring an imagined "plantation" past steeped in Lost Cause legend. In 1959 and again in 1971, student publications reported on staged protest lynchings-in-effigy that included blackface. Virginia attorney general Mark Herring (UVA 1983) admitted to wearing blackface at a 1980 UVA fraternity party,[30] and as recently as 2002, fraternity parties at the University involved students appearing in blackface.[31] A photo from the Eastern Virginia

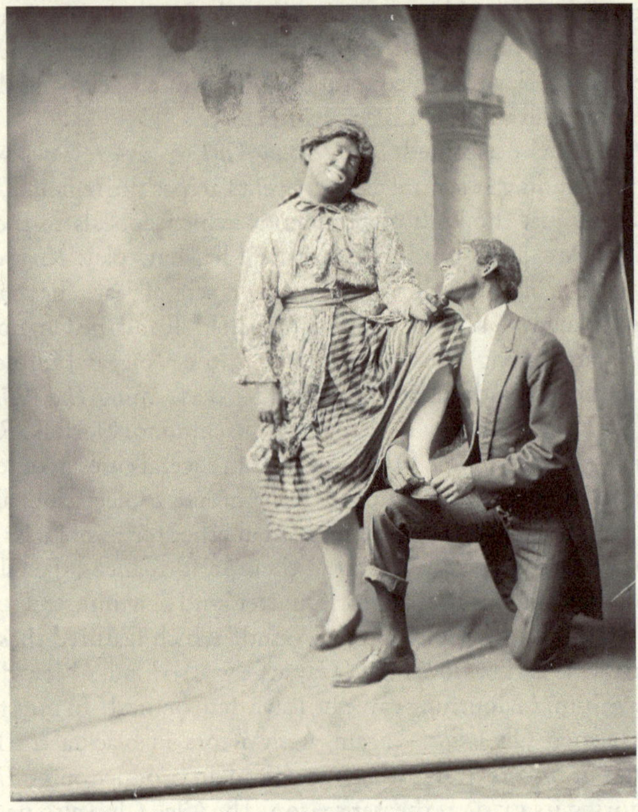

Two University of Virginia Glee Club members posing in blackface at Holsinger Studio in Charlottesville, 1917. (University of Virginia Albert and Shirley Small Special Collections Library)

Medical School's 1984 yearbook surfaced in 2019 that showed Governor Ralph Northam's page, which included a photo of two people in costume: one wore a Klan robe, and the other was in blackface.[32] In 2015, after a Black student was violently arrested by state Alcoholic Beverage Control (ABC) officers, student protesters were greeted anonymously on a social media app with racist comments straight out of the era of Thomas Nelson Page and the Plantation School.[33] Other forms of racial or ethnic stereotyping have occurred as recently as the beginning of the 2019 spring semester, when images circulated depicting students misappropriating Native American and other attire. These serve as a powerful reminder of the persistence of modes of expression that are rooted in older white supremacist ways of thinking. The pervasive racism on display at the University in the early twentieth century is mirrored today as we continue to witness twenty-first-century instances of blackface and racist cultural appropriation.

Notes

1. "Editor's Drawer," *Virginia University Magazine* 6, no. 1 (1867): 45.
2. *Charlottesville Chronicle,* April 25, 1867, as quoted in Joseph Carroll Vance, "The Negro in the Reconstruction of Albemarle County, Virginia" (master's thesis, University of Virginia, 1953), 19.
3. Fairfax Taylor did not support his son in his election bid. During his time at the Convention, the younger Taylor largely voted with the Radical Republicans, including supporting a failed attempt at creating integrated public schools (the schools were officially segregated in 1870). For more information on Taylor's story, see Christopher Brooks and *Dictionary of Virginia Biography,* "James T. S. Taylor (1840–1918)," *Encyclopedia Virginia,* last updated December 22, 2021, https://encyclopediavirginia.org/entries/taylor-james-t-s-1840-1918/.
4. Isabella Gibbons, letter, *Freedman's Record* 4, no. 3 (March 1868): 41–42.
5. "The Future Rulers of the World," *Virginia University Magazine* 6, no. 5 (April 1868): 211.
6. "Editor's Drawer," *Virginia University Magazine* 6, no. 5 (April 1868): 239.
7. "Athletic Sports," *Virginia University Magazine* 7, no. 5–6 (February–March 1869): 282; "Collegiana," *Virginia University Magazine* 10, no. 4 (January 1872): 215; "Editor's Table," *Virginia University Magazine* 12, no. 4 (January 1874): 267; "Collegiana," *Virginia University Magazine* 11, no. 4 (January 1873): 215.
8. "Collegiana," *Virginia University Magazine* 18, no. 5 (February 1879): 305.
9. Eric Lott, *Love and Theft: Blackface Minstrelsy and the American Working Class* (New York: Oxford University Press, 1993), 3.
10. William John Mahar, *Behind the Burnt Cork Mask: Early Blackface Minstrelsy and Antebellum American Popular Culture* (Urbana: University of Illinois Press, 1999), 1.
11. "Collegiana," *Virginia University Magazine* 18, no. 5 (February 1879): 306.
12. "The New Time: From Amid the Shadows of the Old. In Two Parts—Part I," *Virginia University Magazine,* n.s., 12, no. 1 (November 1882): 80.
13. "Plea for a Race Distinction in the United States," *Virginia University Magazine,* n.s., 23, no. 1 (October 1883): 19.
14. "Collegiana," *Virginia University Magazine,* n.s., 13, no. 7 (April 1884): 433.
15. Micki McElya, *Clinging to Mammy: The Faithful Slave in Twentieth-Century America* (Cambridge, Mass.: Harvard University Press, 2007), 12.

16. "The Darkeyad," *Virginia University Magazine*, n.s., 24, no. 8 (May 1885): 482–84.
17. "Editor's Table," *Jefferson Monument Magazine* 1, no. 8 (May 1850): 262; *Virginia University Magazine*, January 1870, 41 and 48. See also William Ramsey, letter to father, undated, Special Collections, University of Virginia Library (Ramsey was a student from 1883 to 1887).
18. McElya, *Clinging to Mammy*, 6.
19. *Corks and Curls*, 1888, 11–12.
20. Brian Roberts, *Blackface Nation: Race, Reform, and Identity in American Popular Music, 1812–1925* (Chicago: University of Chicago Press, 2017), 20.
21. Nevil Gratiot Henshaw, manuscript of *The Visiting Girl* (1907), Accession #8426, Special Collections, University of Virginia Library.
22. Henshaw, *Visiting Girl* manuscript, 17.
23. Deborah Gray White demonstrated that white perception of Black womanhood originated in slavery: "In antebellum America, the female slave's chattel status, sex, and race combined to create a complicated set of myths about black womanhood." One of the most prevalent versions of Black womanhood was the Jezebel, "a person governed almost entirely by her libido" and "in every way . . . the counterimage of the mid-nineteenth-century ideal of the Victorian lady." Deborah Gray White, *Ar'n't I a Woman? Female Slaves in the Plantation South* (New York: W. W. Norton, 1999), 28–29.
24. Henshaw, *Visiting Girl* manuscript, 22.
25. Henshaw, *Visiting Girl* manuscript, 22.
26. For more on these tropes of Black manhood, see Donald Bogle, *Toms, Coons, Mulattoes, Mammies, and Bucks: An Interpretive History of Blacks in American Films*, updated and exp. 5th ed. (New York: Bloomsbury Academic, 2016).
27. "Arcadians Trip Huge Success," *College Topics*, February 13, 1907.
28. Edward N. Main to the Director of UVA Glee Club, March 1, 1936, in Papers of the University Glee Club, 1920–1961, Special Collections, University of Virginia Library.
29. Main to the Director of UVA Glee Club, March 1, 1936. See also, in *College Topics*, the following: "Glee Club to Give Washington Concert," April 24, 1912; "Glee Club Plays to Packed House," April 29, 1916; "Glee Club Will Perform at Sweet Briar Feb 23," February 16, 1918; "Sixteen Performances Booked by Glee Club," September 16, 1920.
30. Jonathan Miller and Alan Blinder, "Second Virginia Democrat Says He Wore Blackface, Throwing Party into Turmoil," *Washington Post*, February 6, 2019, https://www.nytimes.com/2019/02/06/us/politics/virginia-blackface-mark-herring.html.
31. Amy Argetsinger, "2 U-Va. Fraternities Suspended over Photos," *Washington Post*, November 20, 2002, https://www.washingtonpost.com/archive

/local/2002/11/20/2-u-va-fraternities-suspended-over-photos/835418f0-d384-42f5-9cc4-6082637a2ff8/.

32. Rhae Lynn Barnes, "The Troubling History behind Ralph Northam's Blackface Klan Photo," *Washington Post,* February 2, 2019, https://www.washingtonpost.com/outlook/2019/02/02/troubling-history-behind-ralph-northams-blackface-klan-photo/. Established in the spring of 2018, the research team of the UVA President's Commission on the University in the Age of Segregation began documenting racist imagery in student and University publications as one of its first tasks. Soon after the blackface controversies broke in the national media, Rhae Lynn Barnes, a leading subject matter expert and assistant professor of history at Princeton University, came to UVA and contributed to this important conversation with "'A Dangerous Unselfishness': Understanding the Long History of Amateur Blackface Minstrelsy," for Special Collections and the Office of Diversity and Equity, University of Virginia, Charlottesville, Va., April 15, 2019. Those interested in learning more about this subject should look for her forthcoming book *Darkology: When the American Dream Wore Blackface.*
33. T. Rees Shapiro, "Some Virginia Students, School Officials Struggle with Anonymous Bullying and Hate Speech on Yik Yak App," *Washington Post,* May 7, 2015, https://www.washingtonpost.com/news/grade-point/wp/2015/05/07/some-virginia-students-school-officials-struggle-with-anonymous-bullying-and-hate-speech-on-yik-yak-app/.

Response

Uncovering UVA's "Hidden" History

KRISTEN GRAVES

TO BE Black at UVA is a shared experience—but also a unique one for each individual African American student. Our shared circumstances are found in the everyday struggles at UVA and in the ability to unify as a community despite particular obstacles. Whatever it is . . . the Black experience at UVA is both a mixed blessing and a pyrrhic victory. While we may laugh on our way to the Pav and swap weekend stories at the Black Bus Stop, we are also keenly aware of the dark history that brings us closer together and stains our time at the University: UVA's long historic connection to white supremacy and racism.

For me, arriving at UVA was a culture shock. I felt disoriented, as I often was one of the few, if any, Black or minority students in my courses or in my extracurricular activities. I found it hard to relate to my classmates when they described trips to Paris, upbringings in stable, two-parent households, and seemingly predestined pathways to prestigious jobs and internships.

Despite this, I refused to be tokenized or ashamed of my background. I poured my energy into making UVA a more diverse and welcoming place, as I quickly learned the roles that students could take to effect change, ranging from activists who worked for radical change outside of UVA to institutional drivers who worked within UVA's established systems to make incremental advancements.

I decided to find solace in both those spheres. As someone who has always been interested in history, I gravitated toward research opportunities and other means of uncovering UVA's hidden history. My time was spent diving deep into primary sources in our libraries and archives, organizing with professors, and becoming a student leader of the Cornerstone Summer Institute, a camp for high school students that challenged them to confront the often terrible history I was helping uncover in the archives.

During my time investigating those many sources and UVA student publications in particular, I regularly encountered blackface images—and so much more. The publications were often filled with depictions of African Americans as creatures, brute beasts, or "things" more monstrous. As a history major and African American woman, the disturbing illustrations were unsurprising, as I had read about this history already. Nonetheless, viewing them was constantly disheartening. While sifting through all those materials, I became sharply aware of how, through their publications, white students at UVA had spent decades participating in or orchestrating the intellectual foundation for claiming Black freedom and Black citizenship as illegitimate. No wonder my early experiences in classrooms, in activities, and on Grounds were often so alienating.

Reviewing those materials forced me to deeply reflect on how recent this history is and how embedded white supremacy is in UVA's culture and that of the Charlottesville community. We have a lot of work to do. I was forced to see anew the University's historical role as an engineer of violence against Black Americans through its long commitment to white rule. Worse, the unsettling images in those publications reminded me of how this history continues to shape the University's atmosphere and politics. Sometimes, the past is not even the past, especially when we, the UVA community, have not yet really come to terms with it.

I had to act, had to work to make the University live up to its professed twenty-first-century values and make change. To help represent the minority community and educate others and work from within this space, I became an academic and historical tour guide. I felt compelled to use my voice to demonstrate to prospective Black students how they, too, could excel in the face of adversity—how they, too, could reclaim and rewrite the narrative. In that work, I sought to champion the overlooked stories and often forgotten narratives of enslaved laborers and other trailblazers. We must continue to recognize their humanity, their resilience, their vital contributions to the University and to the local community. We must also say their names. So I did just that, over and over, hoping to make it impossible to ever silence their humanity and their agency again.

The history revealed in Ashley Schmidt and Kirt von Daacke's essay on blackface at UVA details only a small subset of the school's long history and culture of hatred, mockery, and violence against African Americans.

It reflects the repeated narrative of UVA's commitment to white supremacy and the dehumanization of Black people in society. From the first bricks laid at "Jefferson's university," to the pseudoscience and racist public policy of the era of segregation, to today—when state leaders, often alumni of UVA, are exposed as having worn blackface in the late twentieth century—UVA has often been a leading force in promoting "Southern" values, whatever they may be. It also has a long and deplorable history of exploiting Black bodies, Black labor, and Black souls. My entire experience at UVA—beginning with the Unite the Right rally in August 2017 and continuing throughout the rest of my undergraduate career—forced me to engage with the complexities of white supremacy. As a Black woman, these events have made me more resilient and dedicated to social causes that create more inclusive and educated spaces. I also have come to understand the indispensable value of contextualizing historical events and effectuating change from a learned history. Education and truth-telling will not solve everything, but we cannot create more diverse, inclusive, and equitable spaces without first confronting the realities of this school's, this state's, and this nation's history. Now, looking back as a recent graduate, I remain hopeful that ongoing projects such as the President's Commission on Slavery and the University and the President's Commission on the University in the Age of Segregation will in fact be critical entities at UVA that can make change from within. As an alumna, I will also demand continuing change from without.

"An Imperfect Sketch" Revisited

Burkley Bullock's Life and Legacy at UVA and Beyond

SCOT FRENCH

In April 1890, an editorial in the University of Virginia's *College Topics* student newspaper suggested reducing petty thefts from student residences by "making all servants in the employ of the University wear badges" and "relieving the grounds of the swarms of darkies of all sizes and descriptions, who now infest the place."[1] The editorial drew a sharp distinction between African Americans employed as trusted servants on Grounds and those who intruded themselves upon public and private spaces reserved for elite white students.

That same year, UVA's *Corks and Curls* yearbook published five brief character sketches of African American men whose daily interactions with students and faculty made them familiar, even welcome, faces on Grounds. The editors introduced "Berkeley Bullocks" as "one of the best known and generally liked" of the "many odd and picturesque characters of the negro race that are to be met with everywhere around the University, but that are now fast passing away before the superior intellectual culture and proud assertion of equal rights on the part of their descendants." They cast Bullock as a living, breathing relic of the "good old antebellum darkey" type popularized in the writings of Thomas Nelson Page and Joel Chandler Harris.

> He is full of cornfield philosophy, reminiscences, folk-lore and quaint observations on men and things, all so well and pithily expressed that it

> is well worth one's while to listen with attention to one of our last surviving representatives of the old plantation hand. . . . He knows well his place, and is never pushing, scorning with holy indignation the growing class of educated, aspiring negroes of our present, justly believing with Uncle Remus that he could "fling more edication in a N____r with a barr'l stave than all the schools twixt this and Michigan." Such is an imperfect sketch of Berkeley, which, if perfect, could scarce be necessary, for we all know him so well that there is hardly a need of anything to bring back to memory what none are likely to forget.[2]

The historical record—painstakingly retrieved from a multitude of sources—presents a far different portrait. Bullock was a literate man who, over the course of a lifetime, freed himself and his mother from slavery, sent his children to school, purchased more than a dozen properties in Albemarle County and the city of Charlottesville, started the Ivy Creek Baptist Church, ran several businesses, and co-founded the region's first industrial and land improvement company "organized by colored men" for the benefit of the African American community.[3]

Burkley (also spelled Berkeley or Berkley) Bullock was born in Louisa County in or around 1830.[4] His parents, Abraham and Cynthia, were enslaved, meaning that young Burkley entered life as chattel in the eyes of state and federal law.[5] The Bullocks belonged to Col. John R. Jones, a wealthy financier and merchant who profited directly from slavery and the slave trade. Jones held a stake in a mercantile firm at Louisa Courthouse; he also did "quite an extensive business" in Albemarle County "and acted as the financial agent of several of the most substantial planters and farmers of the county." Jones owned a "fine mansion" at 109 Jefferson Street, where he raised "a large family of ten children."[6]

According to Bullock family history, young Burkley "performed the duties of a house boy" for the Jones family. "In his mid-teens," his great-granddaughter Jean Henderson writes, Bullock "was assigned head of the commissary when Colonel Jones discovered he could read and perform other learned tasks." It is possible, she adds, that Bullock worked "in Colonel Jones's store" at Court Square.[7] The story of how Bullock learned to read and write provides a glimpse into the social world of the slave community and strategies of resistance shared across households and generations. It was Peter Fossett—once Thomas Jefferson's trusted "footman" at Monticello, sold to Colonel Jones at auction after Jefferson's death—who taught Bullock to read and write.[8] "Peter Faucett [*sic*] taught my father, Burkley Bullock, to read and write by light wood knots in the late hours

Undated photograph of Peter Fossett. (National Museum of African American History and Culture)

of night when everyone was supposed to be asleep," Charles Bullock told an interviewer in 1949. "They would steal away to a deserted cabin, over the hill from the big house, out of sight."[9]

In a late nineteenth-century newspaper interview, Fossett described the power of slave literacy and the threat such knowledge posed in the eyes of his Charlottesville master:

> When I was sold to Col. Jones I took my books along with me. One day I was kneeling before the fireplace spelling the word "baker," when Col. Jones opened the door, and I shall never forget the scene as long as I live.
>
> "What have you got there, sir," were his words.
>
> I told him.
>
> "If I ever catch you with a book in your hands, thirty-nine lashes on your bare back."
>
> He took the book and threw it into the fire, then called up his sons and told them that if they ever taught me they would receive the same punishment.

The Joneses came to value Fossett as a trusted enslaved servant—"notwithstanding that all the time I was teaching all the people around me to read and write, and even venturing to write free passes and sending slaves away from their masters. Of course they did not know this or they would not have thought me so valuable."[10] Empowered with literacy and local knowledge, Bullock engaged in everyday acts of resistance. He ran off at least once, perhaps with the aid of a self-forged pass, getting as far as the Ohio River. Horace Tonsler, an ex-slave from Charlottesville, related the story as he had heard it from Bullock himself:

> Yes, I know of a case of runaway slave. Berkeley Bullock, an' he has two sons living here now. One day he showed me de very road he used when he fust 'scaped. Dis road led to Bath County. He said he traveled at night by the moonshine. Said he would feel 'round de trees an whichever side de moss grew on, he knowed dat was de north direction. Den he said he boarded a stage dat went as far as de Ohio River. Being of yellow complexion he had an old cap pulled over his eyes; he gave de man his ticket, an' kept on walking to the back. . . . Bullock was still on de stage when it got to de Ohio River. Dey caught him dere fo' he could make it cross de river.[11]

When Colonel Jones became "embarrassed by financial troubles" in the mid-1850s,[12] he sold "thirty six valuable slaves" to cover his debts.[13] Bankruptcy sale records indicate that Bullock and his mother were sold to different buyers, "Cynthia" to "Wm. Brand" for $5, and "Berkley" to "S. Maupin" for $1,205. Bullock's likely buyer, UVA professor Socrates Maupin, lived in Pavilion VIII on the Lawn.[14]

Bullock secured freedom for himself and his mother sometime before the end of the Civil War. "Somehow he was freed first and then bought his mother for a few dollars because she pretended to be feeble and not able to work for a so-called master," his granddaughter, Fanny Bowles Leach, wrote in her memoir.[15] An archival source, discovered by historian Gayle M. Schulman, indicates that "Berkeley" seized his freedom during the waning days of the war, after the occupation of Charlottesville by Union troops and the surrender of the University of Virginia. In a letter dated April 7, 1865, Mary L. Minor—the daughter of UVA law professor John B. Minor—informed her aunt that "Dr Maupin lost one of his horses & Berkeley was discovered in the act of riding off the other. He of course went taking his family along. Two other men of the Drs went also."[16]

The military defeat of the Confederacy, followed by ratification of the Thirteenth Amendment and passage of the 1866 Civil Rights Act, placed Bullock and his fellow freedpersons in a new relationship to their former masters. In February 1866, Bullock and William Brown lodged a complaint with the Freedmen's Bureau against William Ross and four other white men. While the details and outcome of the case are not known, the suit affirms Bullock's willingness to assert his right to legal redress through the newly created civil court system.[17]

Like many formerly enslaved persons in Virginia, Bullock saw property ownership as the key to securing independence and economic autonomy for himself and his family. In September 1868, he purchased a half-share in 243 acres of farmland in Albemarle County near Earlysville. Bullock partnered on the purchase with his wife, Mary Ann, and another African American couple, William and Caroline Brown, who used a house and lot they owned in the city of Charlottesville to secure the $3,000 deed of trust.[18]

Banking on their own sweat equity, the Bullocks and Browns hoped to pay down the loan over three years and take full ownership of the property. When the final payment came due in 1871, however, "the depressed condition of the country and financial difficulties in this county and state" left them "unable to pay the whole of the debt secured." William Brown petitioned the Chancery Court to delay a public sale, saying the farm would yield sufficient profits to pay off the notes by the spring.[19] Ultimately, however, the property was sold, and Brown and his family left the state.[20]

Undeterred, Bullock cast down his bucket once again. In December 1871, he purchased a 35-acre Albemarle County lot from John Shackleford, a seventy-four-year-old white farmer, for $435.[21] By 1880, Burkley and Mary Ann Bullock owned 75 acres in the vicinity of Hydraulic and Earlysville Roads. The assessed value of their farm, including land, fences, and buildings, was $1,200; the livestock—including one milk cow, one calf, nine swine, and fourteen chickens—was assessed at $30.[22]

As a farm owner, Bullock enjoyed a measure of economic independence, particularly during hard times. Yet he also had a large family—twelve children of varying ages—and may have relied on outside work for sustenance. At a "Meeting of Colored Laborers of the County" held at the Albemarle Courthouse on June 14, 1879, Bullock joined a committee of eight in drafting a resolution accusing "the farmers"—presumably white property owners who relied on Black labor—of conspiring to reduce wages below subsistence and charging "extortionous" prices for goods and services:

> Whereas the wages received by the laborers of Charlottesville, and the county of Albemarle, are insufficient to make them an honorable living, and the prices of produce, rents, clothing, &c., when compaired [*sic*] with wages are extortionous, And whereas, in various portions of the county the laborers are only receiving 25 cents per day for their labor;

> and whereas there is only offered from 75 cent to a $1.00 for wheat harvest, be it resolved: That we the laborers of the county of Albemarle, do in a mass-meeting assemble, do advise each and every laborer in the county to insist that he shall receive such wages as will make him an honorable living, and a good citizen; and whereas, the farmers have met from time to time, and reduced the wages of labor, in consequence of which we have suffered in winter; and in all our suffering we have submitted, and as a sheep dumb before his shearers, we have opened not our mouths. And whereas times are getting harder, and wages lower, we call upon our employers to give us better wages.

The Colored Laborers used the meeting to address other racial inequities as well. A committee of five—Bullock once again listed among them—was appointed to petition Albemarle County Court judge John L. Cochran to "reconstruct the juries, both grand and petty, so as to place some of our race and color, qualified according to the laws of the State, upon the venire; on the grounds that we cannot expect an impartial trial by jurors wholly alien to us in race and color."[23]

Bullock's willingness to press these civil rights and labor issues on behalf of the African American community, in opposition to powerful white interests, affirms his standing as a well-respected, politically active community leader. He was unanimously elected one of two county delegates to the Republican Party state convention in 1876, which may have helped secure his federal patronage appointment as a "colored" clerk at the University of Virginia (Charlottesville) post office in 1883.[24]

During his roughly twenty years as a resident of Albemarle County's Ivy Creek neighborhood, Bullock built a legacy as a church founder and community leader. Yet, like so many other African Americans of his day, he sought better opportunities for himself and his family in the urbanizing centers of the New South. Sometime around 1888, Bullock and his family moved to the newly incorporated city of Charlottesville, a bustling commercial entrepôt with an established Black community. There, the 1888–89 Charlottesville City Directory listed him as the proprietor of a restaurant at Union Station, opposite the Virginia Midland railroad junction. Wright's Railroad Dining Room, owned by a white man and staffed by African American cooks and waiters, competed for business at a nearby location.[25]

UVA students who frequented Bullock's restaurant described a hardworking man who depended upon his "frolicsome" white clientele for business and indulged them in "exasperating conversation."

Looking east down West Main Street, 1919. Charlottesville's Union Station train depot is on the right. (University of Virginia Albert and Shirley Small Special Collections Library)

No one that has ever come into contact with Berkeley can forget his appearance, his manner, and his habits. . . . His face is furrowed deep by the plough of time, not a little aided by care, in the shape of a large family and business much crippled by "that'ar new fangled rest'rant over thar." But still from under his bushy eyebrows there gleam with unabated brilliancy a pair of furtive, restless eyes, which seem always on the alert for chance, gain or unexpected disaster at the hands of his, alas, too often, riotous customers. When not noiselessly gliding about among his chicken legs and apple pies, Berkeley stands in the corner suspiciously eyeing his customers with folded hands and a pitiable look of resigned dispair [*sic*]. It is evident that he is never certain of his pay and is always haunted with a gnawing fear that the frolicsome students may even make away with his house. But, nevertheless, Berkeley is a kind-hearted man, and when asked for credit—after the meal has been consumed—he acquiesces with a fair show of grace. . . .

Such is an imperfect sketch of Berkeley which, if perfect, could scarce be necessary, for we all know him so well that there is hardly a need of anything to bring back to memory what none are likely to forget.[26]

The students saw what they wanted to see in Bullock—an endearing, somewhat comical example of the "good old ante-bellum darkey," "one of our last surviving representatives of the old plantation hand," a colored man conspicuously lacking in formal education but well-schooled in the etiquette of race relations. They knew nothing of Bullock's hard-won literacy, his escape from bondage, his labor organizing and political activity, his business acumen, his family, his social world, or his interior life as a once-enslaved African American man trying to secure a place for himself and his family in the New South economy. Certainly none acknowledged the enterprising intelligence and work ethic that enabled Bullock to acquire more than a dozen properties, open a restaurant, and establish wood, coal, and ice businesses in the heart of the city.

Bullock's vision of uplift extended well beyond himself and his family. In April 1889, he and eight other African American men from the Charlottesville area formed a joint stock company called the Piedmont Industrial and Land Improvement Company. The charter of incorporation authorized the company to issue up to $100,000 in total stock, to be sold in $50 shares. Principal among the group's stated "objects and purposes" were these: "To purchase, hold, lease, rent, improve, sell, exchange, develop, and otherwise deal in real estate"; "to buy and sell real estate on commission"; and "to extend aid and assistance, financial and otherwise, to persons of limited means in purchasing homes."[27]

The company paid interest and dividends based on its income from the rental and sale of properties, many of them located in and around Charlottesville's central business district. In its first month of operation, the company boasted that it had purchased ten city lots and fifteen or twenty more bordering the city. "Thus you see Charlottesville is blooming," the *Richmond Planet* reported, "and with it blooms the only land Improving Co. organized by colored men, chartered by the law and in successful operation in Piedmont, Va." The article concluded with a triumphant declaration of race pride: "We are coming."[28]

By its third year, the Company had expanded its civic role to include the hosting of events designed to highlight the achievements of African Americans in agriculture and industry and stimulate race pride. In October 1891, the company held what was touted as the first county fair to be organized by African Americans. "Pedestrians by the hundreds and a variety of vehicles indescribable" made their way to the fairgrounds on Brenham's Farm. The president and directors of the company—Bullock included—joined the mile-long grand procession, riding on horseback.[29]

When Bullock died in January 1908, Charlottesville's *Daily Progress*—a white-owned paper that typically paid scant attention to African American social affairs—published the news on the front page: "Berkeley Bullock, a worthy colored man respected throughout this community, died yesterday afternoon at the advanced age of seventy-four. He had been in very bad health for the past two years, suffering mainly from rheumatism which developed into dropsy. Bullock was widely known as a steward at several summer resorts, and for years conducted a restaurant near Union Station, this city."[30]

Bullock's funeral notice, also published in the *Progress*, included additional biographical details: "Bullock had been in failing health for over two years. He died at the advanced age of 77 years and had been a member of the church for 65 years, having joined at the age of twelve. He organized the Old Ivy Creek Baptist church, which is now Union Ridge Baptist Church in the county. He was one of the pioneer business men of the city. For a number of years he conducted a restaurant at the Union Station and later engaged in the wood, coal and ice business."[31]

This respectful salute to Bullock stood in sharp contrast to the stock racial caricatures presented by UVA students in their "imperfect sketch" published in *Corks and Curls*.

Bullock is buried, alongside family members, in the Daughters of Zion Cemetery on Oak Street. Founded by an African American mutual aid society in 1873, the cemetery has been recognized as a city landmark worthy of preservation and commemoration.[32] Every year, on Decoration Day, the Preservers of the Daughters of Zion group lay roses on the graves of all buried there. The story of Bullock's remarkable journey from slavery to freedom is included in an audio tour of the site.[33] Let the true story be recorded here as well.

Notes

1. "Make Them Wear Badges," *College Topics*, April 30, 1890. The editors allowed for the possibility that they had mistakenly attributed some of the thefts to African American "visitants" who—unless employed by white students and faculty as servants—had no business being there. "It is possible that injustice may be done to the aforesaid visitants in putting all the thieving upon them—as it is not likely they would care for law books or boxing gloves—but it is probable that most of it is done by them, and at all events it can do no harm to make the experiment and it will have the salutary effect of relieving the landscape of a very disagreeable feature."

2. "Berkeley Bullocks," *Corks and Curls,* vol. 3 (Charlottesville: University of Virginia, 1889–90), 132–33. Bullock's name is misspelled "Bullocks" in the heading but spelled correctly on first reference immediately below. A digitized copy of this volume is available through HathiTrust: https://babel.hathitrust.org/cgi/pt?id=uva.x030808006&view=1up&seq=168.
3. The author is grateful to Bullock family descendants, particularly the late Jean Henderson, for contributing their research and family memoirs to this revised portrait. Local researchers Edwina St. Rose, Sam Towler, Ann Carter, Bob Vernon, and others provided helpful leads on sources and context. The Carter G. Woodson Institute for African-American and African Studies, under the leadership of then director Reginald D. Butler (1996–2005), provided intellectual and institutional support through its Ford Foundation–funded Center for the Study of Local Knowledge.
4. Bullock's headstone at the Daughters of Zion Cemetery lists his birth date as 1830. His obituary, dated January 27, 1908, gives his age as seventy-seven, which would put his birth date in 1831 or 1832. See "Funeral for Burkley Bullock," *Charlottesville Daily Progress,* January 27, 1908, 3.
5. Fanny Bowles Leach, "Family History," undated, p. 5. Photocopy courtesy of Brenda Calloway.
6. Mary Rawlings, ed., *Early Charlottesville: Recollections of James Alexander, 1828–1874* (Charlottesville: Albemarle County Historical Society, 1942), 20. The house, known as "Social Hall," is still standing.
7. See sketch of Berkley B. Bullock Sr. prepared by his great-granddaughter, Jean L. Henderson, in "Linking the Branches of the Bullock Family Tree to Our Charlottesville Roots, 2000." Used by permission.
8. "Charlottesville, Va. Letter. The Only Surviving Ex-Slave of the Renowned Thomas Jefferson Visiting Once More the Place of His Nativity," *The Colored American,* June 23, 1900, 9. Born at Monticello in 1815, Fossett would have been fifteen years older than Bullock. See entry for "Peter Fossett" in the *Thomas Jefferson Encyclopedia* at the Monticello website, https://www.monticello.org/site/research-and-collections/peter-fossett.
9. Charles W. Bullock Sr., undated, Pearl M. Graham Papers, Howard University. The text of a subsequent letter from Charles Bullock to Pearl M. Graham, dated October 10, 1949, suggests that Graham solicited his recollections of Peter Fossett earlier that same year.
10. "Once the Slave of Thomas Jefferson: The Rev. Mr. Fossett, of Cincinnati, Recalls the Days When Men Came from the Ends of the Earth to Consult 'the Sage of Monticello'—Reminiscences of Jefferson, Lafayette, Madison and Monroe," *New York World,* January 30, 1898, 33.
11. Interview with Horace Tonsler, Charlottesville, Va., date unknown, reprinted in *Weevils in the Wheat: Interviews with Virginia Ex-Slaves,* ed. Charles L. Perdue Jr., Thomas E. Barden, and Robert K. Phillips (Charlottesville:

University of Virginia Press, 1976), 286–87. Original source: *Negro in Virginia*, MS version, draft no. 1, chap. 13, p. 14.

12. On Jones's "financial troubles," see the Reverend Edgar Woods, *Albemarle County, Virginia* (1901; Harrisonburg, Va.: C. J. Carrier, 1978), 239.
13. For bankruptcy sale advertisement, see "Thirty Six Valuable Slaves for Sale," *Richmond Enquirer*, October 30, 1855.
14. For the names of enslaved persons sold at auction and their buyers, see deed of sale dated November 16, 1855, Albemarle County Deed Book 54, pp. 387–88. For speculation on the sale/dispersal of Bullock family members, see Sam Towler's comments on "Still More on Peter Briggs," *Encyclopedia Virginia Blog*, November 5, 2013, https://www.evblog.virginiahumanities.org/2013/04/still-more-on-peter-biggs/ (site now discontinued).
15. Fanny Bowles Leach, "Family History," undated, p. 5. Photocopy courtesy of Brenda Calloway.
16. Gayle M. Schulman, "Slaves at the University of Virginia," unpublished manuscript, 2003, Special Collections, University of Virginia Library.
17. *Berkeley Bullock and Wm. Brown v. William Ross et al.*, February 9, 1866; Freedmen's Bureau Field Office Records, 1865–1872, Register of Complaints, Charlottesville, Va.; database with images accessed via FamilySearch.org.
18. See deed "made this 1st day of September, in the year One Thousand Eight Hundred and Sixty Eight—between Eugene O. Michie of the first part and William Brown & Berkeley Bullock of the 2nd part," Albemarle County Deed Book No. 63, pp. 525–26.
19. *Albemarle County Chancery Cause, William Brown &c. vs. R. R. Prentiss, Trustee*, Index No. 1872–018, Case No. 561 16, Library of Virginia.
20. The Browns moved to Cambridge, Mass.; see 1880 U.S. Census, Middlesex County, City of Cambridge, Mass., Ward 1, 66.
21. The sale was not recorded until thirteen years later, after Shackleford's death. Bullock requested that legal title to the tract be conveyed to him since the money he owed on the property had "long since been paid in full." See deed "dated May 12th 1884, between said Rebecca Shackleford, Richard Shackleford, & Louisa Shackleford, his wife, of the first part, and said Berkeley Bullock of the second part," Albemarle County Deed Book No. 83, p. 383.
22. U.S. Census, 1880, Agricultural Supplement, Schedule 2, Productions of Agriculture in Charlottesville District in the County of Albemarle, State of Virginia, p. 5, Supervisor's District 3, Enumeration District 11.
23. "Meeting of Colored Laborers of the County," *Charlottesville Jeffersonian Republican*, June 18, 1879; Special Collections, University of Virginia Library.
24. On Bullock's election as a delegate to the Lynchburg Convention, see "Grand Republican Rally in Albemarle," *Staunton Valley Virginian*, April 6, 1876. "S. Berkley Bullock (colored)" is listed as one of two clerks at the University of Virginia post office in 1883. While the "S." before the name

raises questions, records show no other "Berkley Bullock (colored)" eligible for such an appointment in that time and place. See *Official Register of the United States, Containing a List of Officers and Employés in the Civil, Military, and Naval Service on the First of July, 1883*, vol. 2, *The Post-Office Department and the Postal Service* (Washington, D.C.: GPO, 1884), 48th Congress, 1st Session, H.Misc.Doc. 4, 1884, p. 734 (accessed via Readex AllSearch).

25. See entries for "Wright's Railroad Dining Room" and "Bullock Berkeley col" under "Restaurants" in *Turner's Annual Directory for the City of Charlottesville, Va.* (Yonkers, N.Y.: E. F. Turner, 1889), 120. Both restaurants were located at the "VM" (Virginia Midland) junction.
26. *Corks and Curls*, 1889–90, 132–33.
27. Charter of the Piedmont Industrial and Land Improvement Co., April 9, 1889; Charter Book 1, Charlottesville City Clerk's Office.
28. *Richmond Planet*, May 17, 1890, 4.
29. *Richmond Planet*, November 7, 1891, 4. For a more detailed account of the company's origins and civic activities, see Gideon French and Scot French, "Introduction," Piedmont Land & Industrial Improvement Company StoryMap, Daughters of Zion Cemetery website, https://storymaps.arcgis.com/stories/ca550fc2743741f8b7ffff358e2da4c7.
30. "Worthy Colored Man Dead," *Charlottesville Daily Progress*, January 25, 1908, 1. This news item misreports Bullock's age as seventy-four; other sources would make him closer to seventy-seven or seventy-eight.
31. "Funeral for Burkley Bullock," *Charlottesville Daily Progress*, January 27, 1908, 4. The funeral notice added three years to Bullock's age (seventy-seven), which comports more closely with the 1830 birthdate on his gravestone.
32. "Grave Concern: Local Group Preserves Black Cemetery," *Cville Magazine*, June 8, 2017, https://www.c-ville.com/grave-concern-local-group-preserves-historic-black-cemetery/.
33. The audio tour featuring the Bullock family is accessible via the Daughters of Zion Cemetery website: https://daughtersofzioncemetery.org/links/.

Response

Learning from Family History

CHERYL BULLOCK-HANNAH

I was born in 1965 in Hackensack, New Jersey, over one hundred years after the emancipation process began in the United States, freeing over four million enslaved people. I have lineage on both sides of my family, dating back to 1790, that includes people who were not in fact enslaved but lived free in New Jersey. I was raised by free people who were raised by free people and so on. I am also a child of the 1970s, when the Black Power movement was everywhere. It was in the media, on television, and in the news. Afros were everywhere, as were dashikis, as Black Americans demanded the full fruits of freedom and embraced African cultural heritage.

For me, family history was not really talked about for various reasons. At that time, my family was forward-looking and progressive, so it was always important that we not rest on our laurels. Instead, we learned to put in the work that we wanted for our lives. I graduated from college, expanded my social world and sphere of influence, and marked an over-twenty-year career in retail business management. I was often the only person of color at work. This was especially the case as I advanced in management. Being the only person of color in the workplace was not my goal, but I had learned to adapt long before, focusing on the work at hand.

I am also a "Bullock," part of a history and past I only knew a little about. Being a Bullock, at least in the Black community, was often a reference to who I was and whom I belonged to, where I came from. In 1934, Charles H. Bullock Jr. married Edna M. Everett, and they opened Bullock Funeral Home in Hackensack. They would later open a second location in Englewood, New Jersey. Charles and Edna were prominent members of their community, involved with the NAACP, The Links Inc. (a volunteer service organization for women of African descent), and Jack & Jill of America (an African American community service organization dedicated to child education and welfare). Upon my grandfather's death, during a visit with his sister Mary, I learned about their father's involvement with the YMCA—and continued to learn my own family history. My greatest takeaway was to learn that he was a gifted storyteller, and this gave me license to improve my storytelling skills. Years later, Mary's daughter, Jean, began to share with us our Charlottesville history and even the possibilities of connections to Thomas Jefferson, a family history I had not known about before. Cousin Jean was losing her eyesight and had someone come in to dictate her notes to, notes that covered her dining room table. As I sat off to the side, alone—allowing my father and nephew time to talk and visit—I looked on the coffee table beside me at the many books on Charlottesville, Thomas Jefferson, and Sally Hemings. I suppose I imagined that opening the doorway to my family history would be as simple as opening up one of those books and seeing my name right there in bold print.

Who am I? Cheryl Bullock, descendant of free Black business owners in New Jersey, descendant of some of those enslaved in Charlottesville and at the University of Virginia, and someone somehow related to Thomas Jefferson. It certainly did not happen that way, yet I knew that our cousin Jean was on to something! Little by little over the years I put the work in to not only uncover and connect the family history but also to fill her shoes as another family historian. As far as the references to Jefferson are concerned, there are quite a few Bullocks who intermarried with Jefferson descendants through Sally Hemings. My family's history is interwoven directly with the "Founding Fathers" of the United States (who held many of my ancestors in bondage!). When relaying the stories in a casual but memorable fashion, I often call him "Uncle Tom" for effect, flipping popular memory of the Harriet Beecher Stowe title character from *Uncle Tom's Cabin* on its head.

Take a seat, "Uncle Tom"—it's time to talk "Bullock" history. I have researched Burkley and many of his descendants. The strength and endurance of those in the Bullock lineage never cease to amaze me. They were strong-minded, humble, family-oriented trendsetters and changemakers. They continue to be so today. It is not uncommon for them to hide their superpowers so as not to draw unnecessary attention or make those around them feel inferior or not worthy. That's the opposite of what slavery tried to do to people. Despite enslavers' best efforts, Burkley Bullock and others remind us that, in fact, ownership of people is inherently impossible. He rose to the top despite every moment of adversity. He learned to read and write by lighted knots in the woods. He ran his enslaver Colonel Jones's commissary despite the fact that Jones originally forbade him to read. Burkley freed himself and his mother, bought property, raised a large family, led a church community, operated a land and improvement company, had a farm and a luncheonette, and—despite everything—showed up in the second edition of *Corks and Curls* (the University of Virginia yearbook). He was so successful, so well known, that even racist white students at UVA could not diminish him.

The real problem lies in the mindset of many in the white community. White privilege is compounded by the creation of spaces that have excluded the truth or omitted the difficult parts. White privilege prohibits us from ever growing by fully understanding our collective American past. In researching my family history, I have also uncovered the history of communities that have not simply endured but have succeeded! It is so obvious that Burkley Bullock had much more in mind for his legacy than meets the eye. Yes, slavery existed in America; it was always evil; and those enslaved universally sought release from the horrors of bondage. Suffice it to say that if Burkley hadn't minded slavery (of course, he hated it!), there would be no story of his escape. After 1865, he sought the full fruits of newfound freedom and was incredibly successful in that. He did not just succeed on his own nor strive to ensure only the success of his family: he sought to uplift his entire community.

Burkley's son Charles was no different—he sought community uplift as a pioneer in the Colored YMCA movement. He won his first secretaryship over 243 other applicants before he was twenty years old, and he then relocated to Brooklyn, New York, then to Louisville, and finally to Montclair in New Jersey. In his community work, he changed lives along the way, including the lives of his descendants, who would go on to build their own lives, attend college, own businesses, and own property. Louise Bullock was the first African American graduate of Rutgers University in New Brunswick, New Jersey; Eleanor Bullock was the first African American to graduate from Holy Name Nursing School in Teaneck, New Jersey; Jean Henderson was the first African American principal in Moorestown, New Jersey; and now we have the works of Bullock descendant and artist Lola Flash being shown at the Metropolitan Museum of Art and the African American Museum of American History and

Culture. We stand on the shoulders of Bullocks, generations of ancestors whose resilience, determination, and hard work paved the way for us.

I think it's wonderful that UVA is addressing the issue of slavery as a part of its past, but there is so much more work to do at UVA, in Charlottesville, in Virginia, and in America. Sure, honestly address the realities of slavery and racism, but take time to honor the humanity and determination of those who came before us. We need more stories like this one about the resilience, determination, and triumphs of Black families in American history.

When the KKK Flourished in Charlottesville

KIRT VON DAACKE AND ASHLEY SCHMIDT

In February 1915, the promotional campaign for D. W. Griffith's blockbuster film *Birth of a Nation* culminated in a special viewing at the White House for President Woodrow Wilson. A Virginian and University of Virginia School of Law alumnus (he attended for one year before withdrawing due to illness), Wilson was familiar with the message portrayed by the film; it was adapted from *The Clansman* and *The Leopard's Spots*, books written by Thomas Dixon Jr., Wilson's friend and classmate from his time in graduate school at Johns Hopkins University. Steeped in the mythology of the "Lost Cause," the film *Birth of a Nation* traces the Civil War era through the competing views of a Northern abolitionist family and a South Carolina planter family. The film reaches a crescendo after the assassination of Abraham Lincoln and feverishly depicts the imagined "failure" of Reconstruction, particularly the election of Black congressmen. The film mocks formerly enslaved African Americans as inferior, less than human, lazy, and incapable of self-governance or citizenship. *Birth of a Nation* concluded by metaphorically reuniting white Northerners and Southerners, and thereby the nation, through a reclamation of white rule and civilization led by the Ku Klux Klan. One of the film's title cards captured the idea succinctly: "The former enemies of North and South are united again in common defence of their Aryan birthright."

After that White House screening, President Wilson reportedly commented that the movie was "writing history as lightning, and my only regret is that it is all so true."[1] Many white Americans appear to have

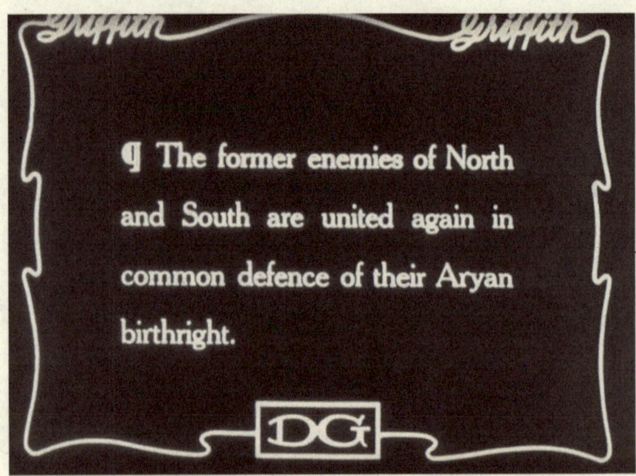

Title card from D. W. Griffith's *The Birth of a Nation*, 1915.

agreed. The Klan's membership surged in the years after the film's release—the mass reorganization of the Klan became more national, and chapters throughout the nation embraced the regalia featured in the movie. By 1924, membership nationwide had spiked to possibly as many as four million people. Charlottesville and the University of Virginia were enthusiastic participants in the national resurgence of public and celebratory white supremacy and the KKK.[2] In fact, the local embrace of the KKK—and with it, white supremacy and Lost Cause mythologizing—was already well underway before *Birth of a Nation*'s release. In 1909, the law fraternity Phi Delta Phi advertised its "annual Ku Klux Klan ride around the University grounds."[3] As a part of the Founder's Day festivities, the Phi Delta Phi Klan ride began on the Rotunda steps and attracted a large crowd. By 1909 it was a venerated tradition, but Klan-informed celebrations were not confined to the University, and the message they sent to Black residents in Charlottesville was understood by all. In 1916, the *Daily Progress* reported on the children parading in costume on Halloween: "a gay battalion of Ku Klux Klan came thundering down from the heights of the Midway, recalling other days. Many a dusky denizen of 'bottom' was seen to shrink instinctively back into the shadows of Preston Avenue."[4] In 1924, Charlottesville's *Daily Progress*, commending a local revival of *Birth of a Nation* and with it the message of the necessity of white rule, would term the film the "greatest spectacle" and "the greatest picture of the age."[5]

Movie poster for Griffith's "mighty spectacle," *The Birth of a Nation*.

This resurgence was not just in rhetoric or symbolic marches; it had real and violent consequences for African Americans in the Charlottesville area, as it had for decades by the time Woodrow Wilson was president. For example, in early April 1880, UVA students "imbued with the spirit of rioting and insubordination" marched down Main Street to "'clean out' the town." Students surrounded the home of a Black man near downtown in the Vinegar Hill neighborhood but "found a large number of negroes ready for the fray." A fight ensued and students used "clubs, stones, and pistols" against their Black neighbors. Police officers arrived and sent the students away after arresting one student for assault.[6] The fact that Black Charlottesvillians were prepared for such an attack speaks volumes about threat of racist terrorism at the time. In that 1880 instance, police arrived and broke up the violence, but they were not in the business of protecting and serving the Black community. In late March 1884, a man visiting Charlottesville recounted what he saw while in town: "It appears that a negro was detected stealing, or attempting to steal, a bundle of laths." After the Black man realized he had been spotted by police, "he immediately started off on a run, pursued by two police officers, but before he had got a hundred yards one of the officers drew his revolver, took deliberate aim, and fired, killing him instantly." The visitor additionally commented: "In view of the fact that the negro was well known in Charlottesville, and could have been arrested without difficulty, and that the offense was so trivial, the shooting was entirely unjustifiable, even had the object been only to cripple the man."[7]

Those acts of violence continued and escalated after the 1880s. In March 1890, a mob including UVA students attacked and attempted to lynch William Muscoe, a Black man accused of murdering a policeman.[8] On October 12, 1892, William Young, a Black man accused of murdering a white man, was lynched by a mob in Palmyra, a town twenty miles southeast of Charlottesville in neighboring Fluvanna County. While Young was in police custody in Palmyra, about twenty men stormed the jail and lynched him in a cemetery for the enslaved across the river.[9] Young's arrest and murder followed an altercation that had actually begun in Albemarle County. Six years later, John Henry James was falsely accused of assaulting a white woman in Charlottesville and quickly arrested. The arrest did not quell white rage, and a mob soon gathered outside the jail, threatening to lynch James. The authorities, seeking to disperse the mob and at least let James face trial, sent him to the Staunton jail for the night. The next morning, the police put James on a train back to Charlottesville so he could stand trial. A new mob of well over one hundred white locals—including UVA students as well as the sheriff and police chief—stopped the train before it arrived in Charlottesville, dragged James from the train, and lynched him on the spot at Wood's Crossing.[10] In 1903, "armed bands" of UVA students, looking for the Black residents accused of assaulting several students, "hunt[ed] negroes" by making "persistent raids upon the negro pool rooms." The Charlottesville police again did nothing to quell the violence, even though the "students are earnest in their threats to hang . . . [the] negroes if found." The only reason that the students did not engage in another lynching was because they were unable to find the alleged perpetrators of the earlier attack. According to one contemporary account, the students were well-versed in orchestrating their lynch mobs: "Leaders have been chosen and the body is under arms and ready to respond at the call." Reports that "the student organization has quite demoralized the negroes and no trouble is anticipated" make it clear that the climate of racial terror was pervasive.[11]

In 1917, just six months after *Birth of a Nation* had debuted in town, Black resident W. T. Clements was arrested and held under suspicion of "attempting to incite a rebellion among negroes of this section."[12] Two days after Clements's arrest, local African American men Hampton Cosby and Richard Jones were caught by a police officer while they were allegedly stealing a ham. A white racist hysteria soon gripped the town as a confusing welter of reporting trickled out. The truth of the officer's struggle with Cosby and Jones remains unclear—newspaper accounts shifted overnight and influenced public opinion with their descriptions. The first report, published on April 13, 1917, indicated that the policeman, Meredith A. Thomas, "was done to death by a brutal attack with a stone, his assailant beating him unmercifully about the head, while he was engaged in a scuffle with Robert Jones, colored, whom he had detected in the act of stealing a ham."[13] Both Black men were arrested within hours, along with John Anderson, who just happened to be at the house where Cosby was arrested.[14] One day later, the newspaper's account changed, allegedly based on the confessions of Cosby and Jones. In this version, Jones "knocked[ed] down the officer's revolver . . . and the weapon was fired by Mr. Thomas at the same instant, the ball making the wound in his left thigh just above the knee." During this struggle, Cosby grabbed a "heavy flint rock" and "started in to help him [Jones] by beating the officer over the head with it."[15] Within four days, the paper was describing the incident in fevered terms: the deceased police officer's life had been "snatched away by murder most foul," as he was "done to death while in the discharge of his duty by two negro housebreakers, who are now on trial for the dastardly crime."[16]

Only five days after the incident, Jones and Cosby were already on trial. A mob of hundreds gathered at the courthouse in response to a rising "spirit of riot and lynching" in Charlottesville. The lynch mob of "some hundreds in the principal throng, many having masks over their faces," attempted to storm the courthouse but were repelled by the police. A second lynch mob formed near where the incident had occurred, soon joining the first mob at the courthouse. The second mob included "a large delegation from the student body at the University . . . in the grand march to seize the men and carry out a spectacular lynching at a tree selected near the place of the killing."[17] Newspapers reported that both mobs ultimately included more than a thousand people. In an eerie similarity to the 1898 John Henry James lynching, Jones and Cosby were temporarily removed to Richmond until the mob dispersed and the trial could resume.[18] This time, Cosby and Jones faced a speedy trial of sorts. They were quickly found guilty by a jury of white men and executed at Richmond, barely two months after they had first been arrested.[19] Racial terror in Charlottesville included the very real threat of murderous mob violence as well as both law enforcement and court practices all geared to maintain white rule.

Meanwhile, nationwide, the Ku Klux Klan continued to expand as new chapters formed and membership in the white supremacist organization swelled. As the Klan grew in influence, local chapters attempted to donate to UVA's Centennial Fund. According to physics professor Thomas F. Ball's recollections decades later, in March 1919, the planning committee began to "hear rumors . . . that the Klu [*sic*] Klux Klan was planning to make a larger contribution" to the fund. At a faculty gathering at Professor William M. Thornton's residence on Monroe Hill, Ball was sent outside to talk to a "mysterious individual" who wanted an interview with someone on the planning committee. Once outside in the cold, the man instructed Ball to walk to the University cemetery. Ball recounts that "after entering the cemetery gate, I found myself immediately surrounded by hooded, white-robed men, all of whom stood in a circle with me at the center." When the robed men spoke to Ball, they informed him that they were "members of the Klu [*sic*] Klux Klan and that they were anxious to have me serve as an intermediary between the Klan and the University in connection with their offer of a contribution to the University's Centennial Fund." The men then handed Ball a check for $10,000. According to Ball, after meeting with President Alderman, that gift was reluctantly returned to the Klan a week later.[20]

Two years later, the Klan did donate money to the Centennial Gymnasium Fund. In March 1921, the Virginia state Klan sent a letter directly to President Edwin Alderman pledging $1,000 to UVA's Centennial Endowment Fund. Alderman publicly "expressed the hearty thanks of the University" for what he termed the Klan's "generosity and good will" for the pledge gift.[21] Though Alderman publicly denied knowledge of the actual persons behind the gift, in his private correspondence, he admitted that the Klan's donation was made by "a local student organization" and that, in his mind, "their purposes were of the highest, in so far as the University was concerned" and that he did "not want to hurt their feelings but they were conferred with and told the embarrassment in the matter, and they very handsomely withdrew their subscription."[22] Part of the "embarrassment" that Alderman refers to is the flood of letters from monied donors (particularly from northern cities) who described their strong objections to the Klan's donation. As Alderman and his committee were racing to secure $1 million in donations for the Centennial, he was also answering letters from people disturbed by the news of a donation from the KKK. In one letter, Alderman seemed exasperated and defensive: "I do not at this time feel inclined to discuss the question of the existence of the Klu [*sic*] Klux Klan in this University. . . . It does exist." But, he continues, "I may, however, say without committing myself as to the wisdom of the re-establishment of any such order at this time, that so far the spirit and activities of this organization have been in the direction of honorable living and good conduct."[23]

A few months later, the *Daily Progress* reported that "the spirit of Nathan Bedford Forrest hovered over Charlottesville recently, and the fiery cross, symbolic of the Invisible Empire and of the unconquered and unconquerable blood of America, cast an eerie sheen upon a legion of white robed Virginians as they stood upon hallowed ground and renewed the faith of their fathers." In a midnight ceremony at Thomas Jefferson's grave that month, "hundreds of Charlottesville's leading business and professional men met . . . and sealed the pledge of chivalry and patriotism with the deepest crimson of red American blood."[24] The Klan's vision of white supremacy was popular with both elites as well as ordinary Virginians. Within a month, the newly formed local chapter posted bulletins across town warning that "law and order must prevail at Charlottesville, Va.," and "all undesirables must leave town." The *Daily Progress* further reported that the Klan bulletins included an invitation to "native-born white Americans" to join if they believed in "White Supremacy."[25] They also held a public address at the courthouse on July 20, 1921, delivered by a Klan promoter from Atlanta.

The following year, the Klan's popularity among white leaders in the area was evident, as the paper reported the group's appearance at the Oakwood Cemetery funeral service for the Albemarle County sheriff.

Section heading image depicting the Ku Klux Klan on the ride, University of Virginia *Corks and Curls* yearbook, 1922. (University of Virginia Albert and Shirley Small Special Collections Library)

According to the *Richmond Planet*, "six white-robed members of the Ku Klux Klan suddenly appeared . . . scaled a high rock wall and forming the figure of a cross, marched in the newly-made grave bearing a large cross of red flowers," which they placed on the grave.[26] By 1922, the KKK had at least two chapters locally. The second, known as "VA. Klan No. 5," was at UVA.[27] This UVA chapter had likely been in existence for at least a year, if not longer, when it threatened to separate from the national organization. The 1922 edition of the student yearbook, *Corks and Curls*, even included an image of the Klan on the ride as the frontispiece for the student organizations section. In August 1922, the Grand Dragon of the state Klan came to Charlottesville and delivered a speech advocating "rigid preservation of white supremacy. The destinies of America shall remain with the white race; they shall never be entrusted to the black, the brown, or the yellow, or to the unclean hands of hybrids and mongrels." In reporting on the speech, the *Daily Progress* added that the "Charlottesville Klan is not the largest in Virginia, but it numbers among its members many of our able and influential citizens."[28]

By the early 1920s, with close to sixty local chapters statewide, visible Klan activity, and with it a broad commitment to racial terror in maintenance of white rule, was part of the fabric of life in Charlottesville and Albemarle. In April and June 1924, another travelling KKK speaker, an attorney from St. Louis, lectured at the courthouse downtown.[29] On a Friday night in May 1924, the Klan burned a large cross atop Montalto; the fire lasted two hours and was visible for miles. The next day, the KKK paraded in full regalia from Belmont down Main Street to the Midway atop the African American Vinegar Hill neighborhood, with thousands lining the sidewalks. That evening, Charlottesville resident Thomas Lafayette Rosser Jr. noted that as the town prepared for a celebration of Confederate veterans and the "unveiling of the Lee statue . . . the Klu Klux had a parade" and "some students pelted them with eggs." The egging did not represent opposition to the KKK or their agenda, just some tomfoolery, as "the students put handkerchiefs over their faces and called themselves 'Klu Klux's' and had a snake dance down Main Street, stopping street cars and all traffic."[30] In the same month, the local KKK demonstrated in Crozet, Keswick, and Scottsville. All three events included cross burnings. The local paper remarked that "the hooded order is quite active here."[31]

Unsurprisingly, the Ku Klux Klan's activities locally, supported by many whites, explicitly promoted and enforced white supremacy. In late June 1924, the *Daily Progress* reported that "fifty klansmen, only about six of them masked," set off "heavy explosions from three bombs" and then burned a large cross on a Saturday night "near the colored church just west of Mechum's River." The paper additionally indicated that the Klan's "action is commended by the people" of the area and "the good citizens of that part of the county."[32] Although the Klan was technically a secret organization, local membership was clearly an open secret—no masks or hoods were necessary. Suzanne Cook Martin remembered that her grandfather, John West, a Black barber who had many white customers and lived at 313 West Main Street, told her and his other grandchildren "to quickly get into the house and stay there. He went out to the front gate of the house and watched a parade of Ku Klux Klan men, completely covered in white sheets, as they marched down West Main Street. Afterwards he came in and said, 'I recognized every single one of them!' He was their barber and knew them all by their shoes!"[33]

Many students at UVA similarly supported the Klan's white supremacist ideology. The student publications during this time centered white power and often degraded Black people through the use of blackface minstrelsy. They romanticized violent white supremacy through drawings, poems, and other fiction pieces but also threatened physical violence toward the local Black community. For example, the student yearbook *Corks and Curls* was often filled with racist imagery at that time—in the 1914 and 1917 editions there were more than thirty instances of derogatory images, cartoons, stories, or jokes, and the 1915 and 1928 edition both had well over twenty such instances. *College Topics* in 1924 blamed Black community members (especially children) for property destruction and stealing from students. They even criticized a University policeman for his purported failure to keep Black locals off the campus, issuing a veiled threat: "Let the students take it in hand and a simple announcement that they intend to see that no negroes come on grounds at night without reason will be all that is required."[34]

Such instances of UVA students claiming policing power over Black locals were not isolated incidents. For example, in 1924, newspapers make it clear that there was a sort of white panic about crime and imagined Black criminality that threatened to erupt in racist mob violence against African Americans. In October 1924, student C. M. Frost threw a firecracker at an unnamed Black man behind a fraternity house, allegedly because he thought the man had been involved in an altercation earlier that day in which he had shot and wounded another African American man. Frost never positively identified anyone, but he threw the firework anyway. Immediately, a small mob of students effectively deputized themselves as "crime"-stopping keepers of the racial order when they chased the unidentified Black man down Madison Lane and onto the UVA campus. The police later joined the manhunt with a bloodhound, but they did not find the man they had been chasing (or anyone else, for that matter).[35] Two weeks later, the authorities claimed that they had located Isaac Brooks, the man wanted for his involvement in the shooting, living in northern Virginia. They additionally claimed that he had fled by freight train.[36] Although no mob violence ultimately occurred that day in 1924, panicked newspaper accounts describing the manhunt demonstrate just how close Charlottesville came to another lynching.

Ku Klux Klan march in Charlottesville, July 2017. (Eze Amos)

Students at the University in the early twentieth century saw themselves as emerging guardians of white supremacy. Law student William Saunders Gibson argued that "if there is in America one college of pure Anglo-Saxon heritage, it is the University of Virginia." Gibson drew on the "Anglo-Saxon conservatism" of Jefferson and Wilson as proof that "in the University of Virginia, the Anglo-Saxon boy can find his true soil."[37] In 1923, UVA alumnus and famous composer John Powell, already a founder of the Anglo-Saxon Clubs of America, organized two posts of the club in Charlottesville, one for the University and one in the community. The purpose of these "scientific" eugenics clubs was to "preserve the purity of the white people . . . [and] maintain the qualities and characteristics of the Anglo-Saxon race," ensuring a "rigid classification of all the citizens of the state as belonging either to the white or to the negro race, no twilight zone being recognized."[38]

The Klan continued to be quite active for a few more years, participating in national events in distant cities as well as appearing publicly at local revivals while still parading and burning crosses regularly.[39] Klan activity locally and in Virginia before 1930 presaged the resurgent violent white reactions to the civil rights movement a few decades later—and even as recently as 2017, when the Klan marched in Charlottesville in July, just about a month before an armed white supremacist demonstration left four people dead in August. Klan membership and influence started to decline in Virginia after 1930, thanks to organizational infighting and white Virginian elite disdain for the Klan's penchant for mob violence. As one scholar noted, the Klan "threatened paternalistic notions of noblesse oblige that formed the foundation of Virginia's claim to friendly race relations. In short, elites considered the Klan crass and embarrassing" but otherwise shared a commitment to white rule with them.[40] Unsurprisingly, broad white Virginian support for white supremacy would live on for decades at UVA and in the surrounding area, particularly in reaction to integration, and remains visible even in the twenty-first century.

Notes

1. See Mark E. Benbow, "Birth of a Quotation: Woodrow Wilson and 'Like Writing History with Lightning,'" *Journal of the Gilded Age and Progressive Era* 9, no. 4 (2010): 509–33.
2. Thanks to the Charlottesville mayor's Blue Ribbon Commission on Race, Memorials, and Public Spaces for their research and the historical timeline published as an appendix to their report, which first gave details about Klan activity in the area from 1917 to 1924 (the appendix starts on p. 71 of the document). The report can be accessed at Cvillepedia: https://cvillepedia.org/images/2016_Blue_Ribbon_Commission_report.pdf.
3. "Phi Delta Phi Public Goating," *College Topics*, April 14, 1909.
4. "Hallowe'en Is Duly Observed," *Charlottesville Daily Progress*, November 1, 1916, 1. Articles from the *Charlottesville Daily Progress* are available online, via the University of Virginia Library, at https://guides.lib.virginia.edu/Daily-Progress-Digital.
5. "At the Theatres," *Charlottesville Daily Progress*, January 24, 1924, 1, and "Avoid the Crowd," *Charlottesville Daily Progress*, January 25, 1924, 1.
6. *Wheeling (W. Va.) Register*, April 5, 1880, [1], accessed via Readex: America's Historical Newspapers.
7. "Brutal Act of Charlottesville Policemen," *Baltimore Sun*, March 25, 1884, suppl., [1], accessed via Readex: America's Historical Newspapers.
8. "That Lynching," *College Topics*, March 26, 1890.

9. Steven Schlanger, "Anatomy of a Lynching," Racial Terror in Virginia, James Madison University, https://sites.lib.jmu.edu/valynchings/anatomy-of-a-lynching/.
10. "John Henry James Lynched in Virginia by 150 Unmasked White Men," Equal Justice Initiative, A History of Racial Injustice, https://calendar.eji.org/racial-injustice/jul/12.
11. "Armed Bands Hunt Negroes," *Roanoake Evening News*, December 21, 1903, 1, https://virginiachronicle.com/?a=d&d=TVN19031221.1.1&e.
12. "Held Under Suspicion," *Charlottesville Daily Progress*, April 10, 1917, 1.
13. "Sub Policeman Is Murdered," *Charlottesville Daily Progress*, April 13, 1917.
14. "Sub Policeman Is Murdered"; "Raise Fund for Officer Thomas' Widow," *Charlottesville Daily Progress*, April 16, 1917, 1.
15. "Cosby Shot Thomas," *Charlottesville Daily Progress*, April 14, 1917, 1.
16. "Cosby Shot Thomas."
17. "Lynching Party Is Dispersed," *Charlottesville Daily Progress*, April 17, 1917, 1 and 8.
18. "Judge Scatters Mob," *Baltimore Sun*, April 18, 1917, 6.
19. "Men Die in Electric Chair," *Charlottesville Daily Progress*, June 20, 1917, 1.
20. Thomas Ball's recollections from Thomas Fauntleroy Ball, "The University Centennial," October 23, 1962, in the Papers of Thomas Fauntleroy Ball, 1962, accession #12711, Special Collections, University of Virginia Library.
21. "J. P. Morgan, the Ku Klux Klan and Youngest Descendant of Thomas Jefferson Contribute to U. of Va. Fund," *Alexandria Gazette*, March 23, 1921, 2, and "Ku Klux Klan Gives a Thousand Dollars to Gymnasium Fund," *College Topics*, March 25, 1921, 1–2.
22. Edwin A. Alderman, letter to David R. Lyman, April 7, 1921, Papers of the President, Accession #RG-2/1/2.472, subseries VI, Special Collections, University of Virginia Library, "Centennial Correspondence" Folder.
23. Edwin A. Alderman, letter to E. D. Sampson, April 12, 1922, Papers of the President, Accession # RG-2/1/2.472, subseries VI, Special Collections, University of Virginia Library, "Centennial Correspondence" Folder.
24. "Ku Klux Klan Organized Here," *Charlottesville Daily Progress*, June 28, 1921, 1.
25. "Ku Klux Klan Issues 'Warning,'" *Charlottesville Daily Progress*, July 19, 1921, 1.
26. "Ku Klux Klan at Thomas Funeral," *Richmond Planet*, February 18, 1922, 1, https://virginiachronicle.com/cgi-bin/virginia?a=d&d=RP19220218.1.1&srpos=1&e=--1922---1922--en-20-RP-1-byDA-txt-txIN-Charlottesville.
27. "U. of VA. Klan No. 5," *Charlottesville Daily Progress*, November 6, 1922, 1.
28. "Ku Klux Klan: Grand Dragon of State Visits Charlottesville," *Charlottesville Daily Progress*, August 23, 1922, 1 and 3.

29. "Klan Speaker Here Last Night," *Charlottesville Daily Progress*, April 26, 1924, 1, and "Klan Speaker Well Received," *Charlottesville Daily Progress*, June 9, 1924, 1.
30. Thomas L. Rosser Jr., letter to his daughter Barbara, May 24, 1924, Special Collections, University of Virginia Library, MSS 1171-g, -h, -j, Box 7.
31. From the *Charlottesville Daily Progress:* "Cross Burned on Patterson's Mountain," May 17, 1924, 1; "Klan Parade Drew Big Crowd," May 19, 1924, 1; "Klan Burns Crosses at Several Places," June 2, 1924, 1; and "Flaming Cross Seen Last Night," *Charlottesville Daily Progress*, June 4, 1924, 1.
32. From the *Charlottesville Daily Progress:* "Klan Burns Cross Near Mechums River," June 23, 1924, 1; "Klan Visits Keswick Church," August 23, 1924, 1; and "Klan Visits Fife Chapel," August 30, 1924, 1.
33. Tenth Anniversary Cookbook, African American Genealogy Group of Charlottesville and Albemarle County, Virginia, June 2005, p. 70, quoted in Charlottesville Blue Ribbon Commission Report, appendix (Historical Timeline), 51.
34. "Keep Em Out," *College Topics*, November 8, 1902.
35. "Man Hunt for Negro Murderer Staged by Students and Police," *College Topics*, October 6, 1924.
36. "Negroe Shooter Finally Located," *College Topics*, October 21, 1924.
37. M. S. Gibson, "Why the Anglo-Saxon Boy Should Go to the University of Virginia," circa 1924, Accession #14545, Special Collections, University of Virginia Library.
38. "Anglo-Saxon Club Founds Two Posts in Community," *College Topics*, October 5, 1923.
39. From the *Charlottesville Daily Progress:* "Ku Klux Klansmen Pour into Capital for Demonstration," August 7, 1925, 1; "Klan to Parade at 8 Tonight," August 22, 1925, 1; "Klan Parade a Big Success," August 24, 1925, 1; "Burning Klan Cross Draws Large Crowd," June 16, 1926, 1; "Ku Klux Klan Attend Revival," June 29, 1926, 1, 9; and "Klan Attends Revival Service," July 2, 1926, 1, 3.
40. J. Douglas Smith, *Managing White Supremacy: Race, Politics, and Citizenship in Jim Crow Virginia* (Chapel Hill: University of North Carolina Press, 2002), quoted in "Ku Klux Klan in Virginia," *Encyclopedia Virginia*, https://www.encyclopediavirginia.org/ku_klux_klan_in_virginia.

Response

Truth Revealed

REV. DR. SUSAN MINASIAN

IT WAS a beautiful weekend in Central Virginia. I was given a tour around Charlottesville as part of my interview weekend for a new pastorate. The driver was intentional about showing me the monuments commemorating the Lost Cause. In the process of doing that, I learned about the Charlottesville mayor's Blue Ribbon Commission on Race, Memorials, and Public Spaces and the movement afoot to take down the monuments.

My first response was, "Why don't they just contextualize them?" Little did I know how I had been shaped to ask that question. I am the product of the Richmond public school system. Like most white people, I was taught a certain narrative about the South, slavery, the Civil War. Going through middle school and high school during "busing" (when leaders tried to reach desegregation goals by busing students to more distant schools, out of their segregated neighborhoods) taught me all I needed to know about race in America . . . so I thought.

That eventual move to Charlottesville in 2017 turned out to be more than a course on correcting history. In many ways it was a transformative experience and a dismantling of the narrative that so many of us have accepted as truth. Now, I know a truth that has been revealed about how white supremacy's legacies are all around us—in parks, in schools, in laws, and in systems. Kirt von Daacke and Ashley Schmidt's essay "When the KKK Flourished in Charlottesville" brings out into full light what was never hidden. It is the long local history of white supremacy that we chose to "forget"—and we have paid a great price for doing so.

In the summer of 2018, I joined a community trip to the Equal Justice Initiative's National Memorial for Peace and Justice in Montgomery,

Stonewall Jackson monument with the Albemarle County Courthouse in the background, Court Square, Charlottesville. (Sanjay Suchak)

Alabama, that was part of a local acknowledgment and atonement process for the 1898 lynching of John Henry James. The Charlottesville Civil Rights Pilgrimage was a powerful journey of truth-telling. As we traveled miles visiting with individuals who were the prophetic voices of the civil rights movement, essays like von Daacke and Schmidt's came to life. Testimonies from those on the front lines of history taught us how the legacy of human enslavement was the beginning of a systemic racism that has only changed in how it is embodied in our country. I have learned how the pandemic of racism has not only remained a living legacy but has mutated into new variants to this day.

As a pastor, I have always believed that confession—truth-telling—is good for the soul. I also believe that truth-telling is the first step toward justice. Without that, reconciliation and repair cannot happen. While von Daacke and Schmidt reveal just how prevalent the KKK and white supremacy have been in Charlottesville, we must also remember that pro-slavery ideologies prevalent in Virginia for decades before 1865 and the white supremacist propaganda of the Jim Crow era will continue to poison us unless we openly acknowledge the history, the difficult reality, of how accepted white supremacist groups and their ideas have been our communities.

The University of Virginia established the President's Commission on Slavery and the University (PCSU) in 2013 and the President's Commission on the University in the Age of Segregation (PCUAS) in 2018.

Jar of soil from the site of John Henry James's lynching in 1898, from the Equal Justice Initiative's Soil Collection Project, housed at the Jefferson School African American Heritage Center, Charlottesville. (Kirt von Daacke)

While those are important steps in exposing the complicity of the University throughout its history, more is necessary. Telling the truth and learning the truth are only the beginning. Implementing institutional changes will demonstrate not only the unveiling of truth but the correctives that are imperative for the dismantling of white supremacy at the University, in the city of Charlottesville, in the Commonwealth of Virginia, and in our nation as a whole.

I am writing this reflection in 2021, four years after the beginning of my own journey of learning the truth—that tour of Charlottesville I took before moving there. I am now living in Philadelphia, Pennsylvania, and just last week, white supremacists marched with tiki torches through Philadelphia on the eve of the Fourth of July. On the fourth anniversary of the KKK rally in Charlottesville in July 2017, I witnessed from afar Charlottesville's removal of many of its monuments to the Lost Cause. In that one week in 2021, there were reminders that the material markers of white supremacy can be removed, but the virus it has created remains.

My hope, and prayer, is that we will do what it takes as a nation to become the truth-tellers. In exposing events and ideas from our past, we have an opportunity to own the state of our nation in the present. The summer 2020 murder of George Floyd by a police officer kneeling on Floyd's neck for nearly nine minutes is an all-too-familiar story about the horror that remains a part of our daily narrative. It is up to us not only to read about the truth, to remove the symbols that remind us of the lies we tell about our history, but also to do as the prophet Micah calls us to: "Do justice, love kindness and walk humbly with God" (6:8).

When truth is revealed, we have an opportunity to live differently. The time for living differently is now. While I am grateful for all that has been revealed through studying historical documents, the true revelation has yet to be embodied. How will the truth change us? How will we become a better people? How will those of us with privilege use our location to repair the world?

Truth-telling is indeed an important step, but it is only the first step. When I lived in Charlottesville, I attended many walking tours led by PCUAS co-chair Dr. Andrea Douglas and Professor Jalane Schmidt. They have been my teachers in the streets of Charlottesville and on that long 2017 community pilgrimage to the Deep South. I left that trip and Charlottesville a very different person than the one who asked, "Why don't they just contextualize them?" Today, I know what I didn't know then, and it is now my call not just to do better but also to be a voice for the dismantling of the evil of white supremacy, wherever my journey takes me.

As a pastor, I believe in redemption and transformation. These days it is hard sometimes to keep believing. Yet I will continue to learn, because that assignment is never complete. I want to be one of the truth-tellers. Maybe if more of us wake up when truth is revealed, that Beloved Community will actually become a reality—and a new day will actually dawn.

Walter Reed and the Scourge of Yellow Fever

DAN CAVANAUGH

AT MIDNIGHT on December 31, 1900, Major Walter Reed, an 1869 alumnus of the University of Virginia, sat down in his quarters in Cuba and wrote to his wife: "Here I have been sitting reading that most wonderful book—La Roche on Yellow Fever—written in 1853—Forty-seven years later it has been permitted to me and my assistants to lift the impenetrable veil that has surrounded the causation of this most dreadful pest of humanity and to put it on a rational and scientific basis—I thank God that this has been accomplished during the latter days of the old century—May its cure be wrought out in the early days of the new century!"[1] Walter Reed had good reason to celebrate that New Year's Eve. He and his colleagues had proven that yellow fever was spread by mosquitoes, providing hope that one day humanity would control one of its most frightening diseases. Today, most Americans have little knowledge of Walter Reed or his role in the fight against yellow fever. However, his story was once widely known.

Walter Reed was born in Virginia in 1851. At the age of fifteen, Reed enrolled in the University of Virginia, and after two years of study earned an M.D. In that time, he took James Lawrence Cabell's course in physiology and surgery, John Staige Davis's course in anatomy, and James Harrison's course in medicine.[2] Beyond a listing of the courses he took at the University, little is known about Reed's time at UVA. Reed continued his studies in New York City, earning a second medical degree from the Bellevue Hospital Medical College. Then, in 1875, Reed became

Walter Reed, 1868. (University of Virginia Albert and Shirley Small Special Collections Library)

a doctor in the U.S. Army Medical Corps, where he spent the rest of his career. For nearly twenty years, Reed served as an army surgeon stationed in various military posts across the western states and territories of the United States. Around the age of forty, Reed abandoned his life as a practicing clinician to focus on biomedical research, and in a short time, he became well respected in the army for his research on a wide range of infectious diseases. At the end of his career, he become famous for his work with yellow fever, a disease that had plagued Americans for centuries.[3]

Yellow fever, like Walter Reed, is not well known in the United States today. In the eighteenth and nineteenth centuries, though, outbreaks of yellow fever were common in this country. While other maladies were more prevalent and more deadly, few could generate as much terror. It spread rapidly and could kill 20 percent of a city's population in just two to three months. A series of yellow fever outbreaks in Philadelphia in the 1790s famously shut down the federal government and killed nearly 10 percent of the city's population.[4] As terrible as those Philadelphia outbreaks had been, they were not even the deadliest in U.S. history. The deadliest outbreak of yellow fever occurred in the summer and fall of 1878, infecting 120,000 and killing between 13,000 and 20,000 Americans in the lower Mississippi Valley.[5] These outbreaks and others in the United States were especially frightening to Americans because no one could explain the cause of yellow fever or how it spread.

At the end of the nineteenth century, a growing community of medical researchers, including Walter Reed, worked relentlessly to provide answers. Most of them believed that yellow fever was caused by bacteria and spread by fomites—objects soiled with human blood and excrement. However, after decades of research, there was no scientific evidence to support this theory.[6] Many white physicians and scientists believed, moreover, that individuals of African descent were less susceptible to the disease than other populations. There was no scientific evidence to support this theory, but it became popular among Europeans in the eighteenth century who were trying to legitimize African enslavement in areas where yellow fever was endemic. African Americans from at least the 1790s onward published several works that dispelled this long-standing race-based theory. While there is evidence that Walter Reed held racist views, it is not yet known what he thought of this idea or other race-based theories.[7]

Meanwhile, at the fringes of the biomedical community, a Cuban physician by the name of Carlos Finlay advocated a radically different theory, arguing that yellow fever was spread by mosquitoes. Finlay was correct, but he could not produce experimental results that were conclusive enough to challenge the beliefs of the mainstream scientific community. He acknowledged the uphill battle he faced, remarking in 1881: "I understand too well that nothing less than an absolutely incontrovertible demonstration will be required before the generality of my colleagues accept a theory so entirely at variance with the ideas which have until now prevailed about yellow fever."[8] Nineteen years later, Reed and his associates on the U.S. Army Yellow Fever Commission would finally provide an "incontrovertible demonstration" to prove Finlay's theory—but only after a U.S. public health campaign in Cuba based on the fomite theory failed to control the spread of yellow fever.

After the Spanish-American War, Spain transferred control of Cuba to the United States, and it was agreed that the island would remain a U.S. protectorate until the United States decided to grant Cuba its independence. During the first U.S. occupation of Cuba, from 1899 to 1902, U.S. authorities on the island prioritized funding for yellow fever in Cuba—committing unprecedented amounts of money to the study and control of the disease. This focus on yellow fever was not altruistic; it served U.S. national interests first and foremost. Historically, while most native Cubans contracted yellow fever as children and survived the disease with a lifelong immunity, adult foreigners in Cuba succumbed to the disease in great numbers. The United States feared that without effective yellow fever controls, the thousands of troops it had stationed on the island were in great peril and might spread the disease to the mainland.[9] The U.S. occupation government, confident that the unproven fomite theory was correct, implemented a massive public health campaign to improve sanitation on the island. Although the campaign facilitated the decline of other infectious diseases in Cuba, it did not impact yellow fever.[10]

In May 1900, the U.S. Army, frustrated by this failure, formed the U.S. Army Yellow Fever Commission to gather data in Cuba that might inspire improvements in the public health campaign. Major Walter Reed, then a medical army researcher, was appointed to lead the group. The army designated three physicians to serve on the commission under Reed's direction: James Carroll, Reed's longtime research assistant; Arístides Agramonte y Simoni, an army contract surgeon who had been studying yellow fever in Cuba since the beginning of the occupation; and Jesse Lazear, another army contract surgeon who was studying the causes of yellow fever outside of Havana. U.S. Army Surgeon General George Miller Sternberg first ordered the commission to investigate potential bacterial causes of yellow fever. In June and July 1900, Reed and his colleagues tested the blood of infected yellow fever patients but could find no bacterial agent. They observed in their studies that exposure to fomites did not seem to have any relation to yellow fever infection. With no evidence to support the popular theories about yellow fever, Reed concluded that "at this stage of our investigation it seemed to me, and I so expressed the opinion to my colleagues, that the time had arrived when the plan of our work should be radically changed."[11]

At this time, most likely at the urging of Jesse Lazear, the commission turned its attention to Finlay's mosquito theory. New discoveries encouraged them to pursue this avenue of research. Recently, it had been proven by Britain's Ronald Ross that malaria was spread by mosquitoes, showing that it might be possible that other diseases were spread by the insect. Another researcher, University of Virginia alumnus Henry Rose Carter, had recently discovered that there was a delay of ten to seventeen days between the first infection of yellow fever in an outbreak and its spread to secondary hosts. Carter's discovery suggested that Finlay's attempts to prove his mosquito theory may have failed because his experiments were not designed to account for this delay.

In August 1900, Walter Reed temporarily returned to Washington, D.C., while Jesse Lazear and James Carroll began conducting experiments

Walter Reed as he sailed to Cuba as part of the U.S. Yellow Fever Commission, circa 1900. (University of Virginia Albert and Shirley Small Special Collections Library)

with mosquitoes in Havana's Las Animas Hospital. After several failed attempts to infect volunteer subjects with yellow fever, Carroll volunteered to feed a mosquito on himself and contracted yellow fever. Carroll survived the infection but would suffer from complications of yellow fever for the rest of his life.[12] Four days after Carroll was bitten, a U.S. soldier, William Dean, volunteered to subject himself to the experiment and contracted yellow fever. Dean would also survive. Dean and Carroll became infected while the other volunteers remained healthy because the commission allowed the disease to incubate longer in the mosquitoes that bit Dean and Carroll, which was consistent with the discovery made by Henry Rose Carter. News of Carroll's and Dean's infections reached

Walter Reed in Washington, D.C. After hearing that Carroll would survive, on September 7, 1900, Reed excitedly wrote to his longtime assistant: "Hip! Hip! Hurrah! God be praised for the news from Cuba today–'Carroll much improved–Prognosis very good!' I shall simply go out and get boiling drunk!" After sealing the letter, Reed scribbled on the envelope one final remark: "Did the Mosquito DO IT?"[13]

Excitement and joy would soon give way to tragedy. Jesse Lazear contracted yellow fever and died from the disease on September 25.[14] For over one hundred years, historians have debated the circumstances that led to Lazear's death. In Lazear's notebook, he records that he administered a bite from an infected mosquito to a test subject known as "Guinea Pig No. 1." It has been argued that "Guinea Pig No. 1" was in fact Lazear himself.[15] The infection of Carroll and Dean suggested that Finlay, long mocked by his colleagues as the "Mosquito Man," was right. However, these preliminary experiments would not be enough to upend the popular fomites theory. After Reed presented the early results at a conference in October 1900, an editorial was published in the *Washington Post* that ridiculed the findings: "Of all, the silly and nonsensical rigmarole about yellow fever that has yet found its way into print—and there has been enough of it to load a fleet—the silliest beyond compare is to be found in the arguments and theories engendered by the mosquito hypothesis."[16]

Walter Reed set out to design a series of experiments that would incontrovertibly prove Finlay's theory. First, Reed ordered the construction of an isolated experimental camp outside of Havana "in order to exercise perfect control over the movements of those individuals who were to be subjected to experimentation, and to avoid any other source of infection."[17] The facility was named Camp Lazear in honor of their deceased colleague.

Then, the commission began to recruit human test subjects for the experiments. Human experimentation at that time was not uncommon in medical research, but the way it was generally practiced in the nineteenth century would be considered abhorrent today. Many researchers experimented on enslaved persons, the incarcerated, orphans, and other vulnerable populations without their consent or knowledge. The Yellow Fever Commission did not engage in these practices. Instead, they put out calls for U.S. soldiers and recent Spanish immigrants to volunteer for the study. The commission wanted nonimmune subjects who had no history of previously being infected with yellow fever. The men who volunteered were informed about the experiments beforehand and compensated monetarily for their contribution. Then, for the first time in history, all of the volunteers were given written contracts to sign that contained the terms of their involvement in the study. The Spanish volunteers were given two copies of the contract, one written in Spanish and the other in English, to ensure that they understood the agreement.[18] The experiments would not begin until all the volunteers had given their written consent.[19]

Nearly everyone involved with the experiments understood the gravity of their work. Several of the U.S. soldiers and civilians who volunteered refused monetary compensation. They exposed themselves to yellow fever to help advance "medical science." Later, in a recommendation for one of these volunteers, John Moran, Walter Reed wrote: "A man who volunteered, as he did, without hope of any pecuniary reward, but solely in the interests of humanity and medical science, to enter a building purposely infected with yellow fever . . . should need no word of recommendation from any one."[20] On November 20, 1900, preparations were complete and experiments began at Camp Lazear. In the first experiment, a group of volunteers received bites from mosquitoes that had previously bitten yellow fever patients. Four of the volunteers contracted yellow fever. In the second experiment, four volunteers were injected with the blood of patients who had been infected with yellow fever. Three of the volunteers contracted yellow fever, suggesting that the disease could be transmitted through direct contact with fresh blood.[21]

In the third experiment, the commission hoped to put the fomites theory to rest. Two buildings, personally designed by Walter Reed, were constructed. In the first building, three volunteers were sealed in a room and asked to sleep in linens covered with the excrement and dried blood of patients who had died of yellow fever and wear the clothes of the deceased patients. Although the three volunteers in this room had a very unpleasant experience, none of them contracted yellow fever. The other building had two rooms. The commission released infected mosquitoes into one room and kept the second room completely empty. Volunteers who spent time in the mosquito room contracted yellow fever, while the volunteers in the empty room did not.[22] Combined, the three experiments provided strong proof for Finlay's theory, and remarkably, none of the infected volunteers died during the study.

The occupation government was now eager to put the findings of the Yellow Fever Commission to practical use. Major William Gorgas, the chief sanitary officer of Havana, admitted that after the preliminary experiments, he was skeptical of the mosquito theory, but the experiments at Camp Lazear convinced him otherwise. In December 1900, as the results at Camp Lazear began to circulate, Gorgas wrote to Henry Rose Carter: "So I think if you want to be in at the killing, you had better come down [to Cuba] this winter. I think we are about to make a historic campaign against yellow jack in Havana next summer, and such a seasoned old veteran as you ought to have a part in such a climax."[23] Gorgas was right—the public health campaign of 1901 was historic. The occupation government instituted an unprecedented mosquito control program in Havana. Brigades of Cuban workers fumigated houses, eliminated sources of standing water, and quarantined infected yellow fever patients in rooms protected by mosquito nets. The results were dramatic. In less than a year, yellow fever had been virtually eradicated in Havana, providing the ultimate demonstration that Finlay's mosquito theory was correct.

In the years that followed, mosquito control campaigns eradicated yellow fever in North America and the Caribbean. Generations of people were spared the terror and suffering that came with a yellow fever epidemic, and the disease has become largely forgotten in Walter Reed's native country. The yellow fever experiments catapulted Reed to the heights of fame. After his death in 1902, he was widely memorialized and soon became more a myth than a man. U.S. journalists, artists, and educators, looking for a single heroic figure to symbolize the promise of modern medicine, embellished their stories about Reed. In the drive to make him a hero, Americans too often diminished the vital contributions of Carlos Finlay, Jesse Lazear, James Carroll, Arístides Agramonte y Simoni, and the experimental volunteers.

Also, too often, popular accounts diminished the serious questions surrounding the use of humans in medical experimentation. When Reed first presented the commission's findings to an audience of his colleagues, he received both praise and criticism. The first comment on the commission's monumental paper came from Dr. Louis Perna of Cienfuegos, Cuba, who "criticized the methods employed by the commission in making experiments on human beings and is entirely opposed to such experiments." Reed's Cuban and American colleagues in attendance strongly defended the commission's experiments against Perna's critique, praising the high standards set by this work. Reed himself defended the commission's efforts by noting that his decision to employ human experimentation was not taken lightly, and he assured those in attendance that "all experiments were performed on persons who had given their free consent."[24]

The experiments that Walter Reed and his colleagues designed did not reach the higher ethical standards that have been established for modern experiments, but they were an improvement over what came before. Their work provided an example of how medical research could be done with greater respect for human dignity. This, with the confirmation of Finlay's theory, is the greatest legacy of Walter Reed's and his colleagues' work in Cuba.

Notes

1. Walter Reed, letter to Emilie Lawrence Reed, December 31, 1900, Philip S. Hench Walter Reed Yellow Fever Collection, 1806–1995, Historical Collections, Claude Moore Health Sciences Library, University of Virginia, Charlottesville, Va. (hereafter Yellow Fever Collection), Box-Folder 22:62.
2. *Catalogue of the University of Virginia, 1868–1869* (Baltimore: The Sun Book and Job Printing Establishment, 1869), 14.
3. For a more comprehensive biography of Walter Reed, see William B. Bean, *Walter Reed: A Biography* (Charlottesville: University of Virginia Press, 1982).
4. Mathew Carey, *A Short Account of the Malignant Fever: Lately Prevalent In Philadelphia . . . To Which Are Added, Accounts of the Plague in London and Marseilles,* 4th ed., improved (Philadelphia: Printed by the author and Jones, Absalom, Richard Allen, and Matthew Clarkson, 1794); *A Narrative of the Proceedings of the Black People, During the Late Awful Calamity in Philadelphia, in the Year 1793: and a Refutation of Some Censures, Thrown Upon Them in Some Late Publications* (Philadelphia: Printed for the authors, by William W. Woodward, at Franklin's Head, no. 41, Chesnut-Street, 1794).
5. Jo Ann Carrigan, "The Saffron Scourge: A History of Yellow Fever in Louisiana, 1796–1905" (thesis, Louisiana State University and Agricultural and Mechanical College, 1961), 184. Other more recent works about the 1878 epidemic include Khaled J. Bloom, *The Mississippi Valley's Great Yellow Fever Epidemic of 1878* (Baton Rouge: Louisiana State University Press, 1993), and Molly Caldwell Crosby, *The American Plague: The Untold Story of Yellow Fever, the Epidemic That Shaped Our History* (New York: Berkley Books, 2006).
6. Walter Reed, "The Propagation of Yellow Fever—Observations Based on Recent Researches," in *Yellow Fever: A Compilation of Various Publications,* United States Senate Document No. 822 (Washington, D.C.: GPO, 1911), 92.
7. Walter Reed, letter to Laura Reed Blincoe, April 4, 1902, Yellow Fever Collection, Box-Folder 140:20.
8. Carlos J. Finlay, "The Mosquito Hypothetically Considered as the Agent of Transmission of Yellow Fever," trans. Carlos J. Finlay, in *Trabajos Selectos del Dr. Carlos J. Finlay: Selected Papers of Dr. Carlos J. Finlay* (Havana, 1912), 42. Originally published in *Anales de la Academia de Ciencias Médicas, Físicas y Naturales de la Habana* 18 (1881).

9. In her study on the relationship between yellow fever and Cuban independence, Mariola Espinosa argued that the U.S. Army occupation government's efforts to control yellow fever in Cuba were largely motivated by a concern about the spread of the disease to the United States. See Mariola Espinosa, *Epidemic Invasions and the Limits of Cuban Independence, 1878–1930* (Chicago: University of Chicago Press, 2009).
10. See V. Havard, "Sanitation and Yellow Fever in Havana, Report of Major V. Havard," in *Civil Report of Major General Wood, Military Governor of Cuba 1900* (Havana: United States Government, 1901), 4:12–13.
11. Reed, "Propagation of Yellow Fever," 94.
12. Walter Reed, James Carroll, Arístides Agramonte, and Jesse W. Lazear, "The Etiology of Yellow Fever—a Preliminary Note," in *Proceedings of the Twenty-Eighth Annual Meeting of the American Public Health Association, Indianapolis, October 22–26, 1900* (Columbus, Ohio: Berlin Printing, 1901).
13. Walter Reed, letter to James Carroll, September 7, 1900, Yellow Fever Collection, Box-Folder 153:12. The originals of these letters remain in a private collection.
14. Fever Chart for Jesse Lazear, September 19, 1900–September 25, 1900, Yellow Fever Collection, Box-Folder 3:47.
15. Molly Caldwell Crosby, *The American Plague: The Untold Story of Yellow Fever; The Epidemic that Shaped Our History* (New York: Berkley Books, 2006), 191–97.
16. "The Mosquito Hypothesis," *Washington Post,* November 2, 1900, 6.
17. Walter Reed, James Carroll, and Arístides Agramonte, "The Etiology of Yellow Fever—an Additional Note," in *Yellow Fever,* 70.
18. For a copy of the Spanish contract, see "Informed consent agreement between Antonio Benigno and Walter Reed," November 26, 1900, Yellow Fever Collection, Box-Folder 70:3 [oversize]. For an English translation of the contract, see "English translation [from Spanish] of informed consent agreement between Antonio Benigno and Walter Reed," November 26, 1900, Yellow Fever Collection, Box-Folder 70:4 [oversize].
19. Walter Reed, letter to Emilie Lawrence Reed, December 2, 1900, Yellow Fever Collection, Box-Folder 22:24.
20. John J. Moran, "Memoirs of a Human Guinea Pig" (unpublished autobiography, ca. 1950), 1. Yellow Fever Collection, Box-Folder 25:71.
21. Reed, Carroll, and Agramonte, "Etiology of Yellow Fever," 71–82.
22. Reed, Carroll, and Agramonte, "Etiology of Yellow Fever," 83–87.
23. William C. Gorgas, letter to Henry R. Carter, December 13, 1900, Yellow Fever Collection, Box-Folder 22:37.
24. Reed, Carroll, and Agramonte, "Etiology of Yellow Fever," 87–89.

Response

Four Black University of Virginia Doctors Discuss Black Virginians, Vaccination, and the Novel Coronavirus Pandemic

ANDREA DOUGLAS

Walter Reed's work on yellow fever in 1901 remains a signature contribution to global public health in helping to save lives and control the spread of a deadly disease. Reed, born in Virginia in 1851, was an 1869 medical graduate of the University of Virginia and, in many ways, a typical white Virginian of his time. He learned medicine at UVA under the tutelage of James Lawrence Cabell and the other race scientists on the medical faculty and attended classes with a number of students who would later become leading eugenicists in the early twentieth century. However, his pathbreaking work on infectious disease has had a profound impact on commitment to ethical practice in medical research. His yellow fever study in many ways pioneered the concept of informed consent—that patients should know their diagnosis and agree to the recommended treatment program. Black Americans, however, for long before Reed's study and long after, were frequently not offered informed consent and instead were experimented on by generations of medical professionals for often dubious reasons—and in the service of even more spurious "studies." Such unethical medical procedures on African Americans were also a hallmark of the pre-1865 era of American slavery. Both before and after 1865, Black Americans could not trust doctors in life and feared grave-robbing of their dead by the same doctors. Fear and distrust of the American medical establishment, at least among African Americans, has a long history rooted in those centuries of intentional medical abuse. Twenty-first-century pandemic responses of Black Americans are shaped, too, by these community memories.

On January 24, 2021, as the COVID-19 pandemic raged through the country, four African American doctors employed at the University of Virginia, along with a community public health worker, came together to alleviate fears that African Americans in Charlottesville might have about receiving their COVID-19 vaccine. At the time of the conversation, the percentage of Black people who had received their vaccine was considerably lower than that percentage of the white population. This reality is rooted in the long history referenced above: the American medical establishment created this intergenerational distrust through centuries of unethical medical practices and procedures performed without consent on Black Americans.

This 2021 discussion by Drs. Ebony Jade Hilton, Michael Williams, Tiffani Dennis, and Markie Fleming suggests the continued intersection of race and health care in shaping both Black access to health care and Black fears about vaccines and health care in the midst of an extreme health crisis. We present here their answers to a single yet all-encompassing question: *Why should the community trust that these vaccines are safe when we have had so many examples in history of Black people being used and abused by the medical community?*

Dr. Ebony Jade Hilton: The example that you are referring to is Tuskegee. We need to unpack what Tuskegee is because oftentimes people think Tuskegee was the government giving us something. This time it was the government *not* giving us something. [The] Tuskegee experiment was conducted from 1932 to 1972. The government, the U.S. public health system, said, "We want Black men who have bad blood, anything from high blood pressure to diabetes." They told them that if they had bad blood they would give them a treatment to cure it. But the truth of the matter is they wanted to find Black men who had syphilis, because they wanted to see: If we do not treat syphilis, what happens to your body? The cure for syphilis was diagnosed in 1947 as penicillin. For thirty years prior to the [end of the] experiment . . . there was a cure available. Twenty-eight Black men died and another one hundred died from complications associated with the disease. Forty wives allowed to be infected and nineteen children born with congenital syphilis because the government decided to not give an intervention. I don't want this to be a Tuskegee 2.0 with Covid, because for the last twelve months we have studied why are Black and brown people dying [at] a higher rate, and we now have an intervention that could save your life. If you could save your life with this vaccine and the government does not give it to you, then that is Tuskegee 2.0. As Black people, we have to demand they give us the intervention that will save our lives because we want to grow old with our children as well. I hope clearing up these two things will alleviate some of the fear.

DR. TIFFANI DENNIS: This is an opportunity for people to take some agency over their health care. There are so many examples of health disparities and those socioeconomic concerns and the systemic issues that are propagated, and those are things that we can't control. The health care for Black and brown people [has] suffered with such examples, such as Tuskegee and the Henrietta Lacks [cells taken without consent for research purposes]—these issues are systemic. This is an opportunity to take agency, if you are offered the tool to improve our health, to level this unleveled playing field. If we see ourselves dying at a disproportionate rate and we are given an opportunity to have the same treatment that everyone else is, we cannot allow our fear and the past experience of racism and racist practice to keep us from taking the opportunity to use that tool.

DR. MICHAEL WILLIAMS: The science behind this is also different than earlier experiences because it has also been tested with Black and brown folks by the thousands. So the clinic trials that I use to convince myself that this is what I wanted to do for myself and my family actually did enroll people who look just like me and have similar life experiences to me along with a bunch of other people who don't look like me. And the fact that both Pfizer and Moderna, the two companies approved in the U.S., those companies were very purposeful that they enrolled the same percentage of African American, Latina, and Latino individuals, as well as other minority groups, as well as white people in their clinical trial so that they could legitimately say that this drug has been tested in the same demographic that the United States is currently. So I think Dr. Dennis's point is extraordinarily well placed in that we have [an] opportunity to use something for our benefit, and that has not been the case in the past, and that does overcome the fact that economic and health care and education and transportation and environmental issues . . . have been used to keep Black and brown people oppressed for so long in this country. We have this single tool that can overturn those health effects, and that is this vaccination. I personally had reservations until I had the information, until I had the knowledge before me so that I could answer all of my questions. I was right behind Dr. Hilton to get the second day's worth of shots here at UVA.

Dr. Tiffani Dennis: I want to add that is an important point—the studies, and the percentage of Black and brown people that were involved in them. That is not typically the case when we study new drugs or therapies. We are not always involved in the trials, so we cannot say how applicable they are. This is an exception.

Dr. Markie Fleming: I wanted to add a tiny detail that might matter to some folks. In my daily conversation with people who are hesitant about the vaccine, when I reveal that a Black woman was part of the team that developed the Pfizer vaccine, Dr. Kizzy Corbett, folks tend to sigh a huge sigh of relief. I think it is important to know that this vaccine wasn't just developed by the white man to experiment on Black and brown individuals, but we had representation at the very top. I think the Moderna vaccine also had at least some brown people on the team. I feel like it is good for us to know that we were part of the development of this technology.

Eugenics, the Racial Integrity Act, Health Disparities

P. PRESTON REYNOLDS

BY THE start of the twentieth century, the University of Virginia had become a center of an emerging new strain of racism—eugenics—that would create and perpetuate myths under the guise of scientific research but ultimately was intended to demonstrate white racial superiority. The goal of eugenic science was knowledge of how various traits—emotional, physical, intellectual—were inherited, so that such information could be applied in order to advance the human race and preserve imagined racial superiority. Eugenic scientists used the census, genealogy, measurement of physiological functions and human anatomy, and intelligence testing as methods of investigation. They believed that the application of eugenic knowledge, through legislation and community practices, would eliminate mental illness, physical disabilities, moral delinquency, crime, and even physical illnesses. They assumed the benefit to society would be a dramatic reduction in the cost of caring for the sick, poor, mentally ill, and incarcerated.

These philosophies flourished during the first decades of the 1900s, as researchers and administrators at the University of Virginia focused on the study of improving humanity through controlled reproduction, all with an eye to promoting "desirable" heritable characteristics and suppressing supposedly undesirable ones. But the foundation of eugenics, and the history of hereditarianism and scientific racism at the University, began much earlier—with the institution's founder, Thomas Jefferson. For Jefferson, racial distinction was an observable, scientific fact. In *Notes on the State of Virginia,* Jefferson described enslaved people at Monticello as "lacking beauty; emitting a very strong and disagreeable odor; were in reason, inferior; in imagination were dull, tasteless, and anomalous; participated more in sensual activity than reflection; never conversed in thought above the level of plain narrative; and were never seen producing even an elementary trait of painting or sculpture."[1] Deeply grounded in the methods of Enlightenment science, Jefferson's observations were regarded as concrete phenomena in part because in this tradition, observation was the tool of natural science. While Jefferson is credited with the language "all men are created equal," he also argued that "any attempt to assimilate [Black people] with the American polity is a greater threat to the integrity of the republic than naturalizing immigrants."[2]

Jefferson paved the way for eugenicists by providing a rationale that harmonized their theories of democratic political ideology. Just as Jefferson argued that "self preservation" was the nation's highest moral imperative and its "first law of nature," later Virginia eugenicists sought to deprive Blacks, poor whites, and the mentally defective of their procreative liberties in order to prevent them from destroying the lives of other Virginians (particularly, affluent whites) through genetic pollution.[3] James Lawrence Cabell received UVA's highest degree, a master's, in 1833. After finishing medical school at the University of Maryland and medical training in Europe, he returned to UVA as its third professor of medicine. During his fifty-two-year tenure at UVA, Cabell rose to serve as chair of the faculty. With the publication of *The Testimony of Modern Science in the Unity of Mankind,* Cabell advanced ideas proposed by Jefferson using his credibility as a physician and leader in public health, arguing that Black people were genetically and biologically inferior to whites, thus providing justification for slavery.

Jefferson's and Cabell's race science transitioned into a full commitment to the science and policies of eugenics with the passing of power from Cabell to Paul Brandon Barringer in 1888. Like his mentor, Barringer cast a long shadow on UVA, first as a faculty member and then as dean of the School of Medicine, where he would build UVA's first hospital in 1901 and lay the foundation for eugenic science among its faculty. While chair of the faculty, Barringer published three treatises that secured his preeminence as a spokesperson on the inferiority of Blacks when compared to whites. According to Barringer, rigid hereditary determinism predetermined the absolute limit of African Americans' biological and social advancement. He argued that with emancipation came

University of Virginia alumnus, faculty chairman, and UVA hospital founder Paul Brandon Barringer, undated. (University of Virginia Albert and Shirley Small Special Collections Library)

The first University of Virginia Hospital, circa 1901. (University of Virginia Claude Moore Health Sciences Library)

a reversion of African Americans to "savage" status, creating a new, degenerate Black generation that could not possibly survive in contact with civilized white society.

Barringer believed that under the conditions of slavery, Black people had advanced beyond their natural selection through selective breeding by slave owners. They were on a path toward extinction, accelerated by an irrational procreation that further exacerbated their genetic inferiority and susceptibility to disease and criminality. The drastically high incidence of tuberculosis, syphilis, and typhoid fever among African Americans (locally and in cities around the country) indicated nothing to Barringer about overcrowded housing, lack of clean water, sanitation, or safe meats and pasteurized milk. Instead, the high morbidity and mortality rates of African Americans proved the genetic unfitness of a "markedly criminal race." Barringer condemned Black people to a life of barbarism and death without white intervention. To him, the "Negro Problem" was more than a political problem; it was a huge public health threat to whites. Barringer's tripartite solution to the "Negro Problem" was political disfranchisement; transferring responsibility for African American education from Black to white teachers; and training Black people to be law-abiding laborers and artisans. As he wrote, "Every Negro doctor, lawyer, teacher or other leader in excess of the immediate needs of his own people is an antisocial product, a social menace."[4]

Eugenics flourished in the first three decades of the twentieth century under the leadership of University president Edwin Alderman as he set out to build the school's research base, recruiting the leading men in eugenic science into schools across Grounds. Those recruits included Harvey Jordan, Robert Bean, and Lawrence Royster in the School of Medicine; George Oscar Ferguson in education; Orland White as director of UVA's biological station; and Ivey Foreman Lewis as chair of biology. Together these faculty created eugenics research and education programs at UVA and throughout the state, and in doing so, they trained UVA students as well as high school and college teachers in eugenic racism. They also collaborated with nationally renowned eugenics investigators and presented their work at international eugenics meetings. Fully immersed in race science, these men contributed directly and indirectly to ethically contemptible laws and policies designed to maintain a culture of white supremacy and exclusionary white privilege.

Jordan, a professor of embryology, genetics, and histology, was one of Alderman's early recruits. Joining the faculty in 1907, he served as dean of the School of Medicine from 1939 to 1949. Believing that Black people inherited a susceptibility to contracting diseases such as syphilis and tuberculosis, Jordan called for the compulsory registration of all who were ill. He argued that proposed eugenic marriage, segregation, and sterilization laws were public and racial health measures that "should form part of the health code, to be administered under the State Police powers." The promise of eugenics as a solution to society's ills—and the power of physicians in solving such problems—was best summed up when Jordan declared, at the First International Congress of Eugenics in 1912, that "the future physician must also take a more active part in helping to shape legislation in the interest of race welfare."[5]

Chair of anatomy Dr. Robert Bean argued that the physical features of African Americans confirmed their inferiority when compared to whites. Furthermore, he asserted that "human types that represent different degrees of susceptibility of disease may be segregated and given differential treatment."[6] Through the core courses at the School of Medicine, Jordan and Bean, combined, taught about 20 percent of the school's curriculum. Along similar lines, George Oscar Ferguson, a professor in the School of Education, used intelligence testing among Black, mixed-race, and white children to conclude, "It does not seem possible to raise the scholastic attainment of the Negro to an equality with that of the white. . . . No expenditure of time or money would accomplish this end, since education cannot create mental power, but can only develop that which is innate."[7]

Eugenics began to shape public policy nationally as early as 1907, when Indiana passed a sterilization law. Two Virginia eugenics laws, both passed in 1924, had a profound impact in the commonwealth and throughout the country. The Virginia Sterilization Act and the Racial Integrity Act not only legalized sterilization of the mentally ill and persons of low literacy but also cemented discrimination against marginalized and vulnerable populations, including African Americans. These laws codified Jim Crow into every aspect of community life, and in doing so, they denied African Americans access to medical care, jobs, and fair wages, as well as higher education and professional training. Simply put, eugenic laws created the "one-drop rule," where one drop of African American blood restricted a person of color to life behind the veil.[8]

A band of eugenics populists, including a UVA alumnus, founded the Anglo-Saxon Clubs and then advocated for passage of the 1924 Racial Integrity Act. Dr. Walter A. Plecker, Earnest Sevier Cox, and John Powell

(UVA 1901) sought to preserve the racial integrity of the white race by defining whiteness, with its "no trace" characterization, and Blackness, with its "one-drop rule"—and then restricting the marriage of any white person only to someone else fully identified as pure white. They ultimately succeeded with legislation passed in 1924 and 1927. With autocratic rigidity, Plecker, as director of Virginia's Bureau of Vital Statistics, used birth certificates to prevent fair-skinned Black people from passing into life in the white community, and he used marriage certificates to stop "miscegenation."[9]

Eugenic racism in health care led to the segregation of African Americans into basement wards at UVA's teaching hospital, where Black men and women, including those with mental illnesses, were housed together, complicating the treatment of all who were sick. The accommodations were horrible, at best, and the treatment many received was often disgraceful. African Americans' extremely limited access to ambulatory and surgical care contributed to much higher rates of morbidity and mortality from contagious and chronic illnesses. A comparison study published by James Barksdale in 1949 of health, education, and welfare services for whites and Blacks in Charlottesville confirmed the impact of eugenics on local policies. The data revealed white leaders' failure to invest adequate resources in the Black community to ensure safe housing, proper sanitation, clean water, and essential education for residents of the city's segregated Black neighborhoods.[10]

UVA alumni, including a surgeon general of the U.S. Public Health Service, Dr. Hugh Smith Cummings, and two assistant surgeon generals, Dr. Taliaferro Clark and Dr. Raymond Vonderlehr, took eugenic racism into the tobacco fields of Alabama. Here they implemented the infamous Tuskegee Syphilis Study, where nearly four hundred Black men identified as infected with syphilis were followed in a longitudinal study from 1932 to 1972 as part of an effort to document how the disease manifested in Black individuals left untreated. The tragedy is that these men were never informed of their disease nor offered curative therapy, even when penicillin became in 1943 a very successful treatment for syphilis.[11] Eugenic science, which flourished at UVA, contributed to the design of structural racism in health care and explicit and implicit racial bias among generations of physicians and other health professionals.[12] Eugenic racism reached beyond medicine into friendships and marriage, the composition of classrooms, the lives of the mentally ill and educationally handicapped, and the provision of essential and mandatory public resources.

Notes

1. Gregory M. Dorr, *Segregation's Science: Eugenics and Society in Virginia* (Charlottesville: University of Virginia Press, 2008), 27.
2. Dorr, *Segregation's Science*, 30.
3. Dorr, *Segregation's Science*, 27–33.
4. Dorr, *Segregation's Science*, 44–45.
5. Dorr, *Segregation's Science*, 63.
6. Dorr, *Segregation's Science*, 81.
7. Dorr, *Segregation's Science*, 85.
8. Dorr, *Segregation's Science*; Paul A. Lombardo, *Three Generations, No Imbeciles: Eugenics, the Supreme Court, and* Buck v. Bell (Baltimore: Johns Hopkins University Press, 2008); Paul A. Lombardo, ed., *A Century of Eugenics in America: From the Indiana Experiment to the Human Genome Era* (Bloomington: Indiana University Press, 2011).
9. J. Douglas Smith, "The Campaign for Racial Purity and the Erosion of Paternalism in Virginia, 1922–1930: 'Nominally White, Biologically Mixed, and Legally Negro,'" *Journal of Southern History* 68, no. 1 (2002): 65–106.
10. James Worsham Barksdale, *A Comparative Study of Contemporary White and Negro Standards in Health, Education and Welfare in Charlottesville, Virginia*, Phelps-Stokes Fellowship Papers 20 (Charlottesville: University of Virginia, 1949).
11. Paul A. Lombardo and Gregory M. Dorr, "Eugenics, Medical Education, and the Public Health Service: Another Perspective on the Tuskegee Syphilis Experiment," *Bulletin of the History of Medicine* 80 (2006): 291–316.
12. P. Preston Reynolds, "Eugenics at the University of Virginia and Its Impact on Health Disparities," in *Charlottesville 2017*, ed. Louis Nelson and Claudrena N. Harold (Charlottesville: University of Virginia Press, 2018), 118–32.

Response

the scholastic attainment of the Negro

JAYLA HART

there is no euphemism for eugenics[1]—
no mild-mannered way of masking jefferson's racism
mirrored in the mouths of medical professors
proclaiming

there is a public health threat—
vignette of a midnight menace marked
by its "savage" nature, note the bigotry[2]
barringer believes

there is a Negro Problem—
proposes that criminality is genetic,
that whiteness is the only intervention for racial inferiority
in class, we argue over the politics of white supremacy but

there is no poetic pardoning for an institution
whose politics perceived my people to be property
whose buildings enshrine the egos of enslavers and eugenicists[3]
whose idols wore white coats to cloak their white hoods

there is no history lesson long enough
to wrap around the untreated wounds of the women

and the men and the children condemned
to the corners of a hospital basement because

there is a belief that Black folks feel less pain,[4]
a myth that morphed into morbid medical practices,
policy prescriptions for sterilization instead of schooling,
segregation structured to silence those who survived, remember

there is no surviving without sharing their stories—
their sorrows that stem from systemic marginalization
this suffering that is not solved by symbolic gestures
or lectures on this university's lurid legacy

there is no silver lining to centuries of ignorance
being misinterpreted as standards for intellect,
we still live with the implications of Tuskegee[5]—
you cannot expect trust from us who know

there is a violence faced only by the vulnerable,
a vicious cycle of investigations into our identities,
inquiries into the legitimacy of our intelligence,
studies that reduce our dignity down to stereotypes
there is a lesson I've learned in my time here,
hatred may not be hereditary
but it is more harmful, more deadly than any disease
and you don't need a degree to diagnose that

Notes

The title of this response derives from George Oscar Ferguson, who said in 1916, "It does not seem possible to raise the scholastic attainment of the Negro to an equality with that of the white. . . . No expenditure of time or money would accomplish this end, since education cannot create mental power, but can only develop that which is innate." Ferguson is quoted in P. Preston Reynolds's essay in this volume, "Eugenics, the Racial Integrity Act, Health Disparities."

1. Passing off an inhumane, illogical ideology as "race science" is as oxymoronic as it is outrageous.
2. "With the savage, however, there is no self-control, and dishonesty gives theft, anger gives murder, and desire rape. This state of being is pathognomonic

of savagery; and the African fills the bill." Paul Brandon Barringer, *The American Negro, His Past and Future* (Raleigh, N.C.: Edwards & Broughton, 1900), 8.

3. See Old and New Cabell, Alderman, Cocke, Garrett, Minor, Newcomb . . . need I say more?
4. Kelly M. Hoffman et al., "Racial Bias in Pain Assessment and Treatment Recommendations, and False Beliefs about Biological Differences between Blacks and Whites," *PNAS* 113, no. 16 (2016): 4296–301.
5. Never forget the nearly four hundred Black men who never gave informed consent or received access to the cure for syphilis. Never deny that UVA alumni actively contributed to this forty-year atrocity.

The George Rogers Clark Statue and Native Americans

CHRISTIAN MCMILLEN

One hundred years ago, when Charlottesville began an eight-year period of monument building, the city wrote a series of historical narratives that have reverberated into the present. Beginning in 1916 and ending in 1924, Charlottesville and the University of Virginia erected four statues across the city: two commemorated the Lost Cause, and two glorified the frontier exploits of Meriwether Lewis and William Clark as well as of George Rogers Clark.

The monuments to Robert E. Lee and Thomas "Stonewall" Jackson are powerful symbols of white supremacy. They were built at a time of resurgent Ku Klux Klan terrorism as well as increased valorization of the myth of the Lost Cause, a pro-Confederate interpretation of history that held that the Civil War was not actually lost and could still be won by new forms of racial proscription and segregation. In ways different from the Lee and Jackson statues, the George Rogers Clark and the Lewis and Clark statues are also monuments to white supremacy. They are instrumental in creating and perpetuating the myth of brave white men conquering a supposedly unknown and unclaimed land.

The Lee and Jackson statues have received considerable attention over the years. Most recently, the controversy over their proposed removal erupted in the hate-filled violence wrought by white supremacists on August 11 and 12, 2017. They are now gone. The memorials to Lewis and Clark and George Rogers Clark did not generate profound and violent controversy, but momentum grew for their removal. In November 2019, the Charlottesville City Council voted in favor of removing the Lewis and Clark statue, and community members submitted a petition to UVA earlier that year urging removal of the George Rogers Clark statue. Both statues came down in July 2021.

Edwin Alderman, who served from 1905 to 1931 as UVA's first president, spoke at the unveiling of both statues. In 1919, at the Lewis and Clark ceremony, Alderman characterized Lewis and Clark's journey as one designed "to break paths through pathless woods, to voyage down vast unsailed rivers, to battle with the savage and the beast, to use science in dominion over nature."[1] Two years later, it was front-page news in the *Daily Progress* when Alderman accepted the George Rogers Clark statue on behalf of the University.[2] In a speech celebrating the gift from Paul Goodloe McIntire—the benefactor responsible for all four of the Charlottesville statues—Alderman praised it as an "epic in metal and stone, of conquest and empire."[3]

The statues articulate a particular version of history. Unlike the monuments to Lee and Jackson—monuments, at the time, to relatively recent events—the monuments to Lewis and Clark and George Rogers Clark had less to do with memory than they did with an imagined past. And that past was built upon two myths: the myth of the lone frontier hero settling the West and the myth of the vanishing Indian.[4] In 1916, when announcing the city's intention to build a monument to Lewis and Clark, an anonymous columnist for the *Daily Progress* quoted the "poet laureate of the Confederacy," Father Abram Joseph Ryan: "A land without monuments is a land without memories; a land without memories is a land without history." And the history being written included Native American people solely as obstacles to progress.[5]

At the dedication ceremonies, the speakers extolled individual heroism, empire building, and the conquest of nature. No one mentioned Native Americans. They did not have to. The statues said it all: Native people submitted. The Lewis and Clark statue features the two men standing erect, gazing sternly into the distance, while Sacagawea, their guide, is on her knees with her eyes to the ground. The George Rogers Clark statue calls Clark the "Conqueror of the Northwest" and features Native people braced for submission. Both are explicit in their valorization of conquest and empire. This should come as no surprise: after all, both the Lewis and Clark expedition and George Rogers Clark's pursuits in the West were about conquest and empire.

When the George Rogers Clark statue was unveiled at the University on November 3, 1921, Albert LeFevre, the Corcoran Professor of Philosophy,

Lewis and Clark monument, West Main Street at the Midway, Charlottesville (removed 2021). (Sanjay Suchak)

Bronze figures on George Rogers Clark monument at the University of Virginia. (Sanjay Suchak)

Unveiling of the George Rogers Clark monument at the University of Virginia, 1921, from the 1922 *Corks and Curls* yearbook. (University of Virginia Albert and Shirley Small Special Collections Library)

told the crowd: "I present to the University of Virginia this monument of pride, enlightenment and inspiration—a monument erected as a memorial to the daring adventures of George Rogers Clark, the conqueror of the Northwest territory. This beautiful work of sculptural genius, like the noble statue of Lewis and Clark, awakens in us just pride, because it makes us ever mindful of the tribute we love to render to those great and heroic sons of the soil of Albemarle, sent forth on their high missions and fateful destinies by the prophetic wisdom of Thomas Jefferson."[6]

Despite the hero worship at the unveiling, to claim that Clark was the "Conqueror of the Northwest" is overblown. The contest over control of the Ohio Country began in the middle of the seventeenth century and would not end until almost the beginning of the nineteenth. George Rogers Clark played a minor role in the centuries-long struggle for control between the French, the English, the Native peoples, and eventually the Americans. Clark was an important strategist and soldier during the Revolution's western phase; he was well connected and adept at gathering intelligence. But the victories he became most famous for—particularly Sackville and Vincennes—were won against weakly fortified enemies and had little bearing on the war's outcome.[7]

Clark's approach to Native American people was Jeffersonian. Jefferson had a scientific fascination with them. But he shared the common view that Native people were a barrier to civilization. During the Revolutionary

War, Jefferson counseled Clark in his dealings with American Indians. In a letter to Clark, Jefferson wrote that the best way to deal with Native people was "total suppression of Savage Insolence and Cruelties." Clark followed Jefferson's advice frequently following attacks on Shawnee villages, for instance, with the destruction of houses and crops. His dealings with the Shawnee at the negotiations over the Treaty of Fort McIntosh in 1785—which the Shawnee rejected—further inflamed American relations with Native people and prolonged military conflict. No conquering occurred.[8]

During the Lewis and Clark unveiling ceremony, there was of course similar rhetoric about the singular achievements of the two men. But added to the myth of Lewis and Clark was the notion that the land west of the Mississippi was empty and free for the taking. When local historian Armistead Gordon spoke at the ceremony, he argued that the Louisiana Purchase and Lewis and Clark's expedition were the singular achievements of Jefferson's presidency. After all, the resources in the West were the bounty of that "inexhaustible conquest." Gordon concluded his remarks by honoring "the immortal names of Meriwether Lewis and William Clark, whose indomitable courage and endurance, defying life and death, carved an empire out of wilderness, and gave to succeeding generations of Americans the inheritance which they conquered."[9]

Lewis and Clark, of course, had encountered nothing like a wilderness—and they would never have claimed such a thing. Nor would Jefferson. On the contrary, Jefferson knew that west of the Mississippi, Native people were in charge. In fact, it was, according to Jefferson, the "immense power" of the Sioux, particularly the Lakota, that would be the biggest barrier to American trade and settlement.[10] The wilderness that Armistead Gordon imagined in 1919 at the unveiling of the Lewis and Clark statue was in fact a region in which Sioux population and power would only increase in the decades after Lewis and Clark passed through.

In the early 1920s, in America and Virginia, worshiping those who settled the American landscape—and erasing the presence, in the past and in the present, of those who were here first—was commonplace. This manifested in several ways. For one, in the decades surrounding World War I, the number of statues memorializing the settlement of the West exploded. The frontier had "officially" closed as of the 1890 census. No longer was the West considered unsettled. Frederick Jackson Turner, in his famous essay "The Significance of the Frontier in American History" (1893), claimed that the frontier was a place of rugged individualism, where societies could be formed anew. But with the closing of the frontier

Postcard of the George Rogers Clark "Conqueror of the Northwest" monument at the University of Virginia. (University of Virginia Albert and Shirley Small Special Collections Library)

and America's increasing urbanization, a key piece of America's identity disappeared. When it did, a newfound interest in the country's pioneer past emerged. At the same time, American Indians had come to be considered a "vanishing race," doomed to extinction. Fueling this notion was a proliferation of "expert" opinions regarding what they argued was the vanishingly low Native population prior to contact with Europeans—an argument used to justify denying Native peoples legal rights to land.[11]

Finally, the American West was reimagined as having been a wilderness, an uninhabited land. The American past was rewritten and Natives were erased. There was no place to recognize, for example, the "immense power" Jefferson knew the Lakota Sioux possessed over a huge swath of the Northern Plains. The West, in this new historical narrative, was empty. The statues dedicated to Lewis and Clark and George Rogers Clark reinforced this historical narrative. The myth-building about the vanishing Indian was not only advanced by monuments; more devastatingly, actual laws harmed Native people and exacerbated discrimination against them for decades.

In 1924, when the General Assembly passed the notorious Racial Integrity Act, Virginia added racial purity to this already toxic mix of ideas. The act redefined racial classification in Virginia. Now, there were two categories: white and black. These categories were strictly defined and meticulously policed by the Bureau of Vital Statistics. Being "Indian" was no longer possible. Native people in Virginia began to disappear from official records such as the census. After all, they no longer existed. By the 1940s, the Racial Integrity Act had greatly diminished the number of official Native people in Virginia. Walter Plecker, the state registrar of vital statistics, was relentless in his pursuit of racial purity. He chased down individuals claiming to be Indian.[12]

In 1940, when explaining why he had returned one man's birth certificate, he wrote the following: "We have learned that none of the native-born individuals in Virginia claiming to be Indian are free from negro mixture, and under the law of Virginia every person with any ascertainable degree of negro blood is to be classed as a negro or colored person not as an Indian." To another person claiming to be Indian, he wrote: "We do not recognize any native-born Indian as of pure Indian descent unmixed with negro blood. According to the law of Virginia any ascertainable degree of negro blood constitutes the individual a colored person." Finally, after assiduous research in 1943, he claimed: "Public records in the office of the Bureau of Vital Statistics, and in the State Library, indicate that there does not exist today a descendant of the Virginia ancestors claiming to be an Indian who is unmixed with negro blood."[13] Therefore, there were no Indians in Virginia.

As the national historical narrative erased Indians, so, too, did Virginia's Racial Integrity Act. The impulse to pass laws like the Racial Integrity Act emerged out of the then-flourishing "science" of eugenics. Eugenics was based on the notion that, through selective breeding, superior racial stock would emerge. By forbidding the races to intermarry, racial purity, and thus white racial supremacy, could be maintained. Eugenics, explored elsewhere in this volume, flourished at the University during the first decades of the twentieth century. During the 1920s, in addition to hiring professors who promoted eugenics, UVA also hired sociologist Floyd House. House completed his PhD at the University of Chicago, studying under Robert Park. He arrived at UVA the same year that Ivan McDougle and Arthur Estabrook published *Mongrel Virginians: The Win Tribe*. Win stood for "white, Indian, negro," and the book was presented as a quasi-ethnographic case study of the nearly apocalyptic consequences of racial mixing. The community *Mongrel Virginians* depicted largely self-identified as Indian.

But not everyone believed in the racist logic of eugenics. Jeff Hantman, professor emeritus of anthropology at UVA and an expert on the

Monacan Nation, has been doing research on House and the history of anthropology at UVA. Hantman's research revealed a fascinating 1928 UVA master's thesis by Bertha Wailes, one of House's students. "Backward Virginians: A Further Study of the Win Tribe" was in many respects a rebuttal to *Mongrel Virginians.* Wailes knew the community well and argued that while they were indeed "backward," their place in the social hierarchy could not be explained by their race. In fact, if race played a role in their social position, it was due to the racial prejudice of their neighbors and not any inherent racial characteristics the so-called Win Tribe possessed. Further, Wailes argued, the Win's "backwardness" could be explained by malnutrition, lack of education, and the social isolation they faced because of their skin color. These are much the same conditions that public health experts today call the social determinants of health. The Racial Integrity Act was a special concern for the Win. Due to their mixed-race history, the Win worried they would be erased. In fact, because they supposedly possessed "negro blood," they were officially "colored" under Virginia law. Were these ideas to ultimately prevail, the people we now know as the Monacan Nation would not exist.

The national narrative of the vanishing Indian and Virginia's extraordinary efforts to erase Indians not only had profound consequences for Native identity but also made it astonishingly difficult for Native people to claim legal rights, land, and tribal recognition. In 1946, just before Congress created the Indian Claims Commission and formalized the process by which Native people could gain compensation for stolen land, Felix Cohen—the legislation's lead author and one of the twentieth century's greatest advocates for Native people—wrote that the Indians' claims were "the backwash of a great national experiment in dictatorship and racial extermination." Cohen was blunt, but right. And yet, despite the extraordinary power of Plecker and the Racial Integrity Act and the myth of the vanishing Indian, as enshrined by the Lewis and Clark and George Rogers Clark statues, there has been remarkable change.

The myth of the vanishing Indian is itself vanishing, though it's not yet disappeared. Perhaps most remarkable of all is that on January 29, 2018, Congress passed, and President Donald Trump signed, the Thomasina E. Jordan Indian Tribes of Virginia Federal Recognition Act. Both the legislation and the reports leading to its passage noted the profound burden Plecker's legacy had on tribal recognition. Nonetheless, changing ideas about race, tribal oral histories and traditions, and the work of numerous anthropologists and historians meant that Plecker's efforts to erase Indians in Virginia were, while damaging and deeply racist, ultimately unsuccessful.

While they have now all been removed, it is worth remembering that the Lee and Jackson statues perpetuated the myth of the Lost Cause and actively distorted American history. The monuments to George Rogers Clark and Lewis and Clark did much the same: they aided in sustaining many of the most destructive myths about American Indians.

Notes

1. Edwin A. Alderman, "Presentation Address," in *The Unveiling of the Lewis-Clark Statue at Midway Park in the City of Charlottesville, Virginia, November Twenty-One, Nineteen Hundred Nineteen, at Three O'Clock in the Afternoon, Being a Record of the Exercises Attending the Unveiling*, edited by W. M. Forrest (Charlottesville, Va.: City of Charlottesville, 1919), 8.
2. *Charlottesville Daily Progress*, November 3, 1921, 1.
3. Edwin Alderman, "Address of Acceptance," *Alumni Bulletin*, 3rd ser., 15, no. 1 (January 1922): 14–15, quote on 14.
4. On the vanishing myth, see Brian Dippie, *The Vanishing American: White Attitudes and U.S. Indian Policy* (Lawrence: University Press of Kansas, 1991).
5. *Charlottesville Daily Progress*, 9 December 1916, 4.
6. Albert LeFevre, "Presentation Address," in *The George Rogers Clark Statue: The Unveiling of the Monument to George Rogers Clark by Robert Aitken* (Charlottesville, Va., November 3, 1921), Special Collections, University of Virginia Library.
7. The history of the conquest of the Ohio Country has been written by many. See, for example, Richard White, *The Middle Ground: Indians, Empires, and Republics in the Great Lakes Region, 1650–1815* (New York: Cambridge University Press, 1991).
8. Among many other sources, see James Fisher, "A Forgotten Hero Remembered, Revered, and Revised: The Legacy and Ordeal of George Rogers Clark," *Indiana Magazine of History* 92, no. 2 (1996): 109–32; Colin G. Calloway, "'We Have Always Been the Frontier': The American Revolution in Shawnee Country," *American Indian Quarterly* 16, no. 1 (1992): 39–52.
9. Armistead Churchill Gordon, "The Lewis and Clark Expedition: An Historical Discourse," in Forrest, *Unveiling of the Lewis-Clark Statue*, 35.
10. Thomas Jefferson to Meriwether Lewis, January 22, 1804, Founders Online, National Archives, https://founders.archives.gov/documents/Jefferson/01-42-02-0285.
11. Christian W. McMillen, *Making Indian Law: The Hualapai Land Case and the Birth of Ethnohistory* (New Haven, Conn.: Yale University Press, 2007).

12. Richard Sherman, "'The Last Stand': The Fight for Racial Integrity in Virginia in the 1920s," *Journal of Southern History* 54, no. 1 (1988): 69–92; J. Douglas Smith, "The Campaign for Racial Purity and the Erosion of Paternalism in Virginia, 1922–1930: 'Nominally White, Biologically Mixed, and Legally Negro,'" *Journal of Southern History* 68, no. 1 (2002): 65–106.
13. All quotes from Mika Endo, "'The Word "Mixed" without the "Indian" Would Be Better': Virginia's Racial Integrity Act and the Destruction of Indian Race in the Early Twentieth Century," *Native South* 7 (2014): 92–107. The originals are in the Papers of John Powell, Special Collections, University of Virginia Library. Many of the Plecker letters have been digitized and can be found here: https://ead.lib.virginia.edu/vivaxtf/view?docId=uva-sc/viu03212.xml.

Response

Nanta ish ikhvna ha? Kucha hoh ilhkoli (What have you learned? Go outside)

KASEY JERNIGAN

I MOVED MY family from New England to Charlottesville mid-summer; the sticky heat of late June rarely let up that month. Having grown up in Oklahoma, I quickly grew accustomed to the heaviness of the humid air and the ways it slowed everything to a particular Southern summer stillness. Those early days in this new town, I would spend my evenings walking on Grounds, acquainting myself with the living landscape. I got to know the half-hearted evening breezes, too weak to carry the lemony scent of the magnolia blooms; I listened to the insects as they casually trilled to each other, lacking any sense of urgency in the thick evening heat; and I learned the spaces where mosquitoes were especially active, where they would aggressively nip at my exposed skin, reminding me that life thrives even in sweltering heat.

My favorite part of those walks was getting to know the plant life on Grounds. Humbled by the size and beauty of certain trees, I would silently offer my greetings, recognizing their unique stillness, especially among the oldest. Their leaves hung heavily, listless, seemingly lifeless, weighed down equally by the humid summer air and the knowledge and stories of the many events they have witnessed; the people they have shaded; the songs they have sung with the winds; and the stories they keep and continue to collect as beings pass through the land, ephemeral in the presence of these knowledge holders.

The living landscape is a knowledge keeper, here before any of us and here long after all of us journey onwards. This land has never been *unknown* or *unclaimed,* as the myth of brave white men conquering it would have us believe. Rather, it is a question of *whose* knowledge is privileged, *whose* claims to the land are recognized, and what counts as *knowing* or *claiming.* This larger project seeks to reveal stories yet to be told, knowledges yet to be shared. For Indigenous peoples, affectively engaging with one's surroundings is an important form of knowledge, whereby the land can be understood as a sort of *spirit-scape* in the sense that it is a place filled with the resonance of our actions from generations past. It has influenced—and has also been influenced by—generations of living beings before us and yet to come. Spaces and places can be known through the senses, that is, one can see, hear, touch, feel, and smell faint traces of the past, but one can imagine futures forward.

Just before the fall semester began, I participated in the new faculty orientation program, which included a specialized historical tour of Grounds. The hour-long tour covered the history of UVA's founding, including Jefferson's vision of an institution of higher education, up to the present day and highlighted key architectural sites such as the Rotunda, the Academical Village, and so on. The tour also included other markers related to UVA's legacies of slavery and discrimination, mnemonics of the few known experiences of enslaved laborers involved in the building and the running of this institution, (re)storying specific spaces and places at the University. The tour moved through many difficult experiences marked on this land, topics that remain relevant today. It was a remarkable tour in that UVA is openly grappling with its complicated legacies, but when I asked our tour guides for information about the Indigenous peoples who lived, worked, or studied here, they said there was none. There was, however, a George Rogers Clark sculpture that includes Native peoples.

The first time I walked by the George Rogers Clark sculpture, I paused to study it, surveying it in its entirety. The bronze figure of Clark mounted on a horse is the central feature, and he towers over a small group of Native people, mostly crouching below the horse. One man, partially wrapped in a blanket, cowers as if he's afraid and in the process of moving away. Another figure, a man with long braids and a stereotypical stoic Indian face, is standing up, facing Clark, embodying the tired noble-savage trope, as if he's accepting his fate; yet another figure appears to be begging Clark. Enveloped in a blanket that covers her head, she is holding onto what resembles a cradleboard, a carrier used for infants. Clark, atop his horse, is reaching back toward men from his expedition who are placed just behind the horse. One appears to be handing Clark a gun, while the other is bent over some sort of barrel. The pedestal reads, "Conqueror of the Northwest." One interpretation of this sculpture is that the barrel is gunpowder, and Clark is reaching for the gun with the intention to fire it upon this group of Native people, including an infant in the cradleboard.

The sculpture was part of the University's landscape, or *spirit-scape*, not as a site of reckoning but as a celebration of settler colonialism, genocide, removal, and erasure. An ode to the Doctrine of Discovery, Manifest Destiny, *terra nullius*, or whichever convenient ideology positions the Indigenous peoples of this land as gone, the Clark sculpture not only attempts to obscure Native and Indigenous histories (and therefore our presence) but actively works to write us out of the narrative entirely. It is a monument that affects what we know about the land and the peoples but also what counts as knowledge, as story, as important, as claim, as Indigenous. It is part of this *spirit-scape* as much as the living beings on Grounds.

I passed the Clark sculpture whenever I walked to my office in Brooks Hall, located just nearby. I always looked at it, wondering, Do people not understand what this sculpture represents? Do they recognize that it was erected intentionally to celebrate our genocide, forced removal, and subsequent scrubbing away? Do they know that this is the only material item at UVA to formally acknowledge Native people? On a living landscape that continuously unfolds and becomes through context and relationality, the sculpture of Clark was celebrated and centered—along with the slippery half-truth about a man and a country that consigned my human and other-than-human ancestors to a conquered people and a conquered land.

The sculpture is coming down exactly 102 years after it was unveiled and praised as an "epic in metal and stone, of conquest and empire."[1] That is over a century of work the sculpture clocked to reinforce the myths of an imagined past, of the vanishing Indian, of a land without memories. It is more than one hundred years of profiting from stolen lands without having to reckon with who was displaced (and in what violent ways) in the first place. These are the teachings my students arrive with in my Native American Indigenous Studies courses. They know only of Indigenous peoples in the past; having been taught that all Indigenous peoples either died or were removed, they struggle to grasp that there are Native peoples living today on the East Coast.

The majority of my work in the classroom right now is undoing what they have been taught, helping them to challenge specific narratives that work to keep Indigenous peoples invisible and erased—and to recognize and celebrate the many contributions Indigenous peoples make to society. Students are shocked, angry, appalled, confused, and curious about how they could have been taught so wrongly. Yet the Clark sculpture is iconic, in that it makes visible just how this work is done: to be an institution of higher education *and* to maintain a sculpture for 102 years that enshrines damaging misconceptions and biases toward Native peoples is to participate in miseducation, dishonesty, and violence. Erasure and invisibility are the modern forms of racism against Native peoples. For many Americans, we no longer exist.

With time, more and more students arrive in my classes carrying accurate knowledge, and I find that I can begin to teach them about Indigenous ways of knowing and being. We can start to challenge what is considered knowledge—and just how knowledge is produced—and work to recognize the many ways of *being* in the world. I have recently begun to take my students outside on the land and to the rivers, using land and water as pedagogy, centering felt knowledge, teaching them the ways that land and water hold memories and stories. They are open to this, acknowledging that many of the ways of previous generations are no longer relevant—harmful, even—and they are eager to learn other ways of knowing and being. These days, as I walk across Grounds, I continue to offer my greetings to my favorite trees, but I've added a special promise of hope and a vision of the future: "lawa kvt chi-afvmmachi, / micha na / yukpa hosh chi-ayukpachi afehna achi hoke . . . [many will meet you, and then, happily they will salute you, very much, indeed]."[2]

Notes

1. Edwin Alderman, "Address of Acceptance," *Alumni Bulletin*, 3rd ser., 15, no. 1 (January 1922): 14.
2. From "Chimilhfiopak," by Henry Willis, quoted in Marcia Haag, "On Translating Choctaw Poems," *New Ohio Review* 14 (Fall 2013); gloss by Marcia Haag.

Winds of Change in the 1950s

BRENDAN WOLFE

Colgate W. Darden was the first University of Virginia president to imagine a student body that extended beyond the top tier of elite white men. After serving in Congress and as Virginia's governor, he came to Charlottesville in 1947 with the idea of democratizing Grounds. "During the next twelve years he rejuvenated the university," historian Ronald L. Heinemann wrote. "Attempting to make it a more democratic institution—over the objections of many students, some of whom burned a cross on his lawn—he encouraged the enrollment of public school students, diminished the role of fraternities, and constructed a student activities building. When a faculty member accused him of trying to make the University 'a catch-all for everybody who wants to go to college in the state,' Darden replied, 'That's what it's supposed to be.'"[1]

But that's not at all what UVA had been in the more than 120 years leading up to Darden's tenure. Instead, the school accepted only "young men from the best families," as another historian put it, and the new president's policies caused anxiety in all corners of the University.[2] To see how that anxiety played out and how it mixed with other historical concerns, consider four consecutive editions of the *Cavalier Daily* student newspaper from the spring of 1954. They throw into sharp relief prevailing attitudes about race, class, and sex while providing some context for events during those years that don't otherwise square with the clean-cut image of 1950s UVA.

Friday, May 14, 1954

Toward the end of the school year, the *Cavalier Daily* published a satirical story that imagined life at UVA in 1960. Headlined "University Transformed into 'State U,'" the piece tells of a 1954 graduate returning to Grounds six years later. He grumbles about how UVA has been "eliminating all out-of-state men and making it a point to let in all the meat balls they could find in the state." There was nowhere left to drink and party, fraternities had begun to atrophy, and too many people were hanging out at the Student Union.[3] The "masses," in other words, had taken over. From this point of view, a "State U" functioned as that dreaded "catch-all," a place anybody could attend—public school kids, African Americans, maybe even women. But UVA, according to the article, had always been different. It had been exclusive. It hadn't, though, always been a great place to learn. In 1937, *Life* magazine took note of the school's "broad gentlemanly attitude" and suggested that it "does not breed or encourage scholars." While UVA "does not enjoy top rank as an educational institute," the magazine wrote, its students "are indisputably among the ablest college drinkers in the country."[4]

Being a university for the elite did not necessarily translate into being an elite university. Darden raised faculty salaries and admission standards and threatened to eliminate the fraternities as a means of changing that. But student pushback proved to be intense. In 1951, students stole a laboratory cadaver and hanged it from a tree in front of the Rotunda to protest administration policies.[5] They also burned crosses on Carr's Hill so frequently that Darden publicly protested the harm the flames had done to a particular oak tree.[6] Students feared change, but their methods of protest suggested concerns that went beyond simply the admission of public-school boys.

Tuesday, May 18, 1954

After a day off on Monday, the next issue of the *Cavalier Daily* addressed these fears. The front page announced the Supreme Court ruling that declared public-school segregation to be unconstitutional.[7] The paper's editor, Frank M. Slayton, wrote, "To many people, this decision is contrary to a way of life, and violates the way in which they have thought since 1619"—or the year that the first enslaved Africans arrived in Virginia. "Because the Supreme Court has said 'Thou Shalt Not,' it does not

Gregory Swanson at the University of Virginia School of Law, 1950. (University of Virginia Albert and Shirley Small Special Collections Library)

follow that the people of the South will adopt a new set of mores as easily as a man changes his coat."[8]

Gregory Swanson, UVA's first Black student, had entered the School of Law three and a half years earlier, in the fall of 1950, and only after winning a lawsuit. At the time, UVA fashioned itself an outpost of the old Confederacy. At football games, the band played "Dixie" and fans waved the Confederate battle flag. Swanson left after the program's required one year in residence and reopened his practice in Martinsville, but neither he nor any other member of his cohort finished the required thesis to receive the advanced degree. Swanson "frequently felt the sting of discrimination outside the lecture hall." When visiting Corner businesses, he found himself the

Gregory Swanson (center) with legal team in Lee Park (now Market Street Park), Charlottesville, 1950. Thurgood Marshall and Oliver Hill are third and fourth from right. (Jefferson School African American Heritage Center)

only University man barred from its restaurants, barbershops, and movie theater, which excluded Black people entirely. In his 1981 history of UVA, Virginius Dabney insisted that "the black"—i.e., Swanson—"was well received," and that in Darden's view, Swanson had not been well enough prepared for graduate work, despite already having a law degree.

For its part, the *Cavalier Daily* ignored Swanson while he was on Grounds and did not mark his departure. In 1952, however, Staige Davis Blackford Jr. became the paper's editor. He was a Rhodes Scholar who supported both integration and Darden's efforts to end UVA's reputation as a "Southern country club."[9] On the newspaper's editorial page, Blackford battled and, some have argued, even bettered the powerful University dean Ivey Foreman Lewis, a longtime segregationist and supporter of eugenics. The editor and his allies argued that UVA must change, while Lewis responded that slavery had benefited African Americans and that integration would lead to race mixing, or, as he derisively put it, "a brown America."[10]

Two years later, when the Supreme Court finally made its ruling, this tempest had died down. The *Cavalier Daily,* now under Slayton's editorship, had returned to referencing the traditions of slavery without reproach. Darden, meanwhile, preferred to mostly stay out of the fight. Had there been more pressure, this might have been impossible, but during the 1950s the numbers of Black students remained low. "Time . . . has a habit of correcting all problems," Slayton wrote in the paper's May 18 editorial. Time having been denied in this case, "we will now have the opportunity of seeing what effect legislative morals will have on a way of life."

Wednesday, May 19, 1954

The next day, another urgent issue occupied Slayton's mind, although it is difficult to understand what exactly had happened just from reading the paper. In an editorial titled "Unwarranted Political Pressure," Slayton mentioned "the dismissal of eleven students from the University," but he did not explain the circumstances. Instead, the editor worried that some of the perpetrators might win appeals of their punishment due to their elite status. Other sources reveal that in April, an all-night party on the East Lawn, attended by twelve men and a nineteen-year-old woman, resulted in what appears to have been a sexual assault. After being contacted by the woman's parents, Darden reported that "the girl had come home that day in a dazed condition, apparently beaten and brutalized, covered with bruises."[11]

The *Cavalier Daily* never reported on the incident. Charlottesville's *Daily Progress* did not publish a report when the incident occurred, either, referring only to a "sex scandal" and that the woman was "struck" by the men, according to the paper's later coverage of the Board of Visitors' deliberations on the incident.[12] The historian Henry Wiencek has argued that the attack is important in part because it highlights the state's hypocrisy. In 1950–51, state officials vigorously prosecuted and executed the Black men known as the Martinsville Seven who were convicted of raping a white woman.[13]

Virginia's attorney general insisted at the time that justice would have looked no different had the accused been white. But at UVA, the local authorities apparently never even investigated the East Lawn assault.[14] Instead, the student council called a mass meeting at Newcomb Hall, claiming (among other things) that Darden was treading on the council's authority by looking into the assault. In one of the speeches delivered that day, a student referenced the satirical "State U" piece that had recently appeared in the *Cavalier Daily*. He said that it rightly noted how UVA had "turned into a 1984—a state of distrust and police action."[15] Darden responded with understatement. "Too many University students who insist on complete liberty are not enthusiastic about self-discipline," he told the paper. The alleged attack and its victim, meanwhile, remained unmentioned.[16]

Thursday, May 20, 1954

The day after Slayton's editorial on political pressure, the *Cavalier Daily* reprinted an essay paying homage to Thomas Jefferson. In a section called "Shadow of One Man," the writer, a history instructor, noted that "Charlottesville has changed much since 1826 when Mr. Jefferson finally left it. But it has changed as he would have wished."[17] That assertion seemed very much up for debate in 1954. Jefferson could hardly have imagined a world in which African Americans and women were guaranteed equality under the law. And many faculty, alumni, and students at the university he founded struggled with opening the gates of UVA any wider than they already had. While some, like Staige Blackford, supported a rethinking of whom the University should educate and how, others thought more like the first-year student who wrote to the *Cavalier Daily* during this time. "A woman's place is not in a gentleman's university," he opined—conjuring up the many complicated dimensions of being a "gentleman" in Virginia.[18]

In the 1920s, on the occasion of UVA's centennial, the historian and alumnus Philip Alexander Bruce published an exhaustive five-volume history of the school. In its pages, Bruce praised "the absolute correctness" of Jefferson's foresight and his willingness to uphold "the general principles of our race."[19] Ironically, where race, class, and sex are concerned, the next century challenged that part of Jefferson's vision. During the 1950s, UVA demonstrated an ambivalence on these issues that sometimes erupted in ways that were disturbing and even violent. Only during the next decade or two would change arrive in full force.

Notes

1. Ronald L. Heinemann and the *Dictionary of Virginia Biography*, "Colgate W. Darden (1897–1981)," *Encyclopedia Virginia*, accessed March 6, 2019, https://encyclopediavirginia.org/entries/darden-colgate-w-1897-1981.
2. Virginius Dabney, *Mr. Jefferson's University: A History* (Charlottesville: University of Virginia Press, 1981), 8.
3. Ogden Ashlawn III, "University Transformed into 'State U,'" *Cavalier Daily*, May 14, 1954, 3, 8.
4. "Virginia Has the Most Beautiful Campus in the Country," *Life*, June 7, 1937, 48.
5. "Cadaver Found Hanging from Tree Outside Rotunda; Believed to Have Belonged to the Medical School," *Cavalier Daily*, March 1, 1951, 1.
6. Dabney, *Mr. Jefferson's University*, 286–87.

7. "Supreme Court Declares Segregation in School Systems Unconstitutional," *Cavalier Daily*, May 18, 1954, 1.
8. "The Decision," *Cavalier Daily*, May 18, 1954, 2. The paper notes that all unsigned editorials are by the editor. A native of South Boston, Slayton later attended the School of Law and served as a judge and in the House of Delegates (1973–85). He died in 2013.
9. Alexander S. Leidholdt, "Showdown on Mr. Jefferson's Lawn: Contesting Jim Crow during the University of Virginia's Protodesegregation," *Virginia Magazine of History and Biography* 122, no. 3 (2014): 268n24.
10. Leidholdt, "Showdown," 249–50. Blackford was the son of the UVA medical professor Staige Davis Blackford (1898–1949) and the editor of the *Virginia Quarterly Review* from 1975 until his death in 2003.
11. Board of Visitors Minutes, May 26, 1954, 351. The minutes are available at Jefferson's University—The Early Life Project, http://juel.iath.virginia.edu/node/343?doc=/juel_display/BOV/1950/bov_19540526.
12. "University Visitors Confirm Penalties for Sex Scandal," *Charlottesville Daily Progress*, May 29, 1954, 1, 19.
13. Henry Wiencek, *The Hairstons: An American Family in Black and White* (New York: St. Martin's Griffin, 1999), 213–14.
14. Wiencek, *Hairstons*, 213–14. "The similarity to the Martinsville case is obvious," Wiencek writes, "but in a final irony, one of the rapists, whose only penalty was expulsion and who never even saw the inside of a jail, was from the family of a judge who helped send the Martinsville 7 to the electric chair." Wiencek doesn't name either the student or the judge.
15. Dabney, *Mr. Jefferson's University*, 286; "Closer Student-Administration Relations Are Asked," *Cavalier Daily*, May 29, 1954, 4.
16. "Students Not Enthusiastic about Self Discipline," *Cavalier Daily*, May 29, 1954, 1.
17. William E. Stokes Jr., "'Mr. Jefferson's Country' Maintains Traditions," *Cavalier Daily*, May 20, 1954, 2, 4.
18. Dabney, *Mr. Jefferson's University*, 381–82.
19. Philip Alexander Bruce, *History of the University of Virginia, 1819–1919: The Lengthened Shadow of One Man* (New York: Macmillan, 1922), 5:429.

Response

Trifling Breezes in the Face of Continuing Bigotry and Systemic Racism

WILLIAM M. HARRIS SR.

IN THE 1950s, did UVA president Colgate Darden make efforts for change that were rebuffed by conservative forces? Were there real winds of change in the 1950s? Was UVA really taking its first halting steps toward becoming a flagship state university that was truly inclusive of all Virginians? It is clear to me, despite the occasional glimmers of those possibilities, that most administrators, faculty, and staff at UVA in the 1950s and well beyond were anti-progressive in matters of justice for African Americans. In addition, the vast majority of white students also strongly supported the racist views, programs, and policies of the University. That, too, did not change for decades (if ever) after the 1950s.

In 1960, my twin brother was one of the first Black students at UVA as it grudgingly and slowly desegregated. He was also one of the first Black students to go out for varsity football. The cruelty that he faced was immeasurable. Of course, he was not permitted to join the team. Again, historical fact is so often lost or stolen at UVA. Wes was a stellar high school football player; he went on to become the first Black honors graduate in the School of Engineering.

Wes and I had not dressed alike since we were twelve years old. We had different friends and different social activities. However, we were very close in mutual support, meeting challenges confronted by one the same as both, and we shared social, political, economic, and environmental beliefs and goals. There was a major turning point when we reached high school: Wes was the superior student and more attentive to academic details. We played football side-by-side, however, for four years at Armstrong High in Richmond, Virginia. Wes was the starting center; I was the right guard. That we protected and supported each other is an understatement. In the summer of 1960, freshly graduated from high school, the Harris twins were off to college!

Excited and encouraged by our high school physics teacher, Eloise Bowles Washington, we both wanted to major in physics. In 1960, however, UVA did not permit African American students to enroll in the College of Arts and Sciences (home of the Department of Physics), so neither of us, if accepted, could major in physics at UVA. Wes chose to attend UVA anyway and instead enroll in the School of Engineering, which had admitted its first Black student just five years earlier. I insisted upon majoring in physics and instead attended Howard University. The Commonwealth of Virginia paid my tuition at Howard University for my initial two years.[1] In late August 1960, I got a friend to drive Wes and me to Charlottesville to unload his belongings into the Bonnycastle dormitory. He never had a white roommate; no white student was willing to share space with him. To reduce his frustration and isolation, I would visit some weekends and enjoy the space and our togetherness.

Almost immediately, Wes was confronted by the fact that only a few undergraduate Black students were actually enrolled in the School of Engineering. Equally, it was made very clear to him by white students (and by many professors and administrators) that he and other Black students were not welcome at "Mr. Jefferson's university." This was especially the case when Wes, who had been recruited to play football at Ohio State, turned out for the UVA football team, a team at that point with the longest losing streak—twenty-eight games—among all colleges. Wes was spat upon, had cigarettes thrown at him, and, of course, was called the "N–word" with greater frequency than we had ever experienced.

For his fourth year at UVA, in 1963–64, Wes was assigned a Lawn room (53 West) reflecting his outstanding academic performance. In 1963, Wes and a white faculty member invited civil rights leader and minister Dr. Martin Luther King Jr. to UVA for a lecture. Demonstrating their singular resistance to civil rights, not a single senior faculty member or administrator attended King's Old Cabell Hall speech in March 1963.[2]

Our family and friends attended Wes's commencement in 1964. I was struck that in speaking to the graduates, President Edgar Shannon spent a great deal of time complaining that the University was being put upon by federal government paperwork. Of course, this flies in the face of the reality that it was federal research support that maintained an average-producing university's research. My take was certainly different than most in attendance. Living in Washington, D.C., and enrolled at Howard University, it was strange for me to observe a college professor and president twist the truth in such a clear manner.

My connection to UVA did not end that spring day when my brother graduated. Contacted and encouraged by Wes over a decade later, I took the job of Dean of African Americans at UVA in 1976 with a joint appointment in the School of Architecture's Department of Urban Planning. I arrived as dean of a new unit (Office of Afro American Affairs, now named the Office of African American Affairs) in the Student Affairs division.

My immediate and subsequent experiences at UVA brought frustration—and even disbelief. At that time, Frank Hereford was the University president. Hereford had been born in Louisiana and had been educated at UVA for all of his college training (in physics). Very conservative, intelligent, and dedicated to the University, Hereford was also a man of character who evinced no outward intent to be aggressive or vengeful toward African American students. He appeared to be personally more open to social justice than his environment permitted. Most faculty, administrators, and white students at that time remained opposed to the goals of the civil rights movement.

The other president under whom I served was John Casteen. As with Hereford, Casteen had been college-educated entirely at UVA. However, to me, he seemed less able to handle views that differed with his and was less open to calls for social justice. I specifically recall using the term "African American" in his presence. He was clearly shocked and asked aggressively, "What is this?" Clearly, he could not understand why I and many other Black Americans preferred this term to older terms from the Jim Crow era. He never intervened to halt the extremely racist behaviors expressed by clerical staff and groundskeepers toward African American faculty and students.

Although he had been forced to create the Office of African American Affairs, Hereford did have that as a legacy of his presidency's institutional response to systemic racism. Hardly "winds of change," but an important development nonetheless. Casteen, inheriting that office, did not move the needle to make UVA a more inclusive space. Nor did he create any structures to abate racist behaviors at the University during his lengthy tenure as president. Reminds me of that old adage about how the more things change, the more they stay the same.

My primary experiences with faculty racism came in the School of Architecture. For more than a decade and a half, my presence was as the *only African American* in the entire school. There was one white faculty member who would come to faculty meetings and literally announce that he was a racist. Other white colleagues never objected to his statements. Another faculty member felt it necessary to look at me and make a biblical reference to the "curse of Ham," itself a tired old trope meant to justify the enslavement of Black people. That same white colleague was earning healthy consulting fees in working with the NAACP Legal Defense Fund (having never won a single case). A white female professor had a habit of moving her purse whenever I sat near her in a meeting.

The students behaved similarly, engaging in racist microaggressions and worse. Not infrequently, white students would rebel and insist upon holding class on their own to avoid my instruction. One law student, apparently angry at having a Black professor, exploded that he did not take my class to hear anything related to professional ethics or social justice. These were not isolated incidents.

The feeling of having a target on my back wherever I went was ever-present. After attending a basketball game at University Hall, I drove my VW Beetle through campus on my way home. A campus cop pulled me over and insisted that I was speeding. He flatly refused to indicate how he knew I had been speeding. For this imagined offense, I was handcuffed and taken to jail. At the trial, the judge asked the officer for proof regarding my alleged speeding through the University. The officer said that he could tell I was speeding because he could hear the car's engine. The judge, dripping with white paternalist noblesse oblige and hoping to demonstrate how well the legal system in the City of Charlottesville cooperated with UVA in maintaining "order," reduced the charge, finding me guilty of "improper driving." I appealed the ruling—in what was the first-ever jury trial in such a case locally—and ultimately won on appeal. Yes, a minor traffic infraction for me necessitated an actual jury trial to clear my name.

In summary, the problem of race at UVA has been less about segregation and mostly about institutional racism. Those so-called winds of change proved to be but trifling breezes in the face of continuing bigotry and systemic racism. My story, of course, is not exceptional. I was not the only African American faculty member at UVA to experience such mean-spirited, cruel, institutionally sanctioned behaviors. The struggle continues.

Notes

1. This program arose during the Jim Crow era in Virginia as a way to redirect African American students who attempted to apply to UVA (and other segregated state schools). The program was still in existence as Virginia haltingly desegregated state colleges and universities.
2. Wes and I were able to have a plaque dedicating that event installed in Old Cabell Hall in 2020.

"A Race So Different"

Asians and Asian Americans in UVA's History

SYLVIA SHIN HUEY CHONG

In 2017, the University renamed two buildings on Grounds that had associations with prominent eugenicists: Lewis House, a dormitory at the International Residential College named after biology professor and College of Arts and Sciences dean Ivey Foreman Lewis, and the School of Medicine's Jordan Hall, named after anatomy professor and School of Medicine dean Harvey E. Jordan. Lewis House was renamed Yen House after W. W. Yen (also known as Yan Huiqing), the first Chinese student to graduate from UVA in 1900.[1] Yen went on to serve five terms as the premier of China during its Republican Era. Jordan Hall became Pinn Hall, named for Dr. Vivian Pinn, a 1967 graduate of UVA's School of Medicine who went on to become the first female African American chair of Howard University's Department of Pathology.

While Pinn would seem to embody a natural rejoinder to these disavowed eugenicists, serving as a living reminder of the failure of their predictions about African Americans, Yen is a more ambiguous case. In Virginia, without a large influx of Asian immigrants, Asians were mostly an afterthought in the racist laws of the era and were barely mentioned in the implementation of the Virginia Racial Integrity and Sterilization Acts of the 1920s. Based on his social class, religion, education, and relative assimilation, Yen had little in common with the Chinese laborers being derided at the time as "coolies," "strike breakers," and even replacements for enslaved people. To borrow a term from contemporary sociologists, Yen may have even been seen as an "honorary white."[2]

But only four years before Yen's graduation from UVA, U.S. Supreme Court justice John Marshall Harlan made a striking comment that reminds us of the role Asians and Asian Americans have always played in the United States' otherwise binary, Black-white racial system. Justice Harlan's famous dissent against the "separate but equal" doctrine in *Plessy v. Ferguson* (1896) contrasts loyal and patriotic African Americans with the Chinese, a "race so different from our own that we do not permit those belonging to it to become citizens of the United States," and goes on to lament that the Chinese could ride in a railcar in Louisiana with whites while Blacks remained segregated under force of law.[3] Jim Crow segregation would often, though not always, group Asians alongside whites, yet those like Harlan saw whites and African Americans as united against the intrusion of these "strangers from a different shore."[4]

To recount the history of Asians at UVA, we must keep in mind this constantly shifting triangulation of Asians between Black and white. While this history is of particular interest to UVA's current Asian American students, staff, and faculty, it is also unclear whether these early Asian students would be understood as Asian American by today's standards, since students like Yen not only saw themselves as distinct from other Asians in the United States but ultimately returned to their home countries for their careers and families. Ironically, many of these Asians who thought of themselves as temporary "sojourners" remained in the United States and established the foundations of the Asian American communities that thrive today. Asians and Asian Americans in the nineteenth, twentieth, and twenty-first centuries are linked by their shared fate of labor exploitation, cultural marginalization, and exclusion from the privileges of legal immigration and naturalized citizenship.

How, then, do Asians and Asian Americans fit into a broader history of race and racism at UVA? The arrival of Chinese laborers in America in the mid-1800s was initially greeted enthusiastically by industrialists and railroad tycoons, and as early as 1866, some former slaveholders considered "coolies as a substitute for Negroes" in Southern industrial agricultural production.[5] Despite that early enthusiasm, Asian immigration to the United States was relatively limited. In the 1900 U.S. Census, with the total U.S. population just under 76 million, the total population of Chinese and Japanese (other Asian groups were not counted) was 114,189, with only 3,839 in the entire South and a mere 253 in Virginia. (Compare

"What Shall We Do with John Chinaman? / What Pat Would Do with Him / What Will Be Done with Him," *Frank Leslie's Illustrated Newspaper,* September 25, 1869. (Library of Congress)

this with the over 8.8 million African Americans and 237,196 Native Americans counted in that same census.)[6]

Those early Chinese in the United States, while few in number, nonetheless sparked violent opposition from the white working class, who saw such "coolies" as undercutting their wages and threatening their jobs. This anti-Chinese racism was most virulent in the Northeast and the West Coast, where Chinese immigrants were the most numerous. Deadly riots were not uncommon, as evidenced by the 1871 Chinese Massacre in Los Angeles, the 1885 Rock Springs Massacre in Wyoming, and the 1907 anti-Japanese riots in San Francisco. Soon, most white Americans, already struggling to comprehend the place of African Americans in society in the years after the Civil War, would join in rigid opposition to Chinese immigration. Local, state, and federal restrictions were drafted to prohibit Chinese people from working in mines (Tuolumne County, California, 1849), attending white public schools (California Assembly Bill 668, 1885), marrying white women (Nevada Territory Laws, chap. 32, sec. 1, 3), and testifying in court against whites (*People v. Hall,* 4 Cal 399 [1854]).

"The Massacre of the Chinese at Rock Springs, Wyoming," drawn by T. de Thulstrup from photographs by Lt. C. A. Booth, *Harper's Weekly*, September 26, 1885. (Library of Congress)

Those hostilities culminated in two landmark moments of anti-Chinese immigration legislation. First, the 1875 Page Act effectively ended the immigration of Chinese women. A decade later, the 1882 Chinese Exclusion Act, which passed Congress with widespread national support, barred all Chinese laborers from entering the United States and created a permanent and isolated underclass of those Chinese already here by denying a pathway to naturalized citizenship and preventing their families from joining them. That legislation stood unchanged until 1943, when China was a U.S. ally during World War II.

Chinese merchants, diplomats, and UVA students such as W. W. Yen and Theodore Wong, who attended UVA before Yen between 1894 and 1897 but did not receive a degree, could still come to the United States during this period of exclusion. Many visiting Chinese elites were insulated from most of the hatred and violence simply by virtue of their class and political status. The late Qing court officially sponsored many of these students starting in 1872, dispatching them to elite institutions such as Yale University, Columbia University, and the Massachusetts Institute of Technology, among others. Although neither Yen nor Wong received

Yan Huiqing (W. W. Yen), the first Chinese graduate of the University of Virginia. (*Hawai'i Times* Photo Archives Foundation, Densho Digital Repository)

such official sponsorship and instead personally funded their foreign educations, both also came from families who converted to the Episcopalian Church, and both attended the Anglican-sponsored St. John's College in Shanghai before coming to the United States. Indeed, upon their arrival in the United States, both Yen and Wong attended the Episcopal High School in Alexandria before matriculating at UVA.[7]

Yen returned to China after graduation and taught English at St. John's for six years before coming back to the United States as part of the Chinese legation in Washington, D.C., when he briefly studied law at George Washington University. He returned to China again shortly before the Republican revolution of 1911 and thereafter served in a variety of governmental positions, including vice minister of foreign affairs; ambassador to the United States, Soviet Union, and Germany; and five terms as premier. In his memoir *East-West Kaleidoscope,* Yen describes no incidents of discrimination during his schooling in Virginia, as his Western clothing, fluency in English, and high status made him welcome in most social circles. During his last year at UVA, Yen recounts proudly, the chairman of the faculty refunded his tuition fee, explaining, "You have been so long in our state that we can consider you a Virginian" (27). However, traces of the national anti-Chinese climate emerge in a story about visiting New York City with the Chinese consulate-attaché and being attacked by street urchins who pulled the attaché's queue (22–23), as well as the suspicion from immigration authorities who surveilled Yen's trip to Canada (29).

Theodore Wong's career followed a similar path of return and remigration. After studying at UVA, he returned to China to take the civil service exam, but he moved back to Washington, D.C., in 1911 to become director of the second iteration of the Chinese Educational Mission (CEM), an organization that funded Chinese students' schooling in the United States. The CEM's staff and headquarters were only a few miles away but a world apart from D.C.'s nascent Chinatown, whose residents were largely Cantonese and had moved from the West Coast to the East Coast in search of jobs and safety, becoming employed as laundrymen, cigarmakers, restauranteurs, and grocers.[8] When Wong was killed, possibly by another Chinese student, in a shocking triple murder in D.C. in 1919, newspapers referred constantly to the "high-caste" status of both the victims and the murder suspects, as if to distinguish these students and diplomats from the alien and unassimilable working-class Chinese.

Yen's idyllic description of his time at UVA must be contrasted with local popular representations of Chinese people. Appearing only a year after his graduation, a short story in the 1901 edition of the *Corks and Curls* yearbook called "The Two Ends of Hi Go" presents a *Mikado*-like parody of Chinese life, including the ridiculously named character Hi Go and his parents, No Go and Miss Tea. The story is accompanied by numerous illustrations depicting them as grotesque, queue-wearing oddities

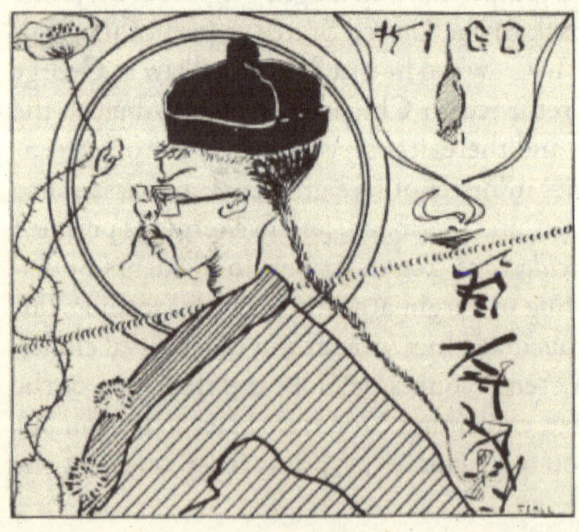

"The Two Ends of Hi Go," University of Virginia *Corks and Curls* yearbook, 1901. (University of Virginia Albert and Shirley Small Special Collections Library)

University of Virginia School of Law students, including Hiraoka Ryosuke (fourth row, center), 1900. (University of Virginia Albert and Shirley Small Special Collections Library)

very similar to the depictions found in racist political cartoons published by the exclusion movement.[9] Even if neither Yen nor Wong encountered such anti-Chinese sentiments, they certainly existed among their fellow UVA students as well as in the United States at large.

Ironically, Chinese exclusion opened the door to a wave of Japanese immigration to the United States, which was encouraged by the new Meiji government as part of a larger effort to modernize Japan through engagement with American and European technologies, politics, and culture. In some ways, the stronger military and diplomatic position of Japan when compared with China—combined with a popular fascination with Japanese culture—resulted in less hatred toward early Japanese migrants. Japan also sent many university students to the United States to acquire knowledge useful to its modernization, and a few of those students came to UVA. The earliest, Itami Jiro, studied law here from 1889 to 1891, while another law student, Hiraoka Ryosuke, overlapped with Yen during his studies from 1898 to 1901. Sugino Kaigiro studied math and science from 1890 to 1894 and even worked briefly for the architectural firm of McKim, Mead & White after the Rotunda fire of 1895.

Despite a fascination with Japanese culture, American popular culture still ridiculed Japanese people as undesirable yellow aliens, indistinguishable in many ways from the hated "coolie." For example, the popular "Hashimura Togo" column in *Collier's Magazine* that started in 1907 was written by white American humorist Wallace Irwin in a yellowface minstrel voice. The title character was named after the Japanese admiral who became famous for his successes in the Russo-Japanese War of 1904, but Irwin's "Togo" persona was hardly laudatory. His Togo was a thirty-five-year-old "schoolboy" who at times also worked as a "houseboy" in the employ of white middle-class women. Irwin's trademark voice for his Japanese doppelganger was a stilted, ungrammatical, pseudo-Chinese accent borrowed from coolie portrayals in the blackface minstrelsy circuit.

The widespread popularity of Togo can be seen in UVA's own rendition in the 1916 *Corks and Curls,* in which an anonymous UVA student adopts Irwin's Oriental masquerade to pen a series of letters entitled "Uniquities [*sic*] of the University, or Letters of a Japanese Schoolboy (With Apologies to Mr. Wallace Irwin)." Togo arrives at UVA—"I leaped from C. & O. local train and disclosed Charlottesville not far from"—and is besieged by fellow students trying to lure him into their "boarding-joints," prompting Togo to reply, "So sorry. . . . 23 meals a day is 20 too much for frugal Japanese" (309). Although the fake letters were likely poking fun at the absurdities of student life rather than at any actual Japanese students (there were none listed for 1916), such painfully awkward language casts even educated and elite international students at UVA as uncivilized rubes.

As the line between "welcome" and "unwelcome" Asians was quite blurred, Chinese and Japanese upper-class subjects attempted to distance themselves from their lower-class countrymen. In *The Four Immigrants Manga,* a Japanese graphic novel published in 1931, author Henry Yoshitaka Kiyama humorously depicts the other side of the Hashimura Togo story, showing how Japanese students felt degraded by being forced into "houseboy" work. Even while proudly declaiming their difference from Chinese coolies and Japanese farmers, these erstwhile servants constantly find themselves being mistaken by white employers and even other Japanese as common laborers.

At the 1904 World's Fair in St. Louis, Wong Kai Kah, a Yale alumnus and imperial vice-commissioner of the Chinese exhibit, lodged a formal complaint with the U.S. government that the distinguished delegates he had encouraged to attend the fair were being treated poorly, like a "coolie . . . detained in the pen on the steamship wharf, or imprisoned like a felon."[10] News of this humiliating incident helped instigate the 1905–6 Anti-American Boycott in China, one of the first modern Chinese mass movements and a precursor to the Republican revolution of 1911, which installed the postimperial government under which W. W. Yen served.

In the segregated South during the early twentieth century, Chinese and Japanese migrants would have occupied a complicated position within the larger Black-white racial binary. While class privilege may have seemingly elevated students like Yen, Wong, Itami, Hiraoka, and Sugino above local African Americans, general sentiments toward Asians in the United States during this period positioned them as even less desirable than African Americans. The pro-labor economic theorist Henry George wrote in 1869 in the *New York Tribune* that while "the Negro" might be characterized as "an ignorant but docile child," the Chinese were "sharp and narrow minded, opinionated and set in character. . . . A population born in China, expecting to return to China, living here in a little China of its own, and without the slightest attachment to this country—utter heathens, treacherous, sensual, cowardly, and cruel."[11]

In a similar vein, the 1916 UVA Hashimura Togo letters casually invoked racist slurs to describe how the members of the Tappa Keg fraternity reacted to Togo's attempt to join them: "Worthy High Grand Stein . . . this resemble yellow peril to me. Who want J— coolies in fraternities?" In the end, the fraternity assents to Togo's membership, but only if he is positioned in rank beneath their "n— janitor" Clarence, a "self-respectful Afro-American" who "knows more fraternity concealments than anybody here," and Togo happily agrees to this arrangement (313). Pacific Islanders were even further denigrated, lacking the veneer of exotic but developed culture to elevate them. A 1917 *Corks and Curls* story called "Saved by the Ray" depicts an UVA alumnus marooned in the South Pacific and about to be boiled by cannibals, who are drawn as primitive, Sambo-like caricatures (378). Filipino Americans were also often likened to African natives, disparaged in an article in the November 1930 issue of the *Cavalier* magazine as "little brown brothers," to borrow the language coined by William Howard Taft when he served as governor-general of the Philippines after the United States annexed the islands as a colony in 1898, after the Spanish-American War.[12]

None of this is to say that Yen, Wong, Itami, Hiraoka, and Sugino were not part of Asian American history. Even if they returned to their

University of Virginia law professor George Yin, grand-nephew of Yan Huiqing (W. W. Yen). (UVA Communications)

countries of origin after studying at UVA, their lives are intertwined with those who elected to stay. In fact, a professor currently at the UVA School of Law—George Yin—is distantly related to both Yen (who was his grand-uncle) and Wong (who was the grandfather of his first cousin).[13] Like Yen and Wong, Yin's father attended St. John's College in Shanghai before coming to the United States for graduate school in the 1930s, and he ended up settling in New York City, where Yen and his siblings were born. But even with their relative privilege and separation from other Asian migrants, George Yin's parents saw their opportunities in the United States limited. Yin's father had a master's in chemistry and his mother studied piano at Julliard, but neither was able to find employment in these fields. To support the family, his father started an import-export business that made use of his language skills in both English and Chinese, and his mother became a clerical worker. Yet their ability to start and support a nuclear family in the era of Asian exclusion (1924–65) also differentiated them from other early Chinese and Filipino Americans, many of whom lived their entire lives in the United States as forced "bachelors" because of the restrictions on female immigration and their own limited economic means.[14]

Even a hundred years later, there are echoes of Hashimura Togo and anti-coolie hostilities for current Asian and Asian American students at UVA and across the country, who may hear backhanded compliments like "Your English is so good" or complaints that their success in STEM fields takes away good grades and job opportunities for "real Americans." The ongoing COVID-19 pandemic has only exacerbated these tensions, as people of Asian descent in the United States have been targets of verbal abuse and violent crimes across the country for their association with the "Wuhan virus" as well as the economic devastation linked to the pandemic.[15] Just a day after UVA president Jim Ryan announced the ending of in-person classes at UVA in March 2020, two Chinese international students reported an incident just outside the Aquatic and Fitness Center in which eggs were thrown at them.[16]

The naming of the Yen House may have been intended to diversify the history of UVA and highlight the achievement of nonwhite students. Much work remains to be done, however, in acknowledging the discrimination and hostility that Asians and Asian Americans have faced over the last two centuries. Furthermore, there is a dangerous continuation of the model minority myth's racial triangulation, as the success of an Asian student is posited as the solution to a racial problem (such as UVA's history of involvement with the eugenics movement).[17] We need to hear about Yen, Wong, Itami, Hiraoka, Sugino, and other exceptional students, but that cannot substitute for a fuller reckoning with UVA's, and the nation's, relationship with Asian Americans and with other people of color.

Notes

1. Chinese and Japanese names are written here with surnames first and given names second, except in cases where the names have already been Westernized and used by non-Asians, such as "W. W. Yen."
2. Mia Tuan, *Forever Foreigners or Honorary Whites? The Asian Ethnic Experience Today* (Newark, N.J.: Rutgers University Press, 1999).
3. *Plessy v. Ferguson*, 163 U.S. 537, 561 (1896).
4. Ronald Takaki, *Strangers from a Different Shore: A History of Asian Americans*, rev. ed. (Boston: Little, Brown, 1998).
5. "Coolies as a Substitute for Negroes," *Debow's Review* 2, no. 2 (August 1866): 215–17. See also the political cartoon "What Shall We Do with John Chinaman?," *Frank Leslie's Illustrated Newspaper*, September 25, 1869, 32, https://www.loc.gov/pictures/resource/cph.3b48686/.

6. Data derived from tables A-1 (Race and Hispanic Origin for the United States: 1790 to 1990), C-10 (Asian and Pacific Islander, for the United States, Regions, Divisions, and States: 1900 and 1910), and 61 (Virginia—Race and Hispanic Origin: 1790 to 1990), from Campbell Gibson and Kay Jung, *Historical Census Statistics on Population Totals by Race, 1790 to 1990, and by Hispanic Origin, 1970 to 1990, for the United States, Regions, Divisions, and States,* Working Paper No. 56 (Washington, D.C.: U.S. Census Bureau, September 2002), https://census.gov/content/dam/Census/library/working-papers/2002/demo/POP-twps0056.pdf.
7. Yen's and Wong's family histories were reconstructed from Yen's memoir, *East-West Kaleidoscope, 1877–1946: An Autobiography* (New York: St. John's University Press, 1974), as well as from an unpublished biographical sketch of Wong compiled in November 2005 by his grandson, Wilfred Ling, which is archived in Special Collections, University of Virginia Library, and with additional assistance by Justin O'Jack, who is the current chief representative of UVA's China Office.
8. Scott D. Seligman, *The Third Degree: The Triple Murder that Shook Washington and Changed American Criminal Justice* (Lincoln: Potomac Books, 2018).
9. The queue (sometimes spelled "cue") was a hairstyle from Manchuria that was worn by men during the Qing Dynasty (1644–1912). The front portion of the head was shaved, with hair toward the back grown long and braided.
10. Wong Kai Kah, "A Menace to America's Oriental Trade," *North American Review,* March 1904, 418–19.
11. Henry George, "The Chinese in California," *New York Tribune,* May 1, 1869, reprinted in *Major Problems in Asian American History: Documents and Essays,* ed. Lon Kurashige and Alice Yang Murray (Boston: Houghton Mifflin, 2003), 99.
12. The offending phrase "little brown brothers" is taken from Lewis Mattison, "Pacific Letter," *Cavalier,* November 1930, 21.
13. See the blog *Inside the Classroom: UVA School of Law* for a feature on Professor George Yin, http://uvalawteach.tumblr.com/post/148495366283/professor-george-yin-grew-up-in-new-york-city-on. See also Eric Williamson, "Professor George Yin Finds Unexpected Family Ties to World Figure, UVA's Past," University of Virginia School of Law, News and Media, 11 April 2018, https://www.law.virginia.edu/news/201804/professor-george-yin-finds-unexpected-family-ties-world-figure-uva%E2%80%99s-past.
14. Personal interview with George Yin, March 26, 2019.
15. As of this writing, there has been a recent spate of killings, assaults, and robberies of Asian Americans in California and New York, including a mass shooting in Atlanta in which six of the eight victins were Asian women. See N'dea Yancey-Bragg, "'Stop Killing Us': Attacks on Asian Americans Highlight Rise in Hate Incidents Amid COVID-19," *USA Today,*

February 11, 2021, https://www.usatoday.com/story/news/nation/2021/02/12/asian-hate-incidents-covid-19-lunar-new-year/4447037001/, and Cady Land, "The Atlanta Shootings Fit into a Long Legacy of Anti-Asian Violence in America," *Time*, March 18, 2021, https://time.com/5947723/atlanta-shootings-anti-asian-violence-america/.

16. Nik Popli, "Chinese International Student Reports Attempted Assault at U.Va.," *Cavalier Daily*, March 12, 2020, https://www.cavalierdaily.com/article/2020/03/chinese-international-student-%20reports-attempted-assault-at-u-va%3E.
17. For more on the history of the model minority myth and racial triangulation, see Kat Chow, "'Model Minority' Myth again Used as a Racial Wedge between Asians and Blacks," April 19, 2017, in *Code Switch: Race and Identity Re-Mixed*, podcast, NPR.com, https://www.npr.org/sections/codeswitch/2017/04/19/524571669/model-minority-myth-again-used-as-a-racial-wedge-between-asians-and-blacks.

Response
We Are Not Invisible

JAY PUN

AFTER READING and digesting Sylvia Shin Huey Chong's essay, which focuses heavily on W. W. Yen and notes his time at the University as having no incidents of discrimination, I am forced to consider my own upbringing in Charlottesville. Like Yen, my acceptance into Charlottesville was because of my distance from stereotypical notions of Asians as different. Yen's description was counter to local popular representations of Chinese people, as in the edition of *Corks and Curls,* which depicts Chinese people as "grotesque, queue-wearing oddities." Such othering images remain pervasive, and while Asians experience a modicum of acceptance, these distortions fuel the present notions of "other," and "sinister," at the heart of anti-Asian racism today.

I grew up in Charlottesville and my family was one of the first (if not the very first) Thai families in town. Both of my parents came over to the States to do their medical residencies with the intention of returning to Thailand, but that never happened. One thing led to another, and they found their home in Charlottesville, starting their respective practices (orthopedics and obstetrics-gynecology) as well as a family. We kept many of our cultural traditions at home, eating sticky rice, noodle bowls, bao, and so on as well as informally practicing Buddhism. In a way, we were like the Thai cultural center for Charlottesville at the time. UVA asked us multiple times to host various Thai students who were going through their medical or law programs, and we happily agreed. It was a familiar place for them to come and get a home-cooked meal from their native land and have some kind of human connection that they were used to.

Outside the house, my mom did everything she could to make sure we felt the same as everyone else. My parents worked hard to be upper middle class, and my mother gave us almost anything we asked for. If I wanted French fries from McDonald's, the new Nintendo game, or the latest recording equipment, she would get it for me. We never had a new BMW or Porsche (my dad liked old sports cars that he'd buy inexpensively and fix up), but we never felt poor—or rich. To help make us feel like we belonged, my mom made a different meal each night. Her dinners ranged from taco night, with the classic Old El Paso seasoning mix, to Pizza Hut on Fridays, burgers, and spaghetti, but my favorite was her native Thai food.

As most Asian parents do, mine sent me to private school, and for the most part, I felt that I fit in relatively well. I had my own clique; I went to their houses and was invited to their country clubs and beach trips many times over. I felt so cool going to their club pool as a guest and getting something to eat at the snack bar, because they didn't have to pay (or at least that's what it seemed like). They just told the cashier a special number and voilà, the "free" food appeared. I figured out later in life that it was billed to their parents, but to me it was like magic. I once asked my mom why we couldn't join the same country club as all my friends, and she said, "Because I don't want to pay for friendships." I didn't understand it at the time, but I'm glad that was one thing she didn't spoil me with.

Once in my middle school history class, as we were studying about enslavement, my teacher said something like, "None of us would know anything about that, because we're all white," and I replied, "Excuse me, I'm not." She then said, "You're white enough." That moment was a turning point for me, as I understood exactly what she meant. No one in the room could have even fathomed what an enslaved person might have felt like, yet my teacher simultaneously kept me invisible, disregarding who I truly was. While my proximity to whiteness was, and still is, evident, that comment stuck with me throughout my life, now giving me the drive to amplify Asian people and their cultures.

These microaggressions are nothing new, nor are they in the same category as the deep and dark hate toward the Black community, but they are real and have marginalized Asian people for years. They include everything from thinking that someone doesn't speak English well before they say a word to thinking ethnic dishes are disgusting without even trying them. In the essay, Chong asserts that some whites considered the Chinese to be a "race so different from our own" that they were not permitted to "'become citizens of the United States'" and that "Jim Crow segregation would often, but not always, group Asians alongside whites, yet those like [Supreme Court justice John Marshall] Harlan saw whites and African Americans as united against the intrusion of these 'strangers from a different shore.'"

When I was in high school, back in 1997, my family opened the first Thai restaurant in Charlottesville. We wanted it to be upscale, marketing it with the phrase "Thai! Simply Exquisite," with white linen tablecloths and a waterfall inside. While we knew Charlottesville hadn't had a Thai restaurant yet, we assumed that many residents were well-traveled enough that it would be a hit. What we didn't expect was how many people would come in asking if we had lo mein or other Chinese dishes. What surprised us most was when we'd get the occasional, "I had such and such at this Chinese place and it had this and that, could you make me something like that?" I now own three Thai/Vietnamese restaurants in Charlottesville and we still get those same questions and requests for the ever-so-popular "duck sauce," which is largely associated with Chinese (American) food but was invented here in the States, not in China.

As the popularity of Thai food (and many other Southeast Asian cuisines) grows, we now start to see food appropriation coming into play more and more regularly. What was once foreign and possibly intimidating food to Americans is now often made by nonethnic people to give their menus some flair. How many times have you seen a deli now make their version of a Vietnamese banh mi sandwich that costs twice as much and is not even close to what it should taste like? Or the fine dining restaurant that serves something "Thai inspired" and simply adds some peanuts and cilantro? Or the food truck serving "Asian fusion" but fails to spell dishes correctly? These practices, while often defended as being inspired by someone's love for another culture, can be felt more like stealing, or food plagiarism, if done without respect to the food's origins.

Charlottesville has been kind to us, as many of us have great careers and fit in well, but we continue to not truly be seen. We occupy the hospital as caregivers, and the restaurants as owners/chefs, but we are also teachers, scientists, artists, activists, politicians, and more. All of these are examples of how Asians are seen as invisible until recognized and lifted by those in power, but we are and should be seen for ourselves first and foremost. We have and hold just as much value as any other group of people. We are NOT a virus. We are NOT a scapegoat. We are NOT the model minority. We are NOT invisible.

I will continue amplifying our Asian community and its individual voices here in Charlottesville and beyond.

Property and Power

BRIAN CAMERON AND ANDREW KAHRL

In early December 2015, a minor act of protest became front-page news in Charlottesville. On the entrance sign to the historically African American neighborhood of Fifeville, vandals spray-painted over its anodyne slogan "Historic, Green, Diverse" the words "Vinegar Hill . . . The Sequel," in reference to the former downtown Black business and residential district infamously destroyed by the city in the mid-1960s as part of an urban renewal project.[1] While workers in the city's Parks and Recreation department quickly removed and repainted the sign, no one could erase Black residents' bitter memories of past injustices or assuage their fears of further displacement at the hands of city and University of Virginia officials. Like many historically Black and working-class neighborhoods in Charlottesville, Fifeville today is undergoing what critics and supporters alike call "gentrification," a process characterized by the redevelopment of older properties into new housing and commercial space that caters to higher-income, and predominantly white, residents. This, in turn, leads to sharp increases in property taxes and rents, making neighborhoods unaffordable to working families and, ultimately, forcing many longtime residents out.

In recent years, local Charlottesville residents and activists have flooded public meetings and taken to the streets to demand action by the city to address its affordable housing crisis. Invariably, they invoke the memory of Vinegar Hill, whose demise has become synonymous with the city's racist past and threats to its working-class and African American populations in the present. While egregious, the destruction of Vinegar Hill, and the reasons offered by local officials for it, was by no means unprecedented.

Vinegar Hill neighborhood with Preston Avenue to the right, viewed from downtown Charlottesville, 1916. (University of Virginia Albert and Shirley Small Special Collections Library)

Rather, throughout the city's history and to this day, African American neighborhoods have borne the costs of the city's—and the University of Virginia's—growth. In some instances, the University played a direct role in the physical destruction of Black neighborhoods and displacement of their residents. At other times, its influence has been felt more indirectly.

Almost from the moment UVA began to expand beyond its original Academical Village, Charlottesville's communities of color faced the threats of displacement and erasure. In the 1830s, free people of color began moving into the area just south of the Academical Village that by the 1860s was increasingly referred to as "Canada," a reference to the free Black people living there. As early as 1833, Catherine "Kitty" Foster—honored today by the Shadowcatcher memorial on the South Lawn—became the first free Black woman to own property in this area, where she lived and worked as a laundress and seamstress primarily serving the University community. By the 1890s, the road separating Canada and the University had been paved and renamed Jefferson Park Avenue, as white developers purchased and built large homes. Thus, Canada became a recurring point of contention for the Board of Visitors, who in 1896 decided to build Old

Downtown Charlottesville, with Vinegar Hill neighborhood visible at center right, circa 1930. (University of Virginia Albert and Shirley Small Special Collections Library)

Cabell Hall so as to close off the Academical Village from "the area immediately to the south of the University's land and in full view . . . filled with unsightly houses." In the early 1900s, the first white property owners moved into the Canada area, and as development intensified through the 1920s, racially restrictive covenants were instated to prohibit the resale of properties to people of color. Nearer to the downtown area, the city purchased and razed McKee Row, an area of African American rental houses, to make way for the Thomas "Stonewall" Jackson monument and Jackson Park, donated by philanthropist Paul Goodloe McIntire.[2]

In 1965, Charlottesville exercised eminent domain to acquire the Vinegar Hill neighborhood and business district, raze it, and attempt to redevelop it for a new thoroughfare and commercial development. The urban renewal scheme for Vinegar Hill followed a blueprint proposed by urban planning firm Harland Bartholomew and Associates, infamous for pioneering racially motivated slum clearance in St. Louis.[3] As was the case in cities across the nation, urban renewal had a devastating impact on Charlottesville's African American community. All told, the city's redevelopment of the area resulted in the forced displacement of more than six hundred Black families and the closing of more than thirty Black-owned businesses that, combined, had generated a gross annual income of $1.6 million.

Like countless other urban renewal projects of this era, the purported benefits resulting from Vinegar Hill's destruction failed to materialize. For years afterward, the cleared site remained vacant as the city struggled to attract new commercial development to the downtown area.[4] "It just stayed like a cemetery," former resident Teresa Jackson Price remarked.[5] For many in Charlottesville's African American community, the slow pace of redevelopment cast the city's stated motives for razing Vinegar Hill into further doubt and deepened their distrust of city leadership.

The displacement of Vinegar Hill's residents coincided with a massive increase in the University of Virginia's student body and expansion of the University's physical footprint. Between 1965 and 1975, UVA's student population doubled from 7,249 to 15,179, fueled by the admission of women (starting in 1970) and the post–World War II baby boom. UVA's growth during these years came at Black Charlottesvillians' expense. During the 1970s, the University Health System encroached upon the Black neighborhood of Gospel Hill with the construction of Jordan Hall, McLeod Hall, and the Claude Moore Health Sciences Library.[6] (Jordan Hall was named for noted eugenicist Harvey E. Jordan and later renamed Pinn Hall in honor of Dr. Vivian Pinn, the School of Medicine's first Black female graduate.) Adjacent to the prior community of Canada, Gospel Hill was originally settled by free Black families in the antebellum era. Through the 1970s and '80s, UVA acquired properties in this neighborhood, razed them, and constructed either parking lots or medical facilities. The Health System redeveloped the last remains of Gospel Hill when it built the new University Hospital in 1984. The University had considered the site of the old Blue Ridge Sanatorium, off Route 20, but ultimately determined that proximity to central Grounds should be a top priority for the site choice.[7] Today, no physical trace of Gospel Hill remains in the built environment of the Health System.[8]

The eradication of these working-class Black neighborhoods paved the way, both literally and figuratively, for Charlottesville's economic reorientation and demographic changes in recent decades. By the early 1980s, Charlottesville was regularly included on lists of the "best places to live" and "best places to retire," and it similarly began ascending the ranks of "best college towns in America."[9] Popular magazines such as *Cosmopolitan* gushed about the city's "beauty" and various amenities and attractions that would appeal to its predominantly white, urbane readership. As high-income earners and retirees flocked to the city, housing prices soared, and growing numbers of residents found themselves priced out.

While UVA's student body swelled, the number of on-Grounds housing units did not. Between 2000 and 2017, UVA's combined graduate and undergraduate enrollment grew by 4,549 students. Of these, 3,920 new students turned to the off-Grounds private rental market for their housing. UVA served only 629 students with new on-Grounds beds added during the same time frame. As more students entered the city's rental market, more of its working-class population left. More affordable residential neighborhoods became extensions of the University and inhospitable to families and children. Landlords reoriented their business around the student housing market, while investors rushed to acquire and redevelop properties to capitalize on the demand.

The growing numbers of students living off Grounds contributed to soaring rents citywide. Between 2012 and 2018, the average apartment rents rose 18.1 percent, jumping by 9.4 percent in 2017 alone. Among the major apartment buildings in the Charlottesville market, average rents were $1,384. This, as one report on the city's housing needs noted, means that "a single person working a minimum-wage job would need to work 147 hours per week" to be able to afford to live in the city. A person earning $15 an hour (the new living-wage standard adopted in January 2020 by the University) would still need to work seventy-one hours each week to be able to afford the average apartment in Charlottesville. At forty hours a week, individuals earning $15 an hour would spend over half their income on housing. That same report found a deficit of 3,318 affordable housing units in Charlottesville for 2017, projected to reach 4,020 by 2040. The latter figure parallels that of UVA's off-Grounds enrollment growth since 2000: 3,920 students.[10]

The growing cost of living in Charlottesville is, in one sense, indicative of the city's prosperity. But the benefits, as well as the burdens, of economic growth have been unevenly distributed and too often come at the expense of Charlottesville's Black residents. Between 2010 and 2017, white median household income in Charlottesville rose from $45,000 to $64,000, adjusted for inflation. Meanwhile, African American median household income actually fell from $31,000 to $28,000. Over the past two decades, the city's African American population has declined from 22 percent to 18.4 percent of the city's total population. These changes have been especially pronounced in the neighborhoods surrounding the University. In the Tenth and Page neighborhood, the African American population dropped 17 percentage points between 2010 and 2017, from 72 percent to 55 percent. Simultaneously, median rent in this neighborhood rose from $666 to $939, median home value increased from $160,300 to $205,800, and overall median household income rose from $17,000 to $38,000. The dwindling number of longtime residents who remain bemoan the loss of community that has accompanied the area's changing racial and socioeconomic demographics, a transformation embodied in the proliferation of fences and walls around properties and new businesses catering to the consumer tastes (and pocketbooks) of students and young white professionals.[11]

In recent years, UVA has taken steps to address the city's affordable housing crisis. In March 2020, the University announced a new goal of supporting the development of one thousand to fifteen hundred affordable housing units in the local market. It also established the Affordable Housing Advisory Group, which seeks to make recommendations and engage with community and housing partners to reach this goal. President Jim Ryan said that the University will allow the use of UVA- or UVA Foundation–owned land for the development of this affordable housing as part of a multiphased approach over the next decade. The University said it will ultimately select development partners through a competitive process. In recent years, UVA has also discussed the possibility of requiring second-year students to live on Grounds. Currently, only first-year students are required to do so. As these efforts proceed, a fuller understanding of this past and the ways it continues to shape and inform the politics of the present will be key to building a more equitable and inclusive Charlottesville community.

Notes

1. Chris Suarez, "Fifeville Sign Vandalized with Reference to Vinegar Hill," *Charlottesville Daily Progress,* December 5, 2015.
2. Sophie Abramowitz, Eva Latterner, and Gillet Rosenblith, "How Charlottesville, Virginia's Confederate Statues Helped Decimate the City's Historically Successful Black Communities," *Slate,* June 23, 2017.
3. Mark Benton, "'Saving' the City: Harland Bartholomew and Administrative Evil in St. Louis," *Public Integrity* 20, no. 2 (2018): 198.
4. Digital Scholarship Lab, "Renewing Inequality," in *American Panorama,* ed. Robert K. Nelson and Edward L. Ayers, accessed July 20, 2021, https://dsl.richmond.edu/panorama/renewal/#view=0/0/1&viz=cartogram.

5. *That World Is Gone: Race and Displacement in a Southern Town*, directed and edited by Hannah Brown Ayers and Lance Warren (Field Studio, 2010), https://www.fieldstudiofilms.com/that-world-is-gone.
6. Brian Cameron, Morgan Feldenkris, and Allie Arnold, "Housing the University: Student Housing and Displacement in Charlottesville, Virginia," May 2018, https://uvalibrary.maps.arcgis.com/apps/MapJournal/index.html?appid=b6c884f9dee140049cd17e4c538874ec.
7. "History of the University of Virginia Hospital from the 1970s to the Millennium," *The University of Virginia Hospital Celebrating 100 Years: A Legacy of Care and a Framework for the Future*, exhibition prepared in 2001 by Hal Sharp and Janet Pearson, Claude Moore Health Sciences Library, Historical Collections, http://exhibits.hsl.virginia.edu/centennial/growth_part3/.
8. Cameron, Feldenkris, and Arnold, "Housing the University."
9. See, among many others, Abby Jackson, "The 20 Best College Towns in America," *Business Insider*, January 14, 2017, https://www.businessinsider.com/best-college-towns-in-america-2017-1#10-bloomington-illinois-home-of-illinois-state-university-11.
10. Form-Based Codes Institute and Partners for Economic Solutions, "Housing Needs Assessment: Socioeconomic and Housing Market Analysis," City of Charlottesville, April 4, 2018.
11. Jordy Yager, "A New Page: Longtime 10th and Page Residents Are Seeing a Shift in the Neighborhood," *C-Ville Weekly*, December 1, 2017.

Response

Ties That Bind

From Covenants to Zoning, a University and City United

JORDY YAGER

IN 2014, Charlottesville community member Karen C. Waters-Wicks meticulously detailed for the first time how Charlottesville's city council came to pass, in 1912, an ordinance requiring the racial segregation of housing locally.[1] In 1917 the U.S. Supreme Court declared the law, and others like it, unconstitutional, but it was Central Virginia's first major citywide attempt at racial zoning. The law's unanimous support by members of the city council testified to how the majority of local white residents viewed the growing and increasingly fortified Black economic base of property and power. Waters-Wicks's article shifted the ground of how we discuss racism in local housing by using seemingly historic and routine government actions to lay bare the deeper and more enduring patterns of structural and systemic racism. Until recently, universities have largely been held in white circles as bearers of knowledge and good to the world. In 2018, however, UVA president Teresa A. Sullivan created the President's Commission on the University in the Age of Segregation to "explore and report on UVA's role in the period of racial segregation." It has been an attempt to pull back the curtain of UVA's past to examine the ways it perpetuated generational harm on local Black residents. Key to this understanding is an honest look at how decision makers held positions of power at both the university and within local government—and how people uphold institutions, which work together to uphold systems.

McKee Row, between Jefferson and High Streets, downtown Charlottesville, ca. 1910. (University of Virginia Albert and Shirley Small Special Collections Library)

In 1912, there were eight white men on Charlottesville's city council, all of whom voted in favor of the racial segregation ordinance. One of those men was a bookkeeper at the woolen mills; another sold building materials and was a part owner of the Charlottesville Lumber Company. A third councilor ran a dry goods store on West Main Street, and a fourth owned a giant Jeffersonian Revival mansion he had built at the top of Gospel Hill, a working-class Black neighborhood near UVA. A fifth councilor, J. H. Montague, operated a furniture store downtown while managing the Levy Opera House in Court Square, just one block away from McKee Row—home to Black porters, laborers, launderers, and domestic workers. Around this time, there were "numerous complaints about the housing on McKee Row crowding up to the courthouse, and about people from the area 'hanging around the Levy Opera House.'"[2] The neighborhood was soon slated for razing, and in 1919 the local newspaper ran the headline "'McKee Block' No More."[3] By the fall of 1921, a giant statue of Thomas "Stonewall" Jackson was erected in its place in a newly landscaped park.

Edward Andrew Balz, a sixth councilor who voted for the 1912 ordinance, was the son of Henry J. Balz, a Confederate army veteran. Edward worked as a ticket agent for the C&O Railway. His brother, Albert G. A. Balz, graduated from and was a professor of philosophy at UVA, where a dormitory today remains named after him. He and his brother played significant roles in creating and maintaining segregation locally. Albert also served as chairman of the Charlottesville school board and oversaw the planning and construction of the largest school building the city had ever seen, the all-white Lane High School on the corner of Preston Avenue and McIntire Road. This, however, was not city-owned property, and in 1938 the all-white city school board seized more than a dozen homes along Pearl Street and Preston Avenue, forcing at least sixteen Black residents to move. Some of these were barbers, laborers, and domestic workers; there was also a painter, a teacher, and a waiter. A few of the homes were rentals, but most were owner-occupied and -built. The homeowners were paid for their property but not given a choice to move, which was legally sanctioned by what has become known as eminent domain, rooted in the "takings clause" of the Fifth Amendment: "Nor shall private property be taken for public use, without just compensation."

That clause is attributed to President James Madison, a member of UVA's first Board of Visitors; he also served as rector from 1826 to 1834. Both Madison and UVA used and profited from Black people's bondage and forced labor, using legal structures to control where and how the people they enslaved lived. In the post-emancipation Jim Crow America of 1938, Madison's words were still being used to control Black people by defining "public use" as whites-only. Further, this forced taking of Black property to build an all-white school dispossessed Black residents of their greatest financial asset and generator of generational wealth at a critical moment: the tail end of the Great Depression, the most catastrophic and far-reaching economic collapse the country had experienced.

A seventh councilor to vote for the 1912 ordinance, Frank M. Huyett, was a real estate agent. In 1918, he bought a property for $2,800 in the Little High neighborhood that contained the clause "the said lot shall never be sold or leased to a negro or negroes." Even as the 1912 racial segregation ordinance cemented white Charlottesville's desire to keep its property from Black residents on a large scale, these racist covenants were the more enduring means white property owners used to carry out their segregationist goals. Research at the Jefferson School African American Heritage Center (JSAAHC) has revealed that the first racial covenants were inserted into property deeds as early as 1893, nearly two decades before the 1912 law. It turns out that the ordinance was a citywide culmination of hundreds of prior attempts to use private individual covenants to restrict Black residents from accessing land. The JSAAHC's Mapping Cville project has so far identified more than two thousand of these racially restricted deeds between 1903 and 1956—a period of the area's largest real estate boom in the twentieth century.[4]

In 1921, the same year the Stonewall Jackson statue was installed atop the predominantly Black McKee Row, Councilor Huyett purchased another property along Emmet Street, directly across from what, three years later, became UVA's Memorial Gym. This property contained the covenant, "No portion of the land hereby conveyed will or shall be sold to any negro person or persons, it being understood and agreed that this covenant shall run with the title to the land." Today this land has been subdivided into seven properties, which are now collectively valued at $13.7 million. Four of these properties make up 88 percent of that value, or $12.1 million, and are owned by the UVA Foundation, the UVA Alumni Association, and the UVA Rector and Visitors.

Through Mapping Cville, the JSAAHC is cataloguing and mapping not only the scale and scope of these covenants but also their impact on property values and their economic impact on people's lives. In the 1930s, when the federal Home Owners' Loan Corporation drew "redlining" maps for every major city in the country, it failed to create one for Charlottesville because it was not large enough. These maps and the practice of redlining were how banks decided whether to lend money to prospective homebuyers. As a result, 98 percent of loans approved by the federal government between 1934 and 1968 went to white applicants.[5] In Charlottesville, despite the absence of a redlining map, these racist covenants show how omnipresent racism was in the local housing market for more than six decades. The 1912 ordinance further demonstrates that white Charlottesville's desire for racial segregation was not just neighborhood-by-neighborhood but citywide.

What's more, the eighth vote in favor of the ordinance was from perhaps the most historically well-known councilor, Rufus W. Holsinger. A renowned photographer, Holsinger was also the director of the National Bank and Trust in Charlottesville, which in the early twentieth century made at least sixty loans to white homebuyers purchasing properties with racist covenants. Though the practice of federally backed redlining may not have been officially orchestrated in Charlottesville as it was in larger cities, through the JSAAHC's Mapping Cville project, we can see the complicit and interconnected networks that allowed for racist financing practices to be enacted on a monumental scale by multiple local banks and financial institutions, including UVA. We can examine our complex history with greater context and honesty and use this new understanding to help undo legacies of harm—and to make better decisions in the future.

Notes

1. Karen C. Waters-Wicks, "An Ordinance to Secure for White and Colored People a Separate Location of Residence for Each Race: A History of De Jure Residential Segregation in Charlottesville and Richmond, Virginia," *Magazine of Albemarle County History* 72 (2014): 107–47.
2. National Register for Historic Places nomination form for the Thomas "Stonewall" Jackson statue, https://www.dhr.virginia.gov/VLR_to_transfer/PDFNoms/104-0251_Thomas_Jonathan_Jackson_Sculpture_1997_Final_Nomination.pdf.
3. *Charlottesville Daily Progress,* February 3, 1919, 1.
4. Mapping Cville—Examining Equity Through History: Mapping Racist Covenants, Infrastructure, and More . . . , https://mappingcville.com/.
5. Richard Rothstein, testimony before U.S. Senate Committee on Banking, Housing, and Urban Affairs, April 13, 2021, https://www.banking.senate.gov/hearings/separate-and-unequal-the-legacy-of-racial-discrimination-in-housing.

Confronting Labor Discrimination

DAN CAVANAUGH

On January 16, 1943, twenty-eight Black women employed at the University of Virginia Hospital staged a walkout after hospital superintendent Dr. Carlisle S. Lentz refused to accept their petition for higher wages.[1] The University employed all of them as "ward maids," a position that the hospital had reserved exclusively for Black women. They assisted nurses, changed linens, and performed other essential work that enabled UVA health care providers to care for hundreds of patients each day. Among the hospital's paid staff, they also earned the lowest wages and worked the longest hours. In response to the walkout, Lentz laid off all twenty-eight women and temporarily replaced them with white women volunteering for the Red Cross and the UVA Hospital Circle of the King's Daughters.[2] While Lentz sought replacements for the ward maids, members of Charlottesville's Black community formed a citizen's committee to discuss a resolution to the walkout with University president John Lloyd Newcomb.[3]

On January 23, the committee—consisting of African American community leaders T. J. Sellers, Rev. E. Lloyd Jemison, and Douglas Edwards—wrote Newcomb to request a meeting and to describe the reason for the walkout: "They [the ward maids] contend that the original petition, asking for a moderate salary increase was made after they had found it impossible to meet the mounting costs of living in our city on their $7.00 per week base pay scale." The committee's letter even detailed the financial straits low wages put Black hospital workers in: "The average maid has to spend $2.00 per week for room rent, $2.50 for food, $1.40 for transportation, 25¢ for uniforms, $1.70 for shoes and clothing. 35¢ for industrial insurance, 25¢

University of Virginia Hospital superintendent Dr. Carlisle S. Lentz, 1933. (University of Virginia Albert and Shirley Small Special Collections Library)

for church dues, 50¢ for recreation, and 35¢ for miscellaneous items, or a total of $9.30 for the basic necessities of life. . . . It is becoming more difficult each day to stretch their paycheck to cover these essentials."[4]

Newcomb declined to meet the citizens' committee.[5] Instead, he spoke with each of the women individually and offered to raise their salaries to $9.00 a week. Lentz could only temporarily rely on volunteers to do the work of the ward maids, and in wartime Virginia's tight labor market, the superintendent would have difficulty hiring other women on a permanent basis to do the job at such low wages.[6] If UVA went much longer without the ward maids and their essential contributions, Lentz and Newcomb would need to close part of the hospital. Thus, they offered the raises in a bid to keep the hospital open. They also likely hoped to deter future work stoppages by declining to engage in any collective bargaining. The new wages offered to the ward maids were still 30 cents less than a living weekly wage. Nonetheless, many of the women accepted the offer to resume their work at UVA Hospital.[7]

The walkout was part of a broader campaign during the 1940s and 1950s that the hospital's Black employees waged for fair compensation and equal opportunities. Their victories were rarely complete, but through this fight, Black men and women made meaningful progress toward dismantling the racism embedded in UVA Hospital at its founding. Nineteenth-century faculty at the University of Virginia dehumanized African Americans and contributed to the development, locally and nationally, of a discriminatory medical culture. When, in the early twentieth century, the University decided to build its own hospital, it created an institution that reflected and reinforced this culture. UVA opened the hospital in 1901 to support the University's medical education program and provide subsidized health care to Virginians who could not afford it. The hospital was also an institution designed to uphold white supremacy. In this foundational period, medical racism flourished at the University, and prominent members of the medical faculty promoted race science as critical to understanding the high prevalence of illness and death among African Americans.

Paul B. Barringer, a professor of medicine, the chair of the University faculty from 1895 to 1903, and the first superintendent of UVA Hospital, was nationally known for a series of abhorrent addresses that promoted white supremacy. In 1900, while spearheading the construction of the hospital, he proclaimed: "I may state that as a Southerner and a physician, I am familiar with the physicians of the South, and it is the almost universal opinion of these men, who should and do know more of the Negro than all classes combined, that the Negro, as a race, is steadily degenerating both morally and physically."[8]

Like many hospitals in the United States, UVA Hospital assigned patients to segregated spaces according to their race, wealth, and gender. By 1907, all male patients were assigned to the hospital's North Pavilion, while women were assigned to the matching South Pavilion. In both buildings, middle-class and wealthy white patients had access to private rooms on the well-lit ground and second floors, while indigent white patients were assigned to open wards on the ground floor. Indigent Black patients were assigned to inferior open wards in the basement, and a few smaller rooms in the basement were made available for paying Black patients.[9] The hospital sorted its employees into a similarly strict hierarchy where race and gender determined opportunity. Administrative positions, medical faculty appointments, and trade positions (such as electricians and carpenters) were reserved for white men. Nursing and clerical positions were reserved for white women. Black men and women could gain employment only as orderlies, cooks, and ward maids.[10]

These men and women were essential to the hospital, but the University did not value Black workers. Positions reserved for white employees

University of Virginia Hospital complex, circa 1915. (University of Virginia Albert and Shirley Small Special Collections Library)

paid more, received better benefits, required fewer hours, and were more prestigious than the jobs reserved for Black employees. This racial division of labor ensured that no white man or woman employed at the hospital earned as little or would be in as desperate a financial situation as those Black women who walked out in 1943. The hospital's discriminatory practices against Black employees remained unchanged until World War II, when developments in the national labor market and the Second Great Migration provided Charlottesville's Black community with new opportunities to fight.

As early as January 1941, Superintendent Lentz reported to President Newcomb that the U.S. mobilization for war was causing a shortage of orderlies, janitors, and maids at UVA Hospital: "We have experienced increasing difficulty in getting the right type of help for this work. While it does not appear to be generally known a great many of the colored population have gone to the larger centers, being attracted by the much

Entrance to the original segregated basement ward for African Americans at the University of Virginia Hospital. (Sanjay Suchak)

higher wages paid in munition factories, etc."[11] Those who remained at the hospital campaigned for better wages and hours. Initially, their efforts were loosely organized. On March 2, 1942, Black men employed as orderlies during the night shift threatened a work stoppage. The next day, Lentz reported the situation to the hospital's leadership team: "At first, they stated that they would quit work unless an immediate pay increase was given them. Notices were placed on the bulletin board, presumably by them, which threatened anyone who took their place. Finally, the night orderlies agreed to work until March 12th but said that they would quit then unless a raise was received."[12]

Lentz and Newcomb seemed to prevent a strike by promising that the University of Virginia would lobby the General Assembly to fund a wage increase.[13] In 1942, they made a similar promise to the ward maids, and in 1943, when it was clear that Lentz and Newcomb would not fulfill their pledge, the twenty-eight maids staged a walkout.[14] After the walkout, Black workers at the hospital continued to act collectively. On March 7, 1944, the men employed as orderlies threatened to walk out unless the hospital immediately reduced their workday from twelve hours to eight hours. To avoid another work stoppage, Newcomb and Lentz hurriedly

University of Virginia Hospital Boys Club, May 1941. (Jefferson School African American Heritage Center)

secured support within four days from the Board of Visitors and the Virginia State Director of Budget for an eight-hour work rule.[15]

In the wake of these early victories, Black employees at the hospital formally organized themselves as Local 550 of the State, County, and Municipal Workers of America (SCMWA-CIO). In 1948, an uncredited author in Local 550's newsletter, "The Beam," described the reasons for forming the union: "It was born here at the University of Virginia during the chaotic days of World War II at a time when many service employees, because of having to work excessively long hours at pitifully small salaries, were quitting in alarming numbers. It was then, that those who had decided to stay and keep the 'ball a-rolling' decided to organize and, through affiliation with the CIO, seek better wages and working conditions." The names of a few of the men and women who formed Local 550 have survived in the University's archives. One of the most prominent, and a figure who loomed large in the history of Charlottesville's civil rights movement, was Randolph L. White. In 1990, Eugene Williams, a leader in the fight to

Randolph L. White (left) at retirement from the University of Virginia Hospital, 1964. (University of Virginia Albert and Shirley Small Special Collections Library)

desegregate Charlottesville's public schools, had this to say about White: "He was a legend. He had the vision to see civil rights when others didn't even want to mention the words."[16]

When White moved to Charlottesville in 1931, he first gained employment as a janitor in UVA Hospital, but he was overqualified for the position, as he had served as a clerk in the U.S. Army's Judge Advocate General's Office and later worked as a machinist.[17] After a short period of time, Superintendent Lentz quickly recognized White's abilities and made him the supervisor of orderlies, ward maids, and janitors—the highest position a Black man could achieve at UVA Hospital.[18] Today, White is more widely remembered as the founder of the *Charlottesville-Albemarle Tribune*, a weekly newspaper that primarily served the region's African American community.[19] White joined other Black employees who risked their livelihoods to form Local 550. They enlisted UVA alumnus F. Palmer Weber (BA '34, MA '38, PhD '40), who was a member of the NAACP's National Board and the CIO's Political Action Committee. Weber, White, and others frequently met to strategize. Years later, White recalled that he participated in the union drive because the established economic and political powers "didn't care nothing about the individual." He added, "Whether you're white or Black, they'll just cut you down, like mowing hay. But when people band together, you can do a whole lot."[20]

In 1944, Lentz knew that the hospital's Black employees held meetings, but it is likely that he did not entirely know their purpose. He reported to President Newcomb: "The orderlies and janitors, numbering variously from 62 to 76, were in an ugly mood on several occasions. There were many clandestine meetings throughout town when they were harangued by members of their own group and outside agitators."[21] After almost a year of organizing, the Virginia regional office of the CIO informed Lentz that the hospital's attendants, orderlies, maids, and janitors had formed Local 550 of the SCMWA-CIO. Union leaders also asked Lentz for a meeting to discuss a collective agreement within the framework of Virginia's public employee laws.[22] Lentz and Newcomb met with the union leaders, but they stalled negotiations in the spring of 1945 while they waited for Virginia's attorney general, Abram Penn Staples, to provide a legal opinion on the right of public employees to unionize.[23] When Staples finally wrote that state law prohibited UVA from recognizing the union, the CIO and the leaders of Local 550 ignored the opinion and continued to demand recognition.[24]

By the summer, Lentz and Newcomb relented and negotiated an agreement that guaranteed better hours, benefits, and wages for the hospital's Black employees.[25] While University leaders stalled negotiations in the spring, Local 550 continued to organize and persuaded the hospital's dietary workers to join the union. After adding these men and women, Local 550 had successfully recruited 80 percent of UVA Hospital's Black workforce into the union.[26] Furthermore, Local 550, through the CIO regional office, developed a relationship with the office of Virginia governor Colgate Darden.[27] If Lentz and Newcomb did not agree to union demands that summer, they might have faced a devastating work stoppage without the support of the governor's office. The University's direct relationship with Local 550 was short-lived. On February 8, 1946, the Virginia General Assembly passed a joint resolution that prohibited state officers and agencies from recognizing public employee unions and prohibited state employees from engaging in work stoppages.[28] It is possible that this resolution, which had been proposed by Virginia's new governor, William Tuck, was a response to the organization of Black workers at

Diners in the segregated University of Virginia Hospital cafeteria, 1954. (University of Virginia Claude Moore Health Sciences Library)

the University of Virginia. At the time, they were likely the only Virginia state employees to belong to a union.[29] Undeterred, Local 550 did not disband. The union survived into the 1950s, and its leaders continued to press for improved working conditions and fair compensation indirectly, through internal "employee committees."[30]

Black workers at UVA Hospital achieved significant victories through collective action. Between 1944 and 1948, their workweek was reduced from seventy-two hours to forty-eight; overtime pay went from nothing to time-and-a-half; holidays with pay rose from four to thirteen days; sick leave doubled; and salaries increased by more than 100 percent. After 1948, they successfully fought to have longtime temporary workers classified as state employees and gained both health insurance and retirement benefits.[31]

Meetings between Black workers and hospital management during this period also brought about changes to UVA Hospital's division of labor. In 1948, Gussie P. Harris and Lucile Blakey were the first Black women to be promoted from ward maid to hospital aide.[32] Three years later, another breakthrough occurred when the hospital looked to the Black community to address persistent nursing shortages. That year the hospital hired its first Black registered nurses: Honor Mobley, Weda Gilmore, and Annie White. UVA Hospital also partnered with Burley High School to develop a program to train Black men and women as licensed practical nurses.[33]

The gains that hospital workers achieved in pay, hours, and opportunities had a significant effect on the overall economic well-being of Charlottesville's Black community. By 1950, UVA Hospital employed over 250 African Americans, and it was likely the largest employer of Black men and women in Charlottesville.[34] Personnel decisions made at the hospital possibly had a more significant impact on the Black community's economic well-being than those of any other employer in the city. In the 1940s and 1950s, Black workers at the hospital made significant progress toward breaking down its racial division of labor, but their victory was far from complete. In 1965, federal investigators responded to a complaint from the NAACP that the hospital was not in compliance with the landmark Civil Rights Act of 1964. When they visited UVA Hospital, the investigators wrote in their report that none of the facility's 170 attending physicians or 196 interns, residents, and fellows were Black. Approximately 5 percent of the hospital's 200 graduate nurses were Black, while about 95 percent of the 90 lower-paid practical nurses were Black. And of the remaining 700 administrative and support staff members, 400 were Black.[35]

Another 1967 report from UVA Hospital's Housekeeping Department shows that the division was racially integrated in the 1960s, but an overwhelming majority of its staff was Black.[36] These two reports show that the racial division of labor established at the hospital in 1901 was still in place in the 1960s. Black men and women were denied opportunities in the hospital's most powerful positions, and they were primarily limited to essential but less valued jobs.

In 1963, twenty years after the citizens' committee asked to meet with President Newcomb, two leaders of Charlottesville's Black community, the Reverend R. A. Johnson and the Reverend James B. Hamilton, met with UVA Hospital director John Stacey. They discussed discriminatory wage scales, unequal employment opportunities, and segregated patient facilities.[37] Soon after the meeting, Stacey dismissed their concerns in a letter. He also suggested that the hospital, not the Black community, should be credited with the hard-fought progress that had already been

University of Virginia Nursing School practical nurse graduates, 1954. (University of Virginia Albert and Shirley Small Special Collections Library)

made. He wrote, "Your committee might wish to recognize the leadership exerted by the hospital in establishing employment opportunities, in providing education and training for the advancement of Negroes, and in accepting the Negro many years ago as an integral member of the hospital team working in behalf of our patients regardless of color."[38]

By 1965, Charlottesville's Black community could not expect University leaders to enact the change needed to eliminate UVA Hospital's racial division of labor. A new generation of activists would need to continue the work of Randolph L. White, Local 550, and the other Black men and women who campaigned for fair compensation and equal employment opportunities more than twenty years earlier.

Notes

1. The present-day University of Virginia Medical Center was called The University of Virginia Hospital or UVA Hospital during much of the twentieth century and is the name used in this essay when referring to the UVA Medical Center. T. J. Sellers, Reverend E. Lloyd Jemison, and

Douglas Edwards, letter to J. L. Newcomb, January 24, 1943, Papers of the President, 1943–1944, RG-2/1/2.541, Subseries I, Box: 7, Folder: Medical Department—Hospital 1943–1944, Albert and Shirley Small Special Collections Library, University of Virginia (hereafter Special Collections).

2. C. S. Lentz, Report of the UVA Hospital Superintendent, January 18, 1943, 8. Annual Reports to the President, 1942–1943, RG-2/1/1.381, Special Collections.
3. Sellers, Jemison, and Edwards to Newcomb, January 24, 1943.
4. Sellers, Jemison, and Edwards to Newcomb, January 24, 1943.
5. J. L. Newcomb, letter to T. J. Sellers, February 2, 1943, Papers of the President, 1943–1944, RG-2/1/2.541, Subseries I, Box: 7, Folder: Medical Department—Hospital, 1943–1944, Special Collections.
6. When asked by a hospital administrator, presumably Lentz, whether they would take over dishwashing from volunteer canteen workers, Mrs. Clemons of the Hospital Circle said that "she wished it clearly understood that the organization did not do this, as the case was definitely a labor situation." Minutes for February 4, 1953, Minute Book of the Regular Meetings of the University of Virginia Hospital Circle, September 1940–June 1945, The University of Virginia Hospital Auxiliary Collection, 1908–2014, MS-13, Box: 1, Folder: 4, Claude Moore Health Sciences Library, University of Virginia (hereafter Moore Health Sciences Library).
7. C. S. Lentz, Report of the UVA Hospital Superintendent, May 4, 1944, 15. Annual Reports of the President, 1904–1958, RG-2/1/1.381, Special Collections.
8. Paul Brandon Barringer, *The Sacrifice of a Race* (Raleigh, N.C.: Edwards & Broughton, 1900), 28.
9. W. Moll and T. L. Savitt, "The Early Years of the University of Virginia Hospital: An Analysis of Patients' Records," *Virginia Medical Monthly* 102 (September 1975): 718.
10. This division of labor is apparent in a report the University of Virginia submitted to the governor of Virginia in 1937. In the report, the term "Negro worker" is used interchangeably with the job titles of "Hospital Orderly" and "Ward Maid." [Personnel Report to the Governor], ca. April 7, 1937, Papers of the President, 1937–1938, RG-2/1/2.491, Subseries III, Box: 12, Folder: Personnel (survey papers), 1937–1938, Special Collections.
11. C. S. Lentz, Report of the UVA Hospital Superintendent, January 15, 1941, 8, Annual Reports to the President, 1940–1941, RG-2/1/1.381, Special Collections.
12. Meeting Minutes of the Executive Committee of UVA Hospital, March 3, 1942, 1, Hospital Executive Director's Office Papers, MS-7, Box: 1, Folder: 27, Moore Health Sciences Library.

13. Meeting Minutes of the Executive Committee of UVA Hospital, March 3, 1942, 1.
14. Sellers, Jemison, and Edwards to Newcomb, January 24, 1943.
15. Lentz, Report of the UVA Hospital Superintendent, May 4, 1944, 15–16.
16. "Local 550 Launches Intensive Campaign for New Members, PAC Determined to Build Up Voting Strength," "The Beam," December 6, 1948, 1–2 (published by Local 550 United Public Workers-CIO). In later years, Local 550 changed its affiliation from SCMWA-CIO to United Public Workers-CIO (UPW-CIO); D. Maurer, "Yesteryears: Randolph White," *Charlottesville Daily Progress*, July 29, 2014.
17. Maurer, "Yesteryears."
18. C. S. Lentz, Report of the UVA Hospital Superintendent, January 18, 1937, 3–4, Annual Reports to the President, 1936–1937, RG-2/1/1.381, Special Collections.
19. Maurer, "Yesteryears."
20. Patricia Sullivan, *Days of Hope: Race and Democracy in the New Deal Era* (Chapel Hill: University of North Carolina Press, 1996), 83.
21. Lentz, Report of the UVA Hospital Superintendent, May 4, 1944, 15.
22. C. S. Lentz, Biennium Report of the UVA Hospital Superintendent, January 16, 1946, 12–13, Annual Reports of the President, 1945–1946, RG-2/1/1.381, Special Collections.
23. J. L. Newcomb, letter to Abram P. Staples, March 12, 1945, Papers of the President, 1943–1945, RG- 2/1/2.541, Box: 18, Folder: Medical Department—Hospital, Special Collections.
24. Superintendent Lentz reported that in the spring of 1945, the attorney general prohibited him from engaging in collective bargaining with the union. Lentz, Biennium Report, January 16, 1946, 12–13.
25. Lentz, Biennium Report, January 16, 1946, 13.
26. Ernest B. Pugh, letter to J. L. Newcomb, May 3, 1945, Papers of the President, 1943–1945, RG-2/1/2.541, Box: 18, Folder: Medical Department–Hospital, 1945, Special Collections.
27. Lentz, Biennium Report, January 16, 1946, 13.
28. Virginia-General Assembly, Regular Session: 985–1056 1946, Senate Joint Resolution No. 12, Unionization of Officers and Employees of the Commonwealth Agreed to February 8, 1946.
29. "CIO Is Refused Contract," *Richmond-Times Dispatch*, January 28, 1946, 5.
30. "Local 550 Launches Intensive Campaign."
31. "Local 550 Launches Intensive Campaign."
32. "Sisters Gussie P. Harris and Lucile Blakey, Appointed Hospital Aides a Precedent," "The Beam," July 19, 1948, 3.

33. R. L. White, "U.Va. Hospital Employs Negro Registered Nurses: Trains Negro Girls for Practical Nursing," *The Tribune,* August 9, 1952, 1.
34. There were 255 regularly employed Black men and women in UVA Hospital's Housekeeping, Attendant, Dietary, and Housekeeping Departments. "210 U.Va. Hospital Negro Employees Win Job Reclassifications, Salary Boosts, Retroactive to July 1, 1948," "The Beam," August 30, 1948, 1.
35. "Report of an Investigation of Compliance with Title VI of the Civil Rights Act on the Part of the University of Virginia Hospital," April 30, 1965, 2–3, Papers of the President, 1964–1965, RG-2/1/2.681, Box: 25, Folder: Medical Center-Hospital 1964–1965, Special Collections.
36. Of the 170 people who worked in the Housekeeping Department, 136 were Black. "Report on the Racial Composition of the Housekeeping Department," November 3, 1967. Hospital Executive Director's Office Papers, MS-7, Box: 21, Folder: 18, Moore Health Sciences Library.
37. Letter from John M. Stacey to Reverend R. A. Johnson, September 24, 1963, 3, Papers of the President, 1963–1964, RG-2/1/2.671, Box: 24, Folder: Medical Center-Hospital-General, 1963–1964, Special Collections.
38. Stacey to Johnson, September 24, 1963, 3.

Response

Can the Damage Done to Blacks Be Repaired?

JANETTE MARTIN

As HISTORIC as the University of Virginia is, and as enamored with its myths and traditions as it is, the reality is that there are still so many stories that desperately need to be told. To once again quote Baptist minister and former Southern Christian Leadership Council leader Fred Shuttlesworth, "If you don't tell it like it was, it can never be as it ought to be." UVA is just beginning to come to terms with the fuller truths about its past, especially in regard to the Black Americans, whether enslaved or free, who built and maintained the University through more than a century and half of slavery and segregation.

One has to wonder: Even if these depressing and dehumanizing stories are researched and shared with the public, can the damage that has been done to Blacks, especially economically, be repaired or compensated for? Would researching these stories to share serve a purpose for those who, as individuals or by family involvement, have an interest? Could future administrators use these stories of the past to try to right a wrong by encouraging equity and fairness in their policies and practices in the workplace? We should hope so.

It is a safe bet to say that there are many who are not aware of labor discrimination at the University in the decades before 1970, and it remains to be seen how these revelations of decades of discrimination at the University (as well as future revelations about racism here) will be received.

"Confronting Labor Discrimination" highlights the struggles of local Blacks working for low wages in segregated Virginia at UVA's segregated hospital. They were protesting and resisting continued victimization at the hands of hospital administrators—victimization that came in many forms, including dangerous or difficult working conditions, unfair treatment, and incredibly low wages. Thanks to the racially motivated and negative attitudes of white administrators, white hospital employees, and white patients, Black workers endured many problems and indignities daily. Black women and Black men working at the hospital waged an uphill but courageous battle against that mistreatment. They fought for decent wages and fair treatment while continuing to work and be responsible for some of the most arduous tasks at the hospital. These Black men and women, however marginalized and mistreated by white administrators, were nonetheless essential to the everyday operations at the hospital. "Confronting Labor Discrimination" also depicts the obstacles that Blacks faced during those years in their efforts to climb the economic ladder and to sustain progress. There was (and is) little disagreement about the fact that economic inequality is problematic. It was true during the fifties and sixties; it had been true locally when the University opened in the early nineteenth century. And to some extent, that trend continues. The past may not even be past.

Black leaders and workers in the 1940s and 1950s were simply trying to improve conditions for themselves and their families as well as the community. Some will say that the struggle for equity was separate from the fight for worker dignity, but it is hard to separate them when revisiting those past struggles.[1] Few problems were as explosive and persistent as state-enforced racial inequality during the earlier years at UVA Hospital. In the face of white supremacy, Black men and women during those tumultuous years engaged in collective action in forming a local union. One leader, Randolph White, was a prominent figure during the Charlottesville civil rights era and became a legend in his pursuit of equity. Mr. White is also remembered in the Charlottesville community as the founder of the local Black newspaper, the *Charlottesville-Albemarle Tribune*. Community and collective action sustained Black Charlottesville during those difficult times—and their names and stories need to be told, this history remembered.

"Confronting Labor Discrimination" also reminds us that leaders and faculty at the University of Virginia often actively contributed to the dehumanization of African Americans, not only in the treatment of hospital workers during the Jim Crow era but also in the discriminatory medical culture that developed and persisted from the University's very founding at least until the 1950s, if not longer. I am glad that we are talking about these realities, but there's much more work to be done. As more stories are revealed, what will be the next step for the University and for the Charlottesville community toward bridging the gap, creating real equity for Black Charlottesvillians and contemporary redress for those many historic crimes?

Notes

1. The Albemarle-Charlottesville NAACP was made aware of the policies and practices Black nurses endured during those years of strife by a member, Mrs. Louella Walker. Mrs. Walker was one of the Black nurses who worked at the hospital. As a means of showing respect and recognition for the work that they did, Black nurses who had attained the status of "Forgotten Nurses" were honored at a 2019 Freedom Fund Banquet. Current University nurses joined in and supported the celebration financially while publicly expressing regrets for the injustices of the past to which Black nurses had been subjected.

The University of Virginia in the Era of Massive Resistance

JAMES H. HERSHMAN JR.

On an August evening in 1956, a racist demagogue threatened an interracial group meeting to promote better race relations in Charlottesville, Virginia. John Kasper, who was fomenting violent resistance to school desegregation throughout the South, denounced the thirty or so members of the Virginia Council on Human Relations (VCHR) who were present. Randolph White, publisher of the local African American newspaper, warned that he was ready to have him arrested. "Mr. Kasper," he declared, "you're on the edge of it!" Upon leaving, the VCHR members were greeted with a burning cross on the lawn of their meeting place, Westminster Presbyterian Church on Rugby Road.[1] Such violent public behavior was unusual for Charlottesville, especially on the doorstep of Thomas Jefferson's university; viewed from the twenty-first century, though, it appears to presage events that would occur sixty-one years later.

The struggle to end racially segregated education dominated the Old Dominion's public life in the 1950s. Much like the dispute over slavery and secession in the preceding century, the school crisis after the 1954 *Brown* decision involved and deeply affected the University of Virginia. The state government under which the University operated was firmly committed to the racial caste system, especially to the maintenance of public school segregation. In their initial reaction to the landmark U.S. Supreme Court rulings, the state's leadership offered a plan strictly limiting, but not totally preventing, any crossing of the color barrier. That course changed markedly in 1956 when U.S. Senator Harry F. Byrd, leader of the powerful

Democratic Party faction that controlled Virginia's government, called for a stand of massive resistance to *Brown*. Virginia, Byrd believed, should defy the federal courts and block desegregation everywhere in the state. Byrd's turn to defiance meant that the University and Charlottesville would be embroiled in a momentous clash of state policy and federal law.

The University's leadership was involved in the first direct challenge to Virginia's "separate but equal" schools. After a 1951 protest strike by Black students in Prince Edward County, NAACP attorneys filed a suit in federal court attacking legally mandated racial separation. The state's attorney general called upon University of Virginia president Colgate W. Darden to testify in defense of the state's practices. In its opinion, the federal court found Darden's testimony convincing; it ruled in favor of segregated schooling, albeit with more attention to the "equal" aspect.[2] On appeal, the Virginia case was grouped with similar cases in three other states. In its 1954 decision, the Supreme Court declared segregation in public education unconstitutional. The implementation decree issued the next year gave an ambiguous directive: to end segregation "with all deliberate speed."

Whites in the University community and Charlottesville reacted to the ruling in three ways. A large but unorganized segment appeared, reluctantly, to accept token desegregation (such as existed at the University), perhaps with a state subsidy for those wishing to send their children for segregated private instruction (a plan Darden advocated). Another group called for unyielding defense of the caste system and the protection of white supremacy. This view found organizational expression in the Defenders of State Sovereignty and Individual Liberties (known as the Defenders), led by University mathematics professor E. J. Oglesby. Under Oglesby's leadership, the Charlottesville-Albemarle Defenders chapter became one of the largest, most active, and well-funded chapters in the state. A smaller group, including Sarah Patton Boyle and members of the VCHR, openly supported *Brown*. They experienced harassment and threats throughout the period.[3]

The active, well-led Charlottesville NAACP chapter took the initiative in responding to *Brown* in October 1955. Representing forty-three African American students, NAACP attorney Oliver W. Hill petitioned the Charlottesville school board to begin implementing desegregation. The board tabled the petition for further study, and after it failed to act by 1956, Hill filed suit in federal court seeking a desegregation decree. Federal district judge John Paul heard the case in July and issued what NAACP lawyer S. W. Tucker termed "a beautiful ruling": that the school

Charlottesville African American students protest against segregation, circa 1958. (Jefferson School African American Heritage Center)

board had to end race assignments of pupils starting in September.[4] Paul's ruling immediately evoked a strident, defiant outcry from segregationists. The Defenders held a mass rally at Lane High School with UVA Board of Visitors member Judge J. Segar Gravatt as keynote speaker. In a fiery address, Gravatt advocated no compromise on segregation; it would be, he declared, a "compromise with evil."[5] The Defenders pledged to use only legal and political resistance, but racist agitators from the Deep South,

Virginia governor J. Lindsay Almond (UVA Law 1923) at a press conference, ending his support for massive resistance to school integration. (University of Virginia Albert and Shirley Small Special Collections Library)

who had made no such commitments, sought to organize in Charlottesville. In August 1956 the city was filled with tension, but a last-minute federal appeal delayed the September deadline.[6]

Even before the Charlottesville suit was filed, Senator Byrd took his stand for the utter defiance of *Brown*—for massive resistance. In late August, Virginia's legislature met in special session to give the new policy legal form. Seeking to influence the special session, Oglesby and the Charlottesville-Albemarle Defenders presented a pro-segregation petition at the state capitol with twenty-two thousand signatures. By contrast, President Darden testified against defying the federal courts and in favor of permitting token desegregation in compliant areas.[7] Supporters of Byrd's massive resistance proved stronger and prevailed, adopting a multifaceted defense of the color line in education. The pivotal law, though, was a mandate that the governor close any school under a federal desegregation order. As the Charlottesville case made its way through the federal appeals process in 1957, a General Assembly investigative committee unsuccessfully tried to intimidate several of the Black parents involved. "The people stayed strong under the pressure," Oliver Hill later recalled, though one parent lost her job in consequence.[8] In addition, the newly elected governor, J. Lindsay Almond Jr., rhetorically doubled down on massive resistance and pledged to enforce the policy.

Appeals and delays in the Charlottesville case ran out in May 1958, when Judge Paul ruled that his original order would take effect when schools opened in September. Through a last-minute series of ostensibly nonracial geographic assignments and tests, the school board attempted to maintain racial separation. Judge Paul, however, directed the admission of ten Black students to Venable Elementary School, a white elementary school located in the University community, and two Black students to Lane High School, the city's only white secondary school.[9] Hoping for some way to avoid the crisis, the school board delayed the fall semester by a week. When the school year began on September 22, Governor Almond ordered the closing of Venable and Lane. In obeying the school closing law, the state was denying education to seventeen hundred white students to block the admission of twelve Black students.

Anticipating the school closings, two groups formed to address the educational needs of the displaced white students. The Charlottesville Education Foundation (CEF), organized months earlier, had ties to the Defenders. CEF's goal was to create private elementary and secondary schools to perpetuate segregation. State grants to parents were expected to cover a portion of tuition charges. Nine mothers whose children attended Venable Elementary School set up the Parents' Committee for Emergency Schooling (PCES) in the weeks prior to the closings. Their declared aim was to operate only until the public schools reopened. CEF held classes in an old estate on Park Street near downtown Charlottesville; PCES conducted classes mostly in the basements of private homes in the community bordering the University. A ruling by Judge Paul in early October illustrated another defining difference between the groups. City teachers could not receive their pay and benefits at the temporary schools, Paul said, if enrollment was based on race. The CEF clearly based enrollment on race; the PCES did not. Hence, most Venable teachers worked for PCES. (None of the African American students applied to attend.) A University engineering professor, Frederick Morton, headed a joint committee to provide education to the high school students.[10] In September, an advocacy group formed to support public schools: the Charlottesville Committee for Public Education (CPE). The group held a large rally at Memorial Gymnasium on the University grounds. CPE was not an interracial group and avoided taking a position on integration or segregation, stressing that its stand was only pro–public education. By November, the Charlottesville group became a chapter in the statewide Virginia Committee for Public Schools.[11]

African American parents and children desegregate Charlottesville's Venable Elementary School, *Charlottesville Daily Progress*, September 8, 1959. (University of Virginia Albert and Shirley Small Special Collections Library)

On the same day in January 1959, state and federal courts ruled the school closing laws unconstitutional. In an unexpected move, Governor Almond backed away from defiance and persuaded the legislature to enable the closed schools to reopen in February. Unlike schools in Norfolk and Arlington, Charlottesville's schools opened with segregation temporarily in place. The school board's attorney convinced the federal appeals court to allow a stay until the September school term. The city needed more time to prepare, he argued, and would give tutoring to the dozen African American students remaining out of school. Finally, as the new school year began in September 1959, nine Black students entered Venable Elementary School and three attended Lane High School without overt incident.[12]

Reopening the schools did not settle the future of desegregation and public education in Virginia. Governor Almond called a special session of the General Assembly and appointed a legislative commission with a mandate to create a plan limiting desegregation. Leon Dure, a retired newspaper editor living in Charlottesville, put forward a concept with the attractive title "Freedom of Choice," which proved popular with the commission and a large cross section of the white public. Dure's plan would subsidize parents wishing to educate their children in segregated private schools. Hardy C. Dillard, a law professor at the University, publicly predicted—accurately, it turned out—that the federal courts would eventually find the proposed state grants an evasive scheme and ban them.[13] In addition to tuition grants, the General Assembly considered other methods, such as a pupil assignment plan and state constitutional amendments to facilitate the creation of private schools.

University economists offered significant—and conflicting—commentary on the proposal to weaken constitutional protections for public education. Lorin A. Thompson, director of the Bureau of Economic and Population Research, issued a report skeptical of substituting a privately operated system for public schools; moreover, the attempt could do lasting damage to Virginia's economy.[14] Two members of the Department of Economics, James M. Buchanan and G. Warren Nutter, provided a study to the legislators holding that a private system could be created without harming the economy. In addition, Buchanan and Nutter followed up with two Richmond newspaper articles summarizing their points while the constitutional change was under General Assembly debate.[15] The attempt at constitutional change failed, but the adopted plan provided generous tuition grants for private education, created a state Pupil Placement Board, and made changes in the local school budgeting process. E. J. Oglesby, Almond's appointee to the Pupil Placement Board, used his position as chairman of the three-member board to slow desegregation to a trickle over the next four years.

The county board of Prince Edward County used the budget changes to close that county's public schools from 1959 to 1964.[16] Subsidized by tuition grants, the CEF created private segregated schools—the Robert E. Lee School and Rock Hill Academy. Dean Ralph W. Cherry of the University's School of Education stated his opposition to tuition grants as a matter of principle but accepted them as a temporary expedient in the current crisis. Leon Dure enthusiastically embraced the new private schools as an expression of "educational choice" and became their chief fundraiser. After retiring from the University, Professor Oglesby taught mathematics in the private high school. In fall 1959, almost one-third of the white students from Venable and Lane attended the segregation academies. Their enrollment, however, steadily waned through the 1960s and fell sharply in 1969, after federal courts disallowed tuition grants as unconstitutional evasions of desegregation. The academies finally closed their doors in 1979.[17]

Sandra Wicks Lewis, Charles Alexander, and Donald Martin—three of the twelve Black students who entered Venable Elementary and Lane High in 1959—on Charlottesville's Lane High School steps, commemorating school desegregation, 2019. (Andrew Shurtleff and *Daily Progress*)

Prodding from additional federal court suits brought more gradual desegregation in Charlottesville's schools. Just as in the University, serious efforts to desegregate did not develop until the late 1960s.[18] The school closing law fell in 1959 and other legal remnants of massive resistance followed a few years later, but its mark was lasting. The divisiveness, ill will, and sheer delay in that period rendered the achievement of true racial integration in Virginia's public schools a far more elusive goal in the years ahead.

Notes

1. "Kasper Says Will Run Human Relations Council Out of Town," *Charlottesville Daily Progress* (hereafter *CDP*), August 24, 1956, 3. Kasper was head of the Seaboard White Citizens Council. There were four cross burnings in Charlottesville during 1956: "Fourth Cross Burned on Charlottesville Lawn," *Washington Post and Times Herald* (hereafter *WP*), December 9, 1956, B6.
2. *Davis v. County School Board of Prince Edward County, Va.*, 103 F.Supp. 337 (1952); Richard Kluger, *Simple Justice: The History of* Brown v. Board

of Education *and Black America's Struggle for Equality* (New York: Alfred Knopf, 1976), 499–500.

3. Dan Wakefield, "Charlottesville Battle, Symbol of the Divided South," *The Nation*, September 15, 1956, 210–13; Paul M. Gaston, *Coming of Age in Utopia* (Montgomery, Ala.: New South Books, 2010), 184–86. On threats to Boyle and her allies, see Kathleen Murphy Dierenfield, "One 'Desegregated Heart': Sarah Patton Boyle and the Crusade for Civil Rights in Virginia," *Virginia Magazine of History and Biography* 104 (1996): 251–84.
4. Benjamin Muse, "Why Charlottesville Is a Racial Test-Tube," *WP*, July 22, 1956, E1; interview with George R. Ferguson, December 4, 1975, Charlottesville, Va.; interview with Oliver W. Hill, October 5, 1976, Richmond, Va.; interview with S. W. Tucker (quote), September 19, 1974, Richmond, Va.
5. "Speech of J. Segar Gravatt of Blackstone, Virginia Before the Defenders of State Sovereignty and Individual Liberties, Charlottesville, Virginia, July 23, 1956," reprint in the Donald R. Richberg Papers, Manuscripts Division, Library of Congress, Washington, D.C., Box 49 (quote); "Mass Meeting Backs Proposal to Ignore Integration Orders," *CDP*, 24 July 1956, 1.
6. James H. Hershman Jr., "A Rumbling in the Museum: The Opponents of Virginia's Massive Resistance" (PhD diss., University of Virginia, 1978), 251–53; Wakefield, "Charlottesville Battle," 212; James J. Kilpatrick, "Alternatives in Charlottesville," *Richmond News Leader* (hereafter *RNL*), August 8, 1956, 12.
7. Tom Hawley, "22,288 Sign Petition Against Integration," *RNL*, August 31, 1956, 1; "Text of Darden's Statement," *WP*, September 2, 1956, A14; Robert E. Baker, "Va. U. President Testifies against Stanley Plan," *WP*, September 6, 1956, 1.
8. Ferguson and Hill interviews (quote); "Brief Case Believed Secret Hiding Place of Tape Recorder," *CDP*, May 17, 1957, 1. E. J. Oglesby, at the time vice chairman of the Albemarle County school board, predicted that Charlottesville schools "will never be integrated": "Charlottesville Official Vows No Integration," *WP*, August 14, 1957, A15.
9. "Integration Set in Virginia Area," *New York Times* (hereafter *NYT*), May 13, 1958, 1; "Judge Paul Refuses Blanket Approval of City School Plan," *CDP*, August 27, 1958, 1. The sequence of actions is outlined in *Dodson v. School Board of Charlottesville*, 289 F. 2d 439 (1961), 441.
10. See Andrew Lewis, "Emergency Mothers: Basement Schools and the Preservation of Public Education in Charlottesville," in *The Moderates' Dilemma: Virginia's Massive Resistance to School Desegregation*, ed. Matthew D. Lassiter and Andrew B. Lewis (Charlottesville: University of Virginia Press, 1998), 72–103; Anthony Lewis, "'Private' Classes Directed to Stop Using Virginia Aid," *NYT*, October 9, 1958, 1; Hershman, "Rumbling in the Museum," 308. A series of editorials and letters to the editor in the

RNL offers perspective on the private school effort: "Random Notes on Private Schools," September 29, 1958, 12; "Purposes of Charlottesville School Groups Vary," October 4, 1958, 8; and "An Answer in Private Schools," October 10, 1958, 10.

11. Lewis, "Emergency Mothers," 88; Hershman, "Rumbling in the Museum," 305–6; interview with Dr. James Bash, April 15, 1972, Charlottesville, Va. Susan McBee's story, "University Remote from School Furor," *WP,* September 22, 1958, B1, presents facts contradictory to the title. The article indicates that the faculty was clearly affected by the school closings.
12. *Charlottesville School Board v. Allen,* 263 F.2d 295 (1959); James H. Hershman Jr., "Massive Resistance Meets Its Match: The Emergence of a Pro-Public School Majority," in Lassiter and Lewis, *Moderates' Dilemma,* 118–19; Don Devore, "Integration at Lane, Venable Carried Out without Incident," *CDP,* September 8, 1959, 1; Lisa Provence, "On Brown's 50th: Why Charlottesville's Schools Were Closed," *The Hook,* April 8, 2004. See also Charles Giametta, "1959 Desegregation: One Step in a Series," September 8, 1979, *CDP,* A1, and Anne Richardson, "'We Want the Same Break for Our Kids,'" September 9, 1979, *CDP,* E1.
13. Hershman, "Massive Resistance Meets Its Match," 127–28; Ted McKown, "When Is a Private School Public? Forum Argues 'Free Choice' Plan," *CDP,* February 20, 1959, 17.
14. Robert E. Baker, "Economic Peril Cited in Closing of Schools," *WP,* December 11, 1958, A17. See also James G. Hershman Jr., "James M. Buchanan, Segregation, and Virginia's Massive Resistance," Institute for New Economic Thinking, November 8, 2020, https://www.ineteconomics.org/perspectives/blog/james-m-buchanan-segregation-and-virginias-massive-resistance, and the December 30, 1984, interview with Lorin A. Thompson conducted by William A. Elwood in the University of Virginia (Alderman) Library, avalon.lib.virginia.edu/media_objects/1r66j1131.
15. James M. Buchanan and G. Warren Nutter, "The Economics of Universal Education," Report of the Thomas Jefferson Center for Studies in Political Economy, February 10, 1959, copy in Special Collections, University of Virginia Library; articles by Nutter and Buchanan in the *Richmond Times-Dispatch:* "Different School Systems Are Reviewed," April 12, 1959, D3; "Many Fallacies Surround the School Problem," April 13, 1959, 7. A proposal, the Wheatley Resolution, to remove constitutional protections for public education was introduced on April 9 and defeated on April 20, 1959. Robert E. Baker, "State's Control of Education Would Be Ended," *WP,* April 10, 1950, D1; "Segregation Bill Loses in Virginia," *NYT,* April 21, 1959, 25.
16. "'Defenders' Chief Heads Pupil Board," *WP,* July 26, 1960, B2; Bash interview. In 1963, the Albemarle County Board of Supervisors removed

Oglesby as school board chairman in a policy dispute: "Albemarle Reinstates 2 School Men," *WP*, July 12, 1963, A5.

17. "Dean Sees Tuition Grants as a Necessary Expedient," *CDP*, July 22, 1959, 15; interview with Ralph W. Cherry, April 20, 1972, Charlottesville, Va.; "CEF to Launch Fund Drive, Leon Dure Is Chairman," *CDP*, April 20, 1960, 13; Gaston, *Coming of Age*, 187; *Griffin v. State Board of Education*, 256 F. Supp 1178 (1969).
18. *Allen v. School Board of Charlottesville*, 203 F. Supp. 225 (1961); interview with S. W. Tucker. Mr. Tucker was the lead NAACP attorney in the cases after 1959. Brian J. Daugherity, *Keep On Keeping On: The NAACP and the Implementation of* Brown v. Broad of Education *in Virginia* (Charlottesville: University of Virginia Press, 2016), 105–46.

Response

Interview with Edward Harris

July 19, 2021

ANDREA DOUGLAS

EDWARD HARRIS: My name is Edward Harris, and I went to Jefferson Elementary School, which was segregated, for grades one through three. For fourth and fifth grade, I went to Burnley Moran and that was on 250 Bypass, which was integrated. Sixth grade, I came back to Jefferson. Because back then Jefferson was where all the sixth graders came to. I was six years old when I started Jefferson, which was probably around 1962.

ANDREA DOUGLAS: So, tell me, if you remember at all, what caused you to leave Jefferson and go to Burnley Moran?

EH: Well, it was a citywide thing that was going on about integrating the schools. So you know, folks [from the NAACP] came around through the community. And they were asking what school would you like to go to? And of course, I wanted to go to Jefferson. But the response was Jefferson's not available.

Mr. [Eugene] Williams was one of the people that came through the community, because, you know, he's well known in the community, and he was active during that period of time with the NAACP. And I remember him coming and talking with my mother and talking with me about the school situation. And you know, what it would be looking like, the next year, you know, a lot of stuff I didn't understand because I was just a kid.

AD: What do you remember about being at Jefferson?

EH: It was like being at home and what I mean by that is that I was comfortable. At Jefferson, my attendance was always good. I was on the honor roll. I was excited about learning. And I was excited about, you know, the environment that I was learning in, you know, it was a connection that felt warm. It felt loving and it felt caring. So, at Jefferson, I remember it being more like community.

AD: How did you get to Jefferson [elementary] school?

EH: Well, sometimes, my mother would drop me off, or I would walk to school with my sister. We would walk to school and then other kids in the neighborhood would join on and we would all walk to school together because the school was right in the neighborhood. Everybody in my family went to Jefferson. All of my siblings went to Jefferson. I used to walk to school with my sister and her friends, to make sure I got to school, and got home, you know, and that's like, the first-grade experience. At times, maybe my mother would pick me up or whatever. But most of the time it was me walking to school with family, friends.

AD: So for the fourth grade, you said, you went to Burnley Moran? How far away from home was Burnley Moran? What was it like to go to school there?

EH: It was quite a distance. I would say a couple miles, seemed like it anyway. It wasn't something that I would just walk to school with my friends. Most of the time I got there because my neighbor's parents gave me a ride. Or, my parents would drop me off. Coming back, it was the bus. Back then the Yellow Cab was in charge of the buses. The bus actually cost fifteen cents to ride back then. And if you didn't have fifteen cents, you didn't ride the bus. That meant you had to walk up the bypass. It was a very unfamiliar area, but you had to, to get home.

At Jefferson, I was an honor-roll student. So in the transition to Burnley Moran, I found myself in classes, being the only Black male in the class. Sometimes it was me and just one other Black girl in the class. And the adjustment was new to me. It's new to the white students. And it's new to the white teachers, you know, so I feel like a stranger in a strange land. It was a culture shock. It was totally different than what I was experiencing at Jefferson. At Jefferson, we were always challenged to learn. At Burnley Moran early on, I felt like I was being ignored. I'd raise my hand because I knew the answer and instead, they'd call on Susie Q, so my unhappiness just started to grow and catapult from there.

The other Black students were in different classes. It was even like that when I got to Jefferson. So for those years—for fifth and sixth grade, there wasn't another Black male in my class. The other students were in other classes, and I'd seldom see them because you stayed with the same core group changing classes. It was like, a real culture shock. You gotta sit up in class, and you can try to relate to folks that don't want to relate to you. Or, you can play like, let me go ahead on and do my thing. And then the teacher may be ignoring you. I was, eight, nine years old, and I was confused because I came from an environment that encouraged me to be the best that I can be. I get in this situation, and it doesn't feel like that no more. It feels foreign. And I know it was foreign to everybody. But as a kid, it felt really foreign to me.

At the beginning of the day you got off the bus, everybody kind of hung outside for a minute until the bell rang. When that happened, it was like stepping out of a Black world and going into a white world. Because I'm coming from the Black community. I'm standing out before school bell with my friends. The bell rings, I go to a classroom, the only Black male in the class, and the culture is different.

AD: What happened if you missed the bus? Or you didn't have your fifteen cents?

EH: I had to walk up the 250 Bypass. I wasn't familiar with the lay of the streets near the school so the bypass would get me up to where I recognized where I was. To walk the bypass you had to pay attention and people would distract you because they were hollering at you, and they threw things at you and it was scary. It was scary. You know, they using the N terminology. "Hey, nigga, go back where you came from." The cars were really loud back then and you could hear them coming and you were afraid. I might be walking with some other youngsters, but the fear was there. You know, we was probably feeding off each other's fear, you know? That fear would have me to where I mean, like, maybe I couldn't even talk. You know what I'm saying? You know, I'm just trying to get to some safety.

AD: Sitting here today, thinking about that period, what do you think were the benefits and the losses of school desegregation?

EH: Well, the only benefit that I can really think of right now is exposure, getting exposed to different things, but I think that would have come. I can't really think of a lot of benefits that came from desegregation. Because I think we lost ourselves. We lost ourselves in that transition. We bought that part that somebody else's ice was colder than ours. We forgot how good we really had things. Now we're reflecting and we're talking about how good it was then. But the gate is open. The horse is gone. You know, so, yeah, I think we lost way more, way more. And now, it's like, we tried to go back and recoup what we lost. So apparently, we lost something that was very vital and important. We bought into the individualism a bit. Oh, you know, and, and that's not who we were as a people, you know, but I think we bought into it to our own demise, sadly enough to say, you know, we bought into it to our own demise. And now we're, we're having to recoup what we already had, you know.

Allies of Integration

PATRICE PRESTON-GRIMES

IN THE summer of 1955, Farmville High School principal James H. Bash spoke at a public meeting of Virginia parents, teachers, and school administrators who had gathered to oppose the desegregation of the Prince Edward County public schools. After raising a series of questions in his prepared remarks about how a county private school system for whites would function, he told the nearly all-white crowd, "I am a public school man and I cannot take any salary from any organization designed to circumvent the ruling of the [U.S.] Supreme Court."[1]

In that moment, the fate of Bash and his family changed forever. With his public opposition to "massive resistance," they were ostracized in the small, close-knit community. Within weeks, Bash stepped down as principal and eventually returned to graduate school at his beloved alma mater, the University of Virginia, devoting the rest of his career to seeking equal education for all. Bash experienced firsthand how efforts to desegregate public schools in Prince Edward County, and throughout Virginia, were painful and slow in the 1950s. In spite of the *Brown v. Board of Education* ruling by the U.S. Supreme Court in 1954 that declared racially separate public schools unequal, and its *Brown II* directive a year later for states to desegregate schools "with all deliberate speed," massive resistance gripped the commonwealth.[2]

The City of Charlottesville also maintained racially separate public schools for Black and white students until the fall of 1958, when Virginia governor J. Lindsay Almond Jr., a Charlottesville native who had earned a UVA law degree, ordered Venable Elementary School and Lane High

School closed and "removed from the public school system," rather than allow Black and white students to attend school together.[3]

Finally, in 1959, school desegregation began peacefully when twelve African American children—who became known as "The Charlottesville Twelve"—were the first students to transfer from their all-Black schools to attend Venable and Lane.[4] The overwhelming majority of Black students, however, continued to attend the nearby all-Black Jefferson Elementary School and Jackson P. Burley High School. Across town, the University of Virginia remained open only to white men through the early 1960s.

As the civil rights movement gained momentum throughout the South, the federal government yielded to political pressures to support desegregation in K-12 public schools and colleges. In 1964, President Lyndon B. Johnson signed into law the Civil Rights Act that included the Title IV provision to provide technical assistance and funding for states to achieve public school integration. Title IV authorized the creation of twenty-seven national education sites to carry out this work. The mission of these sites—known as Consultative Resource Centers, or CRCs—was to support state and local schools on a district-by-district basis during the challenging transition of desegregating K-12 public schools. The centers' goal was to address four key areas: new curriculum development, best practices in school administration, teacher training, and the coaching of school and community counselors in fair and effective student discipline procedures. The Curry School of Education received a CRC grant in 1967. The "Deseg Center," as it came to be called on Grounds, occupied numerous sites, from Peabody Hall and the current site of Madison House to an office on Ivy Road. Its mission was to provide customized technical assistance and in-service training for administrators, teachers, and K-12 school staffs in Virginia and the region. It closed quietly in 1981.

Three School of Education faculty members were central to the CRC's creation, development, and outreach efforts: Bash, the former Farmville High principal; Nathan Edward Johnson; and Howard Webster Allen. Bash was the key architect who wrote the first CRC grant; he credited support from the Phi Delta Kappa Commission on Education, Human Rights, and Responsibilities as crucial to his success with initial grant writing and funding. Bash directed the center for its first four years and hired School of Education colleague Nathan Edward Johnson as the first CRC associate director. Johnson became the first African American faculty member at the University in 1967, after a distinguished career as a public school teacher and administrator in Virginia's Black schools. He

Nathan Edward Johnson (left) and James H. Bash (right), founders of the University of Virginia Curry School Consultative Resource Center for School Desegregation, 1967. (University of Virginia Albert and Shirley Small Special Collections Library)

joined the school faculty after completing his doctoral studies at the University, supported by a Southern Education Foundation Fellowship. Johnson House at Hereford College on Grounds bears his name today, acknowledging his scholarly influence and leadership during the era.

Johnson introduced Bash to Howard "Hank" Webster Allen, who joined the center's team as a full-time staff specialist in 1969. When Bash stepped down as director in 1971, Curry dean Ralph Cherry managed the center until appointing Allen as its director in 1973. Allen led the CRC staff until the center closed in 1981, when the federal government instead funded a regional gender equity center at American University in Washington, D.C. Allen, like Johnson, had a noteworthy career in Black school communities before coming to Charlottesville to complete his educational doctorate. Both Johnson and Allen acknowledged their gratitude to Virginia State University professor Walter Ridley—the first African American to earn a doctorate at UVA and first to receive a degree from a predominantly white university in the South—for paving their way to earn advanced degrees in the School of Education.[5]

The Deseg Center's curriculum, based on the CRC Human Relations Model, was designed to teach participants new interpersonal skills for

Walter Ridley in regalia processing down the University of Virginia Lawn at Final Exercises after completing his Doctor of Education degree in 1953. (University of Virginia Albert and Shirley Small Special Collections Library)

cross-racial understanding, despite their personal differences and prejudices.[6] Over a four-year period, Bash wrote or co-wrote five monographs that the Deseg Center staff delivered personally to local school districts across the region. With these materials, teachers and school personnel participated in small-group discussions and activities, received individual coaching, and gained feedback on developing strategies to deal with teaching Black and white students together in newly desegregated schools.

From the start, gaining access to most local school personnel was challenging. Many districts did not welcome this federally sponsored initiative into their schools, fueled by the pro-segregation climate in counties that promoted "educational choice" as a tool for massive resistance. The Deseg Center staff relied heavily on invitations from school division superintendents to visit local sites and to conduct training workshops within its schools. After gaining access, center staff distributed materials personally during visits to schools and district offices; monographs were also sent to other CRC library sites around the country.[7] Again, Phi Delta Kappa was a valuable resource, advertising the monographs in *The Kappan*, its flagship journal.[8] By 1971, the University of Virginia began publishing some CRC materials, including a paper that Bash co-wrote with Nathan Johnson on human relations as one of a series of educational papers authored by UVA faculty.[9]

Over the next few years, the Deseg Center added a small stream of UVA graduate students to its staff, who provided logistical, research, and/or counseling support. Allen supervised a series of CRC newsletters that were sent periodically to key stakeholders across the commonwealth to spread the word about activities and progress.[10] Yet the Deseg Center struggled to reach many schools, as resistance to change took many forms. The Jim Crow policies of racial segregation remained a part of daily life, especially in rural areas. In the early years, for example, Bash and Johnson planned their business travel carefully. They were mindful of their safety, because a Black and white professional team driving on Virginia back roads or dining together in public spaces could draw unwanted scrutiny and discourage local school personnel from engaging with them. Interviews with CRC staff document a well-crafted approach to maneuvering the de facto segregation policies that prevailed throughout the region.

In a February 1973 speech to center directors at the University of Pittsburgh's Consultative Resource Center, Bash expressed exasperation with the slow pace of change in schools and admonished his colleagues to "quit avoiding the issues and difficulties of intergroup relations and get on with bringing our 'doing up to our knowing.'" Allen, often the most outspoken of the trio, described their constant challenges: "You have Black people in the South, and white people in the South who very seldom communicated with each other. The only time they communicated was when they were working, Black people working for the white folks. There wasn't a whole lot of respect and all." Allen continued, highlighting the difficulty of the project: "And so, now, we're going to desegregate the schools . . . bring all these kids together. Now we've got to do a job to get them to understand what this desegregation process entails."[11]

During Allen's tenure as center director from 1973 to 1981, the CRC cast a wider net to provide services for school systems in Maryland, Washington, D.C., and West Virginia, in addition to the commonwealth. Johnson continued as the CRC associate director until his death in 1980, and Bash remained an active CRC supporter as he taught graduate courses in school administration and supervision and advised students across the School of Education. Throughout the 1970s, the Deseg Center team traveled year-round from UVA to community sites and conducted annual summer institutes, much like the one where Allen met Johnson and Bash. Armed with updated materials and insights from other CRCs, the team presented

University of Virginia education professor Howard "Hank" Allen in 1973. Allen led the Consultative Resource Center for School Desegregation from 1973 to 1980. (University of Virginia Albert and Shirley Small Special Collections Library)

best practices to school administrators, facilitated teacher workshops, and retrained counselors in fair and effective discipline procedures.

Johnson's quiet influence and mediation skills were tested many times in the early years, when school district doors were literally slammed in faces of center directors for their pro-integration stance. Bash often credited Johnson with being the center's moral compass: Johnson kept its mission to achieve a quality education for all students front and center. At the same time, Allen was a member of a small, yet active, group of Black CRC leaders nationally who created informational pipelines that flowed from rural and urban school districts, through the centers, to the federal government (and back). By the late 1970s, a tight network of Black school administrators also emerged from the CRC meetings, buoyed by their involvement in working together on Title IV technical assistance teams.

The new, clandestine communication channels that Black educators formed nationally through their involvement with the consultative centers were very important; this communication helped restore some of the social networks that Black teachers, administrators, and parents lost when racially segregated neighborhood schools closed in response to the

1954 *Brown v. Board of Education* decision. Especially in the South, many Black educators on local and national levels were eager to find new ways to maintain their professional ties and regain their collective agency, as some now taught in predominantly white school settings where they were in the racial minority.[12]

The passage in 1972 of Title IX legislation outlawing gender discrimination in schools created a new set of challenges for the Deseg Center. The federal government's decision to direct the CRCs to investigate gender bias complaints in local schools, as well as continuing to monitor racial inequities, strained center resources and operations. In its last year, the Curry Deseg Center staff served more than ninety school districts and nearly one thousand educators, providing workshops, technical assistance, and training, most often in Virginia and West Virginia. Yet the numbers masked the tensions and contradictions that existed at the time within the center, at the University, and among the school districts about the Deseg Center's impact and how to measure its progress.[13] Some CRC staff viewed the center's effectiveness as mixed at best and felt it remained isolated and invisible at UVA. To this day, many who were in the School of Education at the time do not recall the center's existence on Grounds or its programs, because the work did not take place within the school's Ruffner Hall home (now known as Ridley Hall) or always at University sites. Each center director also expressed frustration with many school district officials throughout the region who ignored numerous invitations from CRC staff to visit sites, conduct teacher workshops, or use the free professional development materials based on the booklets. At the same time, other CRC staff pointed to the climate of massive resistance in local communities and the slow pace of change that prevented them from gaining access to schools and promoting their work.

Still, the Consultative Resource Center for School Desegregation at UVA highlights past obstacles and opportunities to create and sustain educational reform in an oppositional climate. What also emerged from this era were the voices of the University's Black undergraduate students, who were ready to push for the visible change that eluded their elders, using more vocal and direct means of protest.

Notes

1. See Kristen Green's account of the meeting organized by the Defenders of State Sovereignty and Individual Liberties in *Something Must Be Done*

about Prince Edward County: A Family, a Virginia Town, a Civil Rights Battle (New York: Harper Collins, 2015).

2. *Brown v. Board of Education of Topeka* (I), 347 U.S.483 (1954); *Brown v. Board of Education* (II), 349 U.S.294 (1955).
3. John D. Morris, "Almond Orders Charlottesville to Shut 2 Schools," *New York Times*, September 18, 1958, A1, A18. *Locked Out: The Fall of Massive Resistance*, produced by the UVA Center for Politics in 2009, chronicles these events throughout the commonwealth, including the struggle to reopen schools in Norfolk, Prince Edward County, and Warren County.
4. Nine students entered Venable Elementary School in the fall of 1959: Charles E. Alexander, Raymond Dixon, Regina Dixon, Maurice Henry, Marvin Townsend, William Townsend, Sandra Wicks, Roland T. Woodfolk, and Ronald E. Woodfolk. Three students entered Lane High: French Jackson, Donald Martin, and John Martin. See *Charlottesville Daily Progress*, November 20, 2011, A1.
5. In August 1953, E. Louise Stokes-Hunter was the first African American woman to receive an educational doctorate from the University of Virginia.
6. J. P. Dean, A. Rosen, and R. B. Johnson, *A Manual for Intergroup Relations* (Chicago: University of Chicago Press, 1955). At that time, desegregation was broadly defined as "the process by which intergroup practices are changed in an institution or organization" (105).
7. J. H. Bash and R. L. Long, *Effective Administration in Desegregated Schools* (Bloomington, Ind.: Phi Delta Kappa, 1969).
8. Founded in 1906, Phi Delta Kappa International is an association for educators. It has more than six hundred chapters today in North America, and its headquarters is in Arlington, Virginia.
9. J. H. Bash and N. E. Johnson, "A Human Relations Model for a Desegregated Group," Occasional Paper 4 (Charlottesville: University of Virginia School of Education, 1971).
10. *Consultative Resource Center Newsletter: A General Assistance Center* (Charlottesville: University of Virginia School of Education, February 1975).
11. H. A. Allen interview with Jacky Taylor and Liz Sargent, Jefferson School Oral History Project, May 2004.
12. For a detailed account of the transition of Black teachers to predominantly white schools in one Southern state, see Vanessa Siddle Walker's *The Lost Education of Horace Tate: Uncovering the Hidden Heroes Who Fought for Justice in Schools* (New York: New Press, 2018).
13. H. C. Richards, J. H. Bash, and N. E. Johnson, *The Evaluation of Racial Attitudes and Attitude Change* (Charlottesville: University of Virginia School of Education, 1972).

Response

Unfinished Business

LESLIE M. SCOTT-JONES

BLACK CHILDREN have never received an education equal to that of white children. This was the basic argument for the desegregation of schools. The NAACP's lawyers and Black parents alike wanted their children's schools to have the same resources as white schools. But public education all over the country, by linking financial resources to the neighborhoods the schools reside in, was subject to the caste system created during our nation's darkest history. Black parents paid taxes, but it was never enough to raise their children's schools to the level of white schools in neighboring districts. When the NAACP started its public education fight, the goal was to force districts to allocate the money needed to raise Black schools to the level of white ones. White school boards across the country chose to close Black schools entirely rather than invest in them. *Brown v. Board of Education* had little success in creating an equitable system of education. The vagueness and limiting language used in the ruling, the Title IV legislation, and the desegregation centers that followed were not designed to achieve equity.

Years before the landmark case, UVA had its own battle with Black admittance. In 1950, Gregory Swanson sued to gain entry to the UVA School of Law. And in 1951, Booker Reaves became the first Black student from Charlottesville to desegregate the University, ultimately graduating from the School of Education. Eight years later, Robert Bland earned an undergraduate degree from UVA. Each school at UVA has one of these firsts. Although the "Desegregation Center" housed in the Curry School of Education (now the School of Education and Human Development) did necessary and important work as early as 1967, the work is unfinished.

The question of whether the *Brown v. Board of Education* decision succeeded in creating public education that is equal for all children remains. Are public institutions living up to the court's order and their own missions of educating all children? No matter how you look at it, the answer to both questions is no.

The mission of UVA is not all that different from that of any other public university. It aims to be "a public institution of higher learning guided by a founding vision of discovery, innovation, and development of the full potential of talented students from all walks of life." It cannot be denied that for 151 years, UVA did not live up to its current mission, in the same ways that the Declaration of Independence and the U.S. Constitution missed their marks. Using phrases such as "full potential" and "talented students" does not hold UVA accountable for denying the potential and achievement of Black students for 131 years and of women for 151 years. Undoubtedly the current mission is different from the one created at UVA's inception, but Thomas Jefferson's desire to create "citizen leaders" has existed for as long as the school's ties to slavery.

The *Plessy vs. Ferguson* U.S. Supreme Court decision, coupled with the Fourteenth Amendment, averred that by establishing a "separate but equal" standard—in one instance, separate school systems with ostensibly equal resources—America would ensure that Black children received the same quality of education as white children. In reality, that court decision supported Jim Crow laws and Black Codes, which ruled every part of life in a majority of states, guaranteeing that no Black child received the same public education as a white child.

Additionally, when Black schools needed repairs or expansions, instead of allocating necessary funds for their maintenance, white school boards responded by closing schools. Justice Henry Billings Brown, writing the majority opinion in *Plessy v. Ferguson,* stated: "The object of the [Fourteenth] amendment was undoubtedly to enforce the equality of the two races before the law, but in the nature of things it could not have been intended to abolish distinctions based upon color, or to endorse social, as distinguished from political, equality. . . . If one race be inferior to the other socially, the Constitution of the United States cannot put them upon the same plane." Judge Brown believed "separate but equal" meant Black children, and Black communities in general, were inferior and thus not deserving of equality or protection under the Constitution. The lone dissenter, Justice John Marshall Harlan, stated: "Our Constitution is color-blind, and neither knows nor tolerates classes among citizens."

Harlan's voice was a lonely one for decades as Jim Crow America perpetuated white rule and with it an exclusion of Black Americans from the full fruits of freedom.

Years later, the 1954 *Brown v. Board of Education* court decision claimed that schools for Black children were in fact not equal and that segregation violated the "equal protection clause" of the Fourteenth Amendment, which holds that no state can "deny to any person within its jurisdiction the equal protection of the laws." When the Supreme Court sided with Thurgood Marshall, who later sat on that same court, it was heralded as a victory for Black children everywhere who had been forced to be in schools that were not physically safe and many that did not have current or usable textbooks. The court left it to the states as to how this new law would be implemented. In Virginia, schools were closed, in some cases for years. Federal monies were misappropriated, creating charter programs to continue educating white children. When students returned to school, Black children were protected by troops to ensure they were allowed to enter the buildings. At UVA, Mr. Swanson was admitted but was forced to secure his own off-campus housing and forced to eat at different times than his white classmates.

In 1964, almost a decade after the *Brown* decision, Title IV of the Civil Rights Act provided funding to try to heal the strife many integrated students and teachers had been facing. However, the legislation's language made it clear that the goal, as far as the federal government was concerned, was *never* to have schools that were racially balanced and therefore equitable. Twenty-seven national education sites were created to carry out the work of supporting districts as they desegregated schools, focusing on four key areas: curriculum, administration, training, and counseling and discipline.

Locally, the Desegregation Center housed at UVA's Curry School of Education represented a local Virginia support mechanism for desegregation, all thanks to a grant written by James H. Bash. The center staff included Nathan E. Johnson and Howard W. Allen. Johnson later became the first Black UVA faculty member (in 1967) and Allen was hired in 1969, ultimately taking over the program from 1973 until it closed in 1981. The work they were involved in sounds almost identical to today's trend of culturally responsive teaching, with the same aim of engaging white teachers on how to interact with Black children. During its operation, the center was plagued by broad white resistance to its goals and by invisibility at UVA.

Today's trends may be seen as more important, but even now, in the twenty-first century, there are still teachers who resist teaching in a new way or even recognizing that how they treat Black students can be inappropriate at best and criminal at worst. Black children in general, and Black boys specifically, are disciplined more harshly than any other ethnicity in public education. This, unfortunately, is not a trend being curbed by the required culturally responsive teaching initiatives or implicit bias seminars for teachers. In order to create an atmosphere of learning, a student must feel safe, among other things. We have numerous contemporary examples of Black students being forced to cut their hair or face consequences, such as being banned from sports, arrested, or not allowed to graduate even when all academic requirements have been met. Only in 2019 did California's "Crown Law" make it harder for businesses and schools to discriminate based on natural, or non-European, hairstyles. And slowly, localities are removing racist imagery from public spaces while also removing police from schools and shrinking law enforcement budgets and powers. In some ways, not much has changed since the early days of UVA's Desegregation Center.

Unfortunately, the *Brown* decision was not successful in creating an equitable environment in school systems when it comes to enrollment, either. Recent examinations of the progress of desegregation are sobering: "Nine years after Brown . . . 99% of blacks in the South were still in totally segregated schools. Virtually no whites were in historically black schools, nor were black teachers and administrators in white schools. . . . In little more than four decades, enrollment trends in the nation's schools (between 1968 and 2011) show a 28% decline in white enrollment, a 19% increase in black enrollment, and an almost unbelievable 495% percent increase in the number of Latino students."[1] According to the report, New York and California remained the most segregated. Nearly seventy years later, the intended outcome of the Brown decision has not yet come to pass, either nationally or locally.

How did we get here? In 2021, the calls for civil rights and equal access to education continue and the work of the Desegregation Centers likewise remains unfinished. As we often say, the system is not broken; it is working the way it was designed to. In forcing Black children to integrate into white schools, the system of white supremacy gained thousands of new minds to mold to its way of thinking. Black history was all but erased in that transition to schools where "Black history" had never effectively existed in the classroom. Black communities were made weaker as Black teachers lost their jobs and students were bused out of their neighborhoods to schools where they were not welcomed. It is not what Thurgood Marshall and the NAACP had in mind as they fought the legal battles leading up to the 1954 court decision. In the end, we now know—and the history of the Desegregation Center at UVA reminds us—that no desegregation plan conceived by the institutions that created the problem could themselves be the solution. The story of UVA's Deseg Center highlights those sad and enduring realities.

Notes

1. Gary Orfield, Erica Frankenberg, Jongyeon Ee, and Jennifer B. Ayscue, "Harming Our Common Future: America's Segregated Schools 65 Years after Brown," May 10, 2019, The Civil Rights Project / Proyecto Derechos Civiles, www.civilrightsproject.ucla.edu.

Closing Response

I Am My Ancestors' Wildest Dreams

Black at UVA in the Twenty-First Century

TY'LEIK CHAMBERS

I CAN REMEMBER back to my first year at the University of Virginia. I was in my Sociology 1010 discussion block; we were discussing our professor's lecture about white fragility and white violence. I was not very engaged in this conversation. I was one of two Black people in that discussion block. When our TA asked us whether anyone could name a current event that we could tie to either white fragility or white violence, the other Black person raised their hand and answered, "Would August 11 and 12 and the racist Confederate statues count?" This response kicked off a class dialogue where we talked about the statues and the infamous events of the summer of 2017. Many of my white peers continued to exclaim how the removal of statues was "erasing history" and that the statues were "honoring the heritage of the South." At that moment, my energy shifted. I became energized and felt that my input in the conversation was necessary. I spoke and said, "The heritage of the South is the same as the heritage of UVA, white supremacy and racism." As a rising fourth-year looking back, I found myself on many occasions in similar conversations involving discussing UVA's history and perpetuation of racism, eugenics, and anti-Blackness. I have also learned how little students at the University of Virginia often actually know about the history of their alma mater.

For many of my peers at the University of Virginia, their knowledge of UVA's past, and by extension that of Jefferson, is often frankly grade-school level, just scratching the surface of a deep and complicated history.

They come to Charlottesville with the knowledge that Jefferson "built" the school—and yes, enslaved people had a role in the school's construction, but the grounds and architecture are so beautiful, and yes, UVA has Confederate ties, but it's in Virginia, that's to be expected. These talking points negate how active members of the UVA community in the past were as principal architects of white supremacist ideology and Lost Cause ideals. They don't know that the person who crafted the term "Lost Cause" was Edward Pollard, who attended the University of Virginia until 1850. They don't know that the concepts that are at the base of those "heritage" and "erasing history" comments are actually rooted in white supremacy. This ability to engage with bits and pieces of UVA history while omitting other aspects is a luxury many UVA students possess. They can roam the campus from new dorms to Central Grounds, passing a Confederate graveyard and buildings still bearing the names of enslavers, without having to stop and analyze how this type of environment came to be or how it might impact students of color. As one of a handful of Black students that make up roughly 7 percent of the student population, I have had to learn to grapple with these aspects of my college experience.

I could not walk into Cabell Hall for my Italian 1010 classes without the reminder that this building was named after a relative of the enslavers who held my ancestors in bondage. These feelings created a feeling of imposter syndrome and racial battle fatigue. I was tired of constantly having to explain how the microaggressions I experienced attending this predominantly white institution harmed and exhausted me. From having to deal with people describing my hair or my personal ties to my African and Native American ancestry as dirty and unprofessional, to people constantly assuming that I must be an affirmative action case "to be at a school like UVA," I have been bombarded with these daily microaggressions, on top of being expected to be a Black guru to my white peers on everything involving racism. These are feelings that I allowed to dictate my early years at the University of Virginia—until I began to discuss my feelings with one of my African American Studies professors. His words of wisdom forever repeat in my head: "Ty'Leik, you do realize that you are your ancestors' wildest dreams? They were people who were prevented from reading and writing. I'm not saying that being a Black student here is an easy experience, but you will always be able to find people who will support you and want nothing but to see you achieve." His words forced me to take a step back and take in what he had said. I had (and have) a right to be at this school, just as much as anyone else.

That was the day that empowered me to find my voice. I began speaking out against and talking with people about the microaggressions I was personally dealing with. I began protecting my energy and not allowing myself to feel obligated to engage with or teach anyone about racism or white supremacy, when Google is free for everyone. I began connecting and networking more with my Black peers and built a community that was critical to my UVA experience. My success at the University of Virginia is indebted to many of my Black professors, other faculty members, and peers who showed me the importance of choosing myself. These people validated my experience as a Black male at the University of Virginia and gave me the proper resources to make sure that I can still accomplish my college goals! I did not have to allow UVA's history to ostracize me. On the contrary, it motivated me to begin learning about the stories of Black UVA that are never pushed to the forefront while advocating for the University to make its promises of diversity and inclusion a reality. Going into my fourth year at UVA, I have a new strength about me to continue to excel in this space.

The University has made many strides in tackling its history of slavery and racism, attempting to portray and mend the wrongs of the past by creating commissions and organizations such as the PCUAS and the PCSU. Though the efforts are greatly appreciated, it is important that institutions like UVA continue to address and grapple with their history for the sake of their students, in order to show that they are conscious of the environment that they are creating for them—addressing not only issues of the past but problems that arise today as well. It is great to have programs with speakers and big monuments that recognize the contribution and existence of enslaved laborers, but if the climate of the school is still adamantly alienating and ostracizing Black students and other BIPOC students, what benefit does this bring to the students? Many schools complain about low rates of Black or other BIPOC enrollment without ever taking the time to sit and analyze how their schools continue to perpetuate problematic concepts and ideals.

The University needs to really listen to its Black and other BIPOC students if it hopes to truly begin to understand what those students' experiences are like at UVA. The school also needs to put its money where its mouth is when it comes to better supporting student organizations that continue to address and combat injustices and inequities at the University. On top of this, UVA needs to do a better job in mending and building better relationships with the local Charlottesville community. The University owes it not only to itself but to all current and future students to continue to do work. Only then will UVA become a place where *all* students feel that that their voices are heard, respected, and protected. UVA has made significant steps, which should be acknowledged, but the University—like many other institutions—still has a long way to go.

Not everything that is faced can be changed, but nothing can be changed until it is faced.

—James Baldwin, 1962

An America that asks what it owes its most vulnerable citizens is improved and humane. An America that looks away is ignoring not just the sins of the past but the sins of the present and the certain sins of the future.

—Ta-Nehisi Coates, 2014

CONTRIBUTORS

Wes Bellamy, former Charlottesville Vice-Mayor and Albemarle County teacher, is Associate Professor of Political Science and Public Administration at Virginia State University.

Seventh-generation resident of Bergen County, New Jersey, Cheryl Bullock-Hannah is the great granddaughter of Charles H. Bullock Sr. After motherhood slowed down her twenty-year career in ladies' fashion retail management for the Limited, Cache, and Mary Jane Denzer of White Plains, New York, Cheryl was inspired to continue the work of family historian Jean Henderson in telling the incredible story of the Bullock family of Charlottesville, Virginia.

Brian P. Cameron is currently a JD candidate at the University of Virginia School of Law (Class of 2025). He is a 2019 graduate of the UVA College of Arts and Sciences in political and social thought as well as AmeriCorps VISTA alumnus at Habitat for Humanity Virginia.

Dan Cavanaugh is an archivist at the University of Virginia's Arthur J. Morris Law Library.

Ty'Leik Chambers (UVA BA 2018) is the Community Outreach Coordinator for the Getting Word African American Oral History Project at Monticello.

Sylvia Chong is Associate Professor of English and American Studies at the University of Virginia. She is the author of *The Oriental Obscene: Violence and Racial Fantasies in the Vietnam Era* (Duke University Press, 2012).

Dr. Andrea Douglas is the executive director of the Jefferson School African American Heritage Center. She holds an MA and PhD in art history from the University of Virginia and an MBA in arts management and finance from Binghamton University. Douglas has taught graduate and undergraduate classes in African American contemporary and art theory and has published exhibition catalogues and scholarly articles. From 2004 to 2010 she was Curator of Collections and Exhibitions and Curator of Contemporary Art at the University of Virginia Art Museum.

Scot French (UVA PhD 2000), former Associate Director of the Carter G. Woodson Institute for African-American and African Studies and Director of the Virginia Center for Digital History, is Associate Professor of History at the University of Central Florida. He is the author of *The Rebellious Slave: Nat Turner in American Memory* (Houghton Mifflin, 2000) and several site-specific studies on locations including Charlottesville's Vinegar Hill urban renewal district; Booker T. Washington's birthplace in Franklin County, Virginia; and Zora Neale Hurston's "native village" of Eatonville, Florida.

Kristen Graves is a 2021 University of Virginia graduate who majored in government and history. Kristen works in the compliance industry and continues her interest in fostering community development as a legal-aid volunteer and a Virginia State Department of Criminal Justice volunteer.

William M. Harris Sr. is a twin born in Richmond, Virginia. He is Professor Emeritus of Urban Studies and Planning at the Massachusetts Institute of Technology, Martin Luther King Visiting Professorship. Earning an undergraduate degree in physics at Howard University, he completed his master's and doctoral degrees in urban planning at the University of Washington. He is the author of *African American Community Development: A Path to Self-Determination* (Mellen Press, 2012).

Jayla Rose Hart is a writer, poet, and policy researcher. She was born in New York City and raised in Las Vegas, Nevada. An alumna of University of Virginia (CLAS 2022, Batten MPP 2023), Jayla's poetry explores identity development, freedom dreaming, and communal belonging. Her writing has been featured in *V Magazine, Flux Literary Magazine,* and the *Virginia Literary Review.*

James H. Hershman Jr. (UVA PhD 1978) is a former Senior Fellow of the Government Affairs Institute and Emeritus Faculty in Graduate Liberal Studies at Georgetown University. His writings on Virginia's massive resistance period have appeared in numerous publications, including online in the *Encyclopedia Virginia.*

Countess Hughes (UVA 1986 and 1988) found her passion for working with college students as a student leader at the University of Virginia and has worked in student affairs at colleges thoughout the South for thirty-five years.

Kasey Jernigan, a citizen of the Chocktaw Nation of Oklahoma, is Assistant Professor of Anthropology and American Studies at the University of Virginia.

Andrew Kahrl is Professor of History at the University of Virginia. He is the author of *Free the Beaches: The Story of Ned Coll and the Battle for America's*

Most Exclusive Shoreline (Yale University Press, 2018) and *The Land Was Ours: How Black Beaches Became White Wealth in the Coastal South* (UNC Press, 2016).

Janette Martin, a retired award-winning Charlottesville educator, is currently President of the Albemarle-Charlottesville NAACP.

McGregor McCance is Executive Editor of *UVA Today*. He joined the UVA Office of University Communications in 2012. Previously, he spent twenty years in the newspaper industry, where he served as a reporter and editor at newspapers across Virginia including the *Charlottesville Daily Progress*, the *Richmond Times-Dispatch*, the *Roanoke Times*, and the *Lynchburg News and Advance*. He earned his bachelor's degree in Mass Communications at Virginia Commonwealth University in 1991.

Christian McMillen is Professor of History at the University of Virginia, where he has taught since 2004. He is the author of three books, including *Making Indian Law*. He is currently teaching a course called Treaties, Time, and Power in UVA's new Engagements curriculum.

The Rev. Dr. Susan A. Minasian is an ordained clergywoman in the United Church of Christ. She has served in congregational and noncongregational contexts of ministry with a focus on liturgical art, social justice, and spiritual practices.

Louis P. Nelson is Professor of Architectural History and the Vice Provost for Academic Outreach at the University of Virginia. He is a specialist in the built environments of the early modern Atlantic world, with published work on the American South, the Caribbean, and West Africa, and is a leading advocate for the reconstruction of place-based public history.

Patrice Preston-Grimes is Associate Professor Emerita at the University of Virginia, where she was a member of the President's Commission on Slavery and the University. She has received the Exemplary Research in Social Studies Award from the National Council for the Social Studies (NCSS) and has published articles in peer-reviewed journals including *Theory and Research in Social Education*, the *Journal of Social Studies Research*, *Teacher Education Quarterly*, and the *Peabody Journal of Education*.

Jay Pun is a Charlottesville native who returned to the area in 2003 after graduating from Berklee College of Music (BM in professional music) in Boston. Jay is a music teacher at Renaissance School and a restaurateur. He serves on the Advisory Board of the Eko Ise Music Program at the Jefferson School African

American Heritage Center. He is also the author of the forthcoming children's book *Som Tum and Sticky Rice* about the popular dish from Thailand.

P. Preston Reynolds is Professor of Medicine in the Division of General, Geriatric, Palliative, and Hospital Medicine at the University of Virginia. She is the Department of Medicine's Associate Chair for Professionalism and Diversity.

Ashley Schmidt is the Assistant Director of the Gibbons Project at the University of Virginia and staffs the Universities Studying Slavery consortium. She earned her PhD in U.S. History from Tulane University in 2018.

Leslie M. Scott-Jones is Curator of Learning Engagement and Public Programs at the Jefferson School African American Heritage Center. She is the author of plays (*Desire Moments, Thirty-Seven*), novellas, short stories, and *Book Ends,* her first novel.

Kirt von Daacke is Assistant Dean and Professor of History and American Studies at the University of Virginia. He cochairs the UVA President's Commissions on Slavery and the University and the University in the Age of Segregation, serves as managing director of the Universities Studying Slavery consortium, and directs UVA's Gibbons Project. His publications include *Freedom Has a Face: Race, Identity, and Community in Jefferson's Virginia,* the President's Commission on Slavery and the University 2018 Report, and essays in *Educated in Tyranny: Slavery at Thomas Jefferson's University.*

Elizabeth R. Varon is Langbourne M. Williams Professor of American History at the University of Virginia and a member of the Executive Council of UVA's John L. Nau III Center for Civil War History. Her most recent book, *Armies of Deliverance: A New History of the Civil War,* won the 2020 Gilder Lehrman Lincoln Prize and was named one of the *Wall Street Journal*'s best books of 2019.

Brendan Wolfe edited *Encyclopedia Virginia* at Virginia Humanities from 2008 to 2019 and is the author of *Finding Bix: The Life and Afterlife of a Jazz Legend* and *Mr. Jefferson's Telescope: A History of the University of Virginia in 100 Objects.*

Jordy Yager is the Director of Digital Humanities at the Jefferson School African American Heritage Center in Charlottesville, Virginia. An Emmy-winning career journalist, Yager launched the JSAAHC's Mapping Cville project, the region's first mapping of racial covenants. He also helps run the JSAAHC's Central Virginia Black Land Repository program and its advocacy-focused Center for Local Knowledge.

INDEX

Italicized page numbers refer to illustrations.